Eugene Rembor

# Turnaround and Crisis Management

Managing Quick, Dramatic and Sustainable Turnaround in a Crisis

MANAGEMENT
LABORATORY
PRESS

Eugene Rembor

## Turnaround and Crisis Management

Managing Quick, Dramatic and Sustainable Turnaround in a Crisis

1st edition, 2011

Published by MLP Management Laboratory Press, Luetkensallee 41, 22041 Hamburg, Germany. Copyright © 2011 by Eugene Rembor.

Disclaimer:

This book is not to be seen as an investment advice. The real company names and examples are only to illustrate the theory explained in the text. The author, editor or publisher is not reliable for any losses incurred based on this text.

Publication date: September 2011, Hamburg, Germany

Registered with:
Copyclaim: #10001881, #10001882
U.S. Copyright Clearance Center (CCC)

ISBN-3941579991 Agentur für die Bundesrepublik Deutschland in der MVB Marketing- und Verlagsservice des Buchhandels GmbH

Bibliografische Information der Deutschen Nationalbibliothek:
Die Deutsche Nationalbibliothek verzeichnet diese Publikation in der Deutschen Nationalbibliografie; detaillierte bibliografische Daten sind im Internet über http://dnb.d-nb.de abrufbar.

Front Cover Picture:

Graphs: public domain , if not otherwise specified.

# About the Author

Eugene Rembor, MBA, born 1962, studied in Mannheim / Germany, Barcelona and Cambridge. An international career followed, holding Managing Director and CEO positions within Top Fortune 500 and FTSE 100 corporations. Since the beginning of his career Eugene specialised in turnaround, change and transformation and his 32 years of turnaround experience make him one of the longest serving professionals in this industry.

Eugene is an expert in rapid bottom line improvement and turnaround management. He has published three books and writes business columns for various magazines and newspapers. He regularly accepts international speaking engagements. Part of the UKTI envoy, he spoke in Abu Dhabi and Qatar, at NEOCON in Chicago, Hong Kong, Oslo and London. He is a lecturer at the National Enterprise Academy, lectures at various Chambers of Commerce and Embassies on international business and is a member of the Institute of Directors in London, the Turnaround management Association and the Turnaround Management Society.

Eugene can be contacted through his homepage:

http://www.remborpartners.com/

# Content

# Turnaround Situations: A Definition

„The definition of a turnaround situation depends on which role player you ask."

Like beauty lies in the eye of the beholder, views on what constitutes a turnaround situation are coloured by who you ask.

As a troubled company's situation deteriorates over time, more stakeholders and turnaround profession disciplines (and professionals who don't have turnaround in mind at all) enter the arena.

Each party, often myopically, not only looks at the turnaround situation from the perspective of the managerial, financial and legal aspects associated with the particular stage of decline it is involved in, but also from the perspective of the rights and interests of the constituency it presents, and its own professional background and education.

For instance, managers, investors and board of directors are involved right from the start when early signs of decline becomes evident or when a company starts underperforming.

They often bring management consultants and turnaround practitioners on board to help with corporate renewal, business transformation and turnaround initiatives.

Banks and other lenders too enter the equation when a company's situation has deteriorated to the point where their lending exposures become too high.

Lawyers, acting on behalf of creditors, are also drawn into the situation at this point in time. Then, as insolvency occurs, insolvency practitioners, other lawyers and government business rescue legislators join the party too.

With so many possible different role player views, what then constitutes a turnaround situation?

Views on turnaround situations:

### Narrow view of a turnaround situation

„Facing imminent failure ..."

In narrow terms, a turnaround situation is a distressed company normally facing imminent failure due to a cash or solvency crisis. Although they acknowledge the wider view of turnaround, turnaround gurus Slatter and Lovett provide a good description of the narrow view. They state that turnaround situations are „firms whose financial performance indicates that the firm will fail in the foreseeable future unless short-term corrective action is taken."

The narrow view represents the classic turnaround view, often involving making use of business rescue legislation to save the distressed company from failure.

## Wider view of a turnaround situation

„To turn around the trend of results from down to up ..."
Modern thinking, however, leans toward the need for turnaround before a distressed situation has developed.
World-wide, the banking industry has for long influenced their troubled clients' affairs through informal creditor workouts, which often involves turnaround action.

Furthermore, more demanding boards of directors, often prompted by shareholder activism, are increasingly placing pressure on management to improve results before the banks get concerned.
The classic view of a turnaround situation therefore needs to be widened.
Moreover, organisations with benevolent shareholders such as government institutions, or those that are subsidiaries of strong groups, will hardly fail even if in dire financial distress.

Yet, organisations in such conditions are in need of turnaround too. Accordingly, there is the need for a wider view of a turnaround situation as a company that is underperforming or in distress.

A good example of the wider view is „to produce a noticeable and durable improvement in performance, to turn around the trend of results from down to up, from not good enough to clearly better, from underachieving to acceptable, from losing to winning."

## Broad view of a turnaround situation

„Restoration of corporate value ..."
The advent of the corporate renewal and business transformation philosophies added a new dimension to the scope of turnaround.
These philosophies, and the professional disciplines they spawned, help management revitalise and reinvent their companies in a changing business environment.
Typically, they help companies to proactively react to changes in industry drivers of a political, economic, social, technological, legal and environment (PESTLE) nature.

By timeously reacting to early warning signals of decline, they effectively represent pre-emptive turnaround action.
Moreover, by helping management to resolve underperformance due to past inaction by means of remedial business transformation / corporate renewal, these approaches enter the realm of turnaround when marginal underperformance has set in.

By extending the wider view, we can therefore adopt a broad view of a turnaround situation as a company that exhibits symptoms of decline, or which is underperforming or in distress.

A more elegant broad definition of a turnaround situation can be construed from the Turnaround Management Association statement that its members are a community of turnaround and corporate renewal professionals who strengthen the economy through the restoration of corporate value.

A turnaround situation can therefore be viewed as a company in need of restoration of corporate value.

This all-encompassing view covers all stages of corporate decline, whether exhibiting symptoms of decline, underperforming or in distress.

Note, however, that not all organisations in need of a turnaround are companies or even firms. For instance, non-profit organisations, a government programme or school may be in need for a turnaround, not to restore corporate value, but to achieve certain results. For these type organisations, a turnaround situation is probably best described in terms of the wider view as above.

## Seriousness of a turnaround situation

If follows from the aforegoing that the later the stage of corporate decline, the lower the Z-Score and the more difficult a turnaround becomes.

The financial situation worsens and the ability to attract funding decreases.

Externally, customers stop buying and suppliers stop supplying.
Internally, management and staff leave, systems stop operating.
Costs increase because more role players enter the arena.

Creditors start controlling the agenda by virtue of the threat of invoking formal insolvency, and eventually formal insolvency processes eventually kick in, followed by liquidation if not viable.

We regard both business transformation and turnaround as dimensions of corporate renewal.

However, in practice, turnaround practitioners tend to be engaged only once a crisis has developed.

Invariably, action is triggered by lenders or a board of directors, rather than by management.

While no turnaround is easy, turnaround situations that have management and systems intact are easier to address.

Deep turnarounds, where good managers have left and where systems are broken, present the most difficult challenge to turnaround practitioners.

## Seriousness of a turnaround situation - 1

| Type of turnaround situation | Degree of financial distress | Leadership | Systems |
|---|---|---|---|
| Turnaround or remedial transformation of underperforming business | Under-performance | Management intact - focus on leadership alignment | Systems intact |
| Turnaround of a distressed company | Financial crisis | Management intact - possible leadership changes | Systems intact |
| Deep turnaround | Deep financial crisis | Good managers have left - new management | Broken systems |

## Seriousness of a turnaround situation - 1

| Type of turnaround situation | Emergency management | Stakeholder management | Pace |
|---|---|---|---|
| Turnaround or remedial transformation of underperforming business | Create burning platform based on the need to stabilise end rectify decline | Internally directed at management and employees | More measured pace |
| Turnaround of a distressed company | Severe crisis stabilisation | Also externally directed at investors, lenders, suppliers and customers | Rapid, incisive action |
| Deep turnaround | | | |

# Turnaround Situations: Root Causes

- Start-up that hadn't reached break even sales
- Acts of God – Natural disasters, terrorism, war
- Bankruptcy of a holding company
- Fraud / theft
- Weak economy
  - Budget cuts by public clients
  - Decreasing or stopping consumer spending
    - i.e. car industry
    - real estate agents
    - Local manufacturing outcompeted by China
- Competition
- Disappearance of key customers
- Poor Management
  - Lack of expertise / experience / education
  - Weak management
  - Insufficient resources
  - Poor business model
  - Poor understanding of the market
  - Unsuccessful R&D or M&A projects
  - Poor vision
    - Overly optimistic sales projections
  - Poor strategic choices
  - Poor execution of a good strategy
    - Sales declining
- Poor financial administration
  - Lack of control over cash-flow
    - High operating costs
    - High fixed costs
    - Cash flow crisis
    - Overinvestment
    - Fixed price tenders were unprofitable
  - Bad debt following contract dispute
  - Investments which hadn't taken off as fast as expected
  - Attempts to raise funds had failed
  - Losses mounting
  - Creditor pressure
  - Overdraft guaranteed by director
  - Bank concern about overdraft
- Board level arguments
- Non-Supportive shareholders

However, the single most common root cause for disaster is projecting the future based on past experience.

MY HOBBY: EXTRAPOLATING

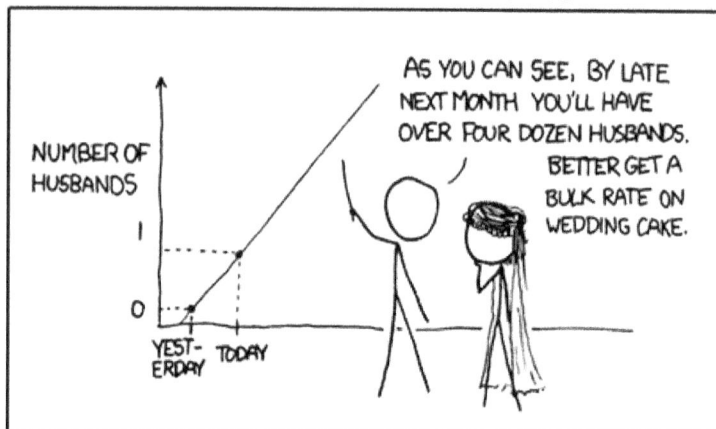

NUMBER OF HUSBANDS

1

0

YEST-ERDAY  TODAY

AS YOU CAN SEE, BY LATE NEXT MONTH YOU'LL HAVE OVER FOUR DOZEN HUSBANDS. BETTER GET A BULK RATE ON WEDDING CAKE.

Projecting the future based on past experience can lead to errors.

When Thomas Watson, the founder of IBM, observed that success lies on the far side of failure, he was preaching a double sermon. The first lesson is the need to persevere through all setbacks. The second is equally important: learn from your mistakes.

They can yield far more value than rejoicing in success. That's why another American entrepreneur, Royal D. Little, entitled his book How to Lose $100 Million and Other Useful Information. The ability to analyse one's own errors, and correct them, is an indispensable, highly instructive part of the entrepreneurial kit.

Sometimes this means making the best of what initially seems a very bad job - like the company whose brand-new product, thought certain of success, was losing money heavily, making no impact in the market and causing extreme stress and overwork. The disaster flowed from a common error: extrapolation of the past into the future.

That can prove fateful even when the future is very recent. The company had experienced strong demand in this particular market segment in the preceding months. As the new product, designed to cream off more boomtime sales, was launched, the market went dead flat. The company had been misled by looking only at its own sales.

In its resulting predicament, thorough homework, wrongly absent before, showed that of three alternatives - battling on regardless, closure, or tweaking - only the third made economic sense. By scaling down production and attacking a different market segment, first-year losses would be kept to £50,000. Breakeven next year would be followed by £100,000 profit in the third.

So it transpired. Better still, the product surged on to dominate its segment and become a highly profitable market leader. The plans could be scaled down without loss of opportunity - simply because the original segment offered none. So beware of extrapolation - and never neglect that homework.

In another, sadder case, though, efforts to recover from unwise extrapolation became self-defeating. The start-up, a service business, had expanded to the limits of its existing offices. Market conditions looked buoyant, and a move to larger premises seemed sensible. But instead of cutting overheads, by moving to a cheaper area, the company took on much bigger and dearer offices. (Sounds familiar?)

Is your choice of office driven by status or ego? Honest?

Recession, hitting its business and savaging the value of London offices, delivered a double whammy. The more the firm tried to cut insupportable overheads, by subletting and cutting staff, the more its business suffered. (Sounds familiar?) It was chasing its own tail - the same fate that's overtaken some major companies, which have become leaner and meaner, all right, but also less able to compete.

So keep the ratio of fixed costs to turnover as low as possible. The attack on overheads is easily relaxed when business is booming, and the boom is being extrapolated into the future. If the breakeven point where income covers costs rises too high, not only will profits be inadequate, but the business will be highly vulnerable to any downturn.

On the other hand, having low-cost offices over a pub, say, with tiny staff and big ambitions has dangers of its own. As in another real-life example, it encourages the proliferation of low-profit activities. This company was undertaking far too much activity (Sounds familiar?) at far too tiny a return. So, even though the breakeven was low, it couldn't get past the vital mark - and failed accordingly.

So always work to high gross margins. The two latter examples provide another warning. There wasn't enough room to learn from failure and proceed to its far side, success. It's hard for a small company, especially when going well, to ask what's the worse that could happen, and what must be done if the worst (as it sometimes will) comes to the worst.

That isn't the same as prudent budgeting. Time and again, boards accept budgets which look immensely prudent compared to the previous year's wonderful rise in sales and profits. But the budgeters have merely aimed off from the extrapolated past. Just as dangerous, they're still in an upside mentality, which affects decisions as well as costs.

Nobody likes to present pessimistic forecasts. But adverse future trends won't disappear for being ignored. Nor will past failures - so exploit them. After all, they've cost plenty.

The best way to avoid too pessimistic and too optimistic forecasts at all is to read the economy and make realistic forecasts that meet the current economic climate.

If they don't, the danger is that you might increase capacities because you anticipate a boom, or you reduce capacities because you expect a downturn. But how do you predict the economy without relying on a crustal ball?

The answer is: "The Economic Clock". Like any other life cycle, economic cycles too have been watched, analyzed and described for decades in not centuries. The result is a tool used for many years by bank economists and stock market experts:

## THE ECONOMIC CLOCK

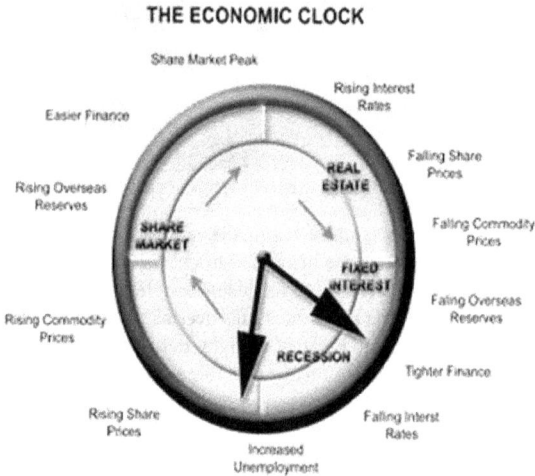

Just look at the economic clock and determine where the economy stands right now – and you have a predication what happens next. You might not know exactly when things happen but usually cycles change within a span of 6-9 months and towards the end of this year (this report is written in 2011) we will have a long lasting boom that will last more or less 8 years. How do I know? Because it has always been hat way and will repeat itself.

What do we learn from this? What we learn is to be aware that it just might be that while we are still reducing our capacities and make redundancies, we meet rock bottom and experience an upswing, where we soon after having downsized, might need to upsize again. If this feels odd – it's not, it's normal. Even if you know that life is a swing and not a flat line (unless you're dead), it is quite normal to upsize, rightsize and downsize, because you cannot simply do nothing and sit and wait, burning money until the next boom sets in. You must manage your company and that often includes a constant change, which is, well, philosophically speaking, anyway what life is: A constant flux.

# Turnaround Situations: How The Institutional Imperative Causes Crisis

Individual managers usually take educated and rational decisions. As soon as they enter the halls of corporate power, however, the institutional imperative phenomena kicks in and very often starts a downward spiral.

1. The organisation resists any change in its current direction.
2. In the same way as work expands to fill available time, corporate projects or acquisitions will materialise to soak up available funds.
3. Any business craving by the leader, however foolish, will quickly be supported by detailed rate of return and strategic studies prepared by his troops.
4. The behaviour of peer companies, whether they are expanding, acquiring, setting executive compensation or whatever, will be mindlessly imitated.
5. Managers cannot control their lust for activity, leading to activism, takeovers, fixing what's not broken and eventually to disaster.

Only extremely grounded and disciplined managers with a healthily small ego will resists to fall victim to the syndrome and not become a lemming following others to the cliffs.
When you are a leader, beware of the danger. When you are a turnaround manager, understand the psychology of leaders.

## Turnaround Situations: Challenges

* Design: What type of restructuring is appropriate for dealing with the specific challenge, problem, or opportunity that the company faces?
* Execution: How should the restructuring process be managed and the many barriers to restructuring overcome so that as much value is created as possible?
* Marketing: How should the restructuring be explained and portrayed to investors so that value created inside the company is fully credited to its stock price?

How to tackle these challenges? Many people say "you have to be creative", but can creative management techniques help you survive the recession?

The present economic crisis is about 30% real and arising from toxic securities (unmanageable). Then there is 50% panic and fear caused by media hype. Finally there is about 20% of 'games playing'. That means parties who take advantage of the situation.

For example, if a corporation has long wanted to sack ten thousand staff, this could not easily be done at other times because it would have severely depressed the share price. But with the excuse of the recession, this sacking now becomes possible. And if others are doing it too, that makes it even easier.

Better thinking is never a luxury. Better thinking is an absolute necessity in difficult times. This better thinking includes creativity. There is a need for creativity in order to look at things in a different way and open up new perceptions. This can mean looking at problems as opportunities.

None of that is easy because we are trained to look at things in the first and obvious way - which is usually enough.

The other need for creativity is in design. We need to design the way forward. You can analyse the past, but you have to design the future. Creative thinking is never instead of information and other forms of thinking, but in addition to these other forms. Under certain circumstances, such as difficult times, creative thinking becomes more important, since nothing else will change things.

Creative thinking works well when there is a well-defined focus. The focus can be very tight and narrow, or it can be general and broad. Any objective is really a package of values.

Creativity can then be applied to the focus itself: do we really want to achieve this? Creativity is then applied to ways of delivering the required values.

Traditionally, creative thinking has been seen as a group process. This can be used, but it does not have to be a group process. An individual can sit down with a focus and a lateral thinking tool kit and develop new ideas entirely on his or her own. These ideas can then be discussed with others with a view to improving them.

## Turnaround Situations: Stages

- Situation Analysis – evaluating prospect of survival, formulating strategies, i.e.
  - Turnaround
    - Change of management
    - Divestment
    - Revenue increase
    - Cost Reduction
    - Strategic Acquisition
    - Or any combination thereof
  - Abandonment
    - Liquidating
    - Selling
    - Asset Strip
    - Playing end game
- Emergency Action Plan – achieving positive cash flow ASAP by stopping

leaks and driving revenue

- Business restructuring – ensuring sustainable positive cash flow, implementing strategic plans, improving operations, optimising product mix and positioning
- Return to normality – profitability achieved, changes implemented. Stakeholders regain confidence and emphasis is placed on growth

# Turnaround Management: Tools

- Creditor management
  - Dealing with aggressive creditors
  - Bailiffs
  - Litigation
  - Debt collectors
  - Negotiating with creditors
  - Banks
  - HMRC
  - Landlords
  - Council & service providers
  - Finance companies
  - Bond holders
  - Mezanine
  - PIKs
  - Refinancing
- Cashflow improvement
  - Cash management
  - Creditor management
  - Standstill agreement
  - Payment plans
  - PAYE and VAT arrears
  - Key and non-core suppliers
  - Debt collection
  - Sales ledger finance
  - Asset based lending
  - Rescheduling finance agreements
  - Payroll reduction and staff redundancies
  - Balance sheet restructuring
  - Formal
  - Company Voluntary Arrangement (CVA)
  - Pre-pack sales
  - Informal
  - Debt reduction/write-off
  - Refinancing
- Operational reorganisation

- Staff reduction
- Contract termination
- Lease termination
- Corporate restructuring
  - Liquidation
  - Hive-downs
  - Scheme of arrangement
- Personal protection
  - Informal payment plan
  - Deed of arrangement
  - Individual Voluntary Arrangement (IVA)
- Asset protection
- Planning & presentation
  - Preparing financial forecasts
  - Preparing RESCUE PLANS
- Directors Guide

# Turnaround Management: How To Get Help

TMA (Turnaround Management Association)
http://www.tma-uk.org/ (UK)

TMS (Turnaround Management Society)
http://turnaround-society.com/ (Europe)

Institute For Turnaround (ift)
http://www.instituteforturnaround.com/ (England)

Turnaround Management TV (helpful information)
http://www.turnaround-management.tv

The Turnaround Management Blog
http://turnaround-manager.blogspot.com/

Vince Cable announced a new 40,000-strong network of business mentors at the launch of Global Entrepreneurship Week in January 2011, and called on more businesses to join up.

Vince Cable wants to see as many business people as possible sign up to mentor new and growing businesses. To make it easier for people to get the mentoring help they need, the Business Secretary outlined the Government's plans for a new single network of mentoring providers. This network of experts will help start-ups, growing companies and businesses seeking financial mentoring.
Each year, some 120,000 businesses in the UK become a turnaround case and

go bankrupt. That's more than 300 per day. No other figure demonstrates more clearly the need of an army of turnaround specialist to help saving these organisations.

For the first time, business mentoring networks are joining forces to improve access to mentoring provision for both mentors and those looking for mentoring support. More mentors will be encouraged to commit to the network over the coming months.

Business Secretary Vince Cable said:

"The best people to advise new entrepreneurs and existing businesses are those who have already started and run successful companies. Mentoring is a very effective way of promoting start-ups, higher productivity and growth amongst established businesses, so I am delighted to announce this new network.

"I also want to encourage more businesses to sign up and offer their support and guidance. We need as many successful mentors as possible to guide the next generation of entrepreneurs and businesses."

Business and Enterprise Minister Mark Prisk said:

"In the current economic climate, it has never been more important to promote an enterprise culture in the UK, and mentors play a crucial role in advising, supporting and encouraging entrepreneurs and small businesses. This new mentoring network will be invaluable for businesses all over the country."

From summer 2011, with the support of the British Bankers' Association and UK mentoring providers, there will be a single online gateway to mentoring provision for mentors and for those seeking mentoring.

The mentoring network has been developed in response to the needs of entrepreneurs and small business across the country. The Annual Small Business Survey 2007/08 found that businesses which used external advice in the last 12 months were twice as likely to have grown their workforce and over 50 per cent more likely to be aiming to grow their business in the next two to three years than those that had not used advice.

Already, over 40,000 mentors of all ages, skills and location will be available for guidance. Organisations such as Horsesmouth and Ecademy have pledged mentors to the network, and for the first time mentors and mentees will have the confidence that every organisation in the mentoring network is signed-up to a shared code of conduct.

Vince Cable and Mark Prisk outlined details of the new mentoring network at the launch of Global Entrepreneurship Week at Google Headquarters in London. Global Entrepreneurship Week is a joint initiative developed and led through a partnership between the Department for Business, Innovation and Skills (supported by Enterprise UK) and the Kaufmann Foundation in the US.

GEW is a key focal moment in the drive to build a strong enterprise culture, with competitive open markets and the pursuit of global trade and investment. Events held as part of GEW aim to inspire, inform and support both budding and relatively new entrepreneurs.

# Turnaround Help:
# How To Get The Most Out Of Your Mentor

Many business owners like to seek advice to help steer them through difficult trading periods or to plan their firms' development. A business mentor can help you come to the right decisions for your firm. Find out when turning to a mentor makes sense.

Just because you run your own enterprise, it doesn't mean you can also be an expert on turnaround management or have the answer to every challenge that comes your way. There will be times when you are uncertain which route to take and need a listening ear or a second opinion  – this is when a mentor can be invaluable.

Restructuring a business is time-consuming, so you rarely get a chance to step back and identify improvements. It's easy to concentrate on the urgent things rather than the important issues — a mentor can help you focus and prioritise.

## A mentor's role

Mentors are not consultants and won't sort out day-to-day issues or teach technical competence. However, they can act as a sounding board for working out dilemmas and thinking strategically about your business. If you want someone to fix your IT or write your finance plan, it's not a mentor that you need.

But a mentor might ask you difficult questions and help you to recognise issues that hadn't occurred to you. They may also introduce you to professional networks, but don't treat it just as a door-opening exercise.

A typical mentoring session might cover both strategic issues and immediate concerns. You'll probably spend half the time talking through the worries at the forefront of your mind -such as your debts - and the other half addressing longer-term issues, such as how to bring in a new management structure.

## Find the right mentor

Bear in mind that not all mentors have to be formally established. Friends, family and business contacts can all become involved in unofficial mentoring. It is also worth noting that from summer 2011 the UK Government is bringing in a new online network of mentor providers.

When talking to potential mentors, ask yourself whether they are listening enough and if you feel you could work with them. The ideal small business mentor is someone with experience of running a small firm, as well as broader business knowledge.

## Get the most from a mentor

Importantly, mentoring is a two-way relationship. It's not just an opportunity to pick the brain of a more experienced business contact. However, you can decide between you how formal or frequent your contact should be.

Some business owners just call or email their mentors as and when they need to, while others schedule regular face-to-face meetings. Most mentor-mentee relationship typically last 12 months, but they can be longer. The costs can also vary substantially - some mentors offer their services for free, but others will charge between £500 and £600 per day.

To get the most out of your mentor, prepare for the sessions and follow up on them. Before you meet, think about what you want to get out of the session, and afterwards reflect on how you can use any insights.

Importantly, you'll only benefit from using a mentor if you're open to being challenged about what you do, and are willing to respond to criticism.

# Turnaround Diagnostics: How To Recognize Distress

- Your gut feeling
- Bills you can't pay
- Outstandings you are chasing
- Unhappy / indifferent customers
- Stagnating / declining sales
- Growing costs

# Turnaround First Aid: Your Survival Pack

- Talk to your bank / investors
  - In person
  - Explain reasons, be truthful, honest, straight
  - Explain action plan
  - Ask for help
- Talk to staff
  - In person
  - Explain situation truthfully, honestly and straight
  - Manage expectations
  - Give clear orders
- Stop spending
- Drive efficiency
  - Can you do more with less?
  - Can you do better?
  - Can you do less? (Reducing capacity)

- Can you do different?
- Can you outsource?
- Reduce cost
  - Leasing / renting vs. buying
  - Outsourcing
  - Not doing it (advertisement / training / new office furniture)
  - Negotiate with suppliers / re-tender
  - Downsizing (staff / space)
  - Reduce inventory
  - Sell of surplus equipment
- Drive quality
  - Higher quality gets market share = more business

Do it in that order!

> Admitting that your company needs help doesn't make you a bad manager in the just the same way as admitting that you need a doctor doesn't make you a bad man. It makes you a sensible person.
>
> Eugene Rembor

There are many reasons that can lead to a situation of corporate distress, but there is only one reason why companies won't be saved: Ego. As a company director the buck stops with you, and this puts a special responsibility onto you to recognise when things are turning sour and when help is needed. You have to be able to stand above things and not to cover up failures, neither your own nor the ones of anyone else, but to act to the best of the company and get expert help.

Calling for expert help doesn't make you a bad manager the same way as it doesn't make you a bad man when you recognise that you need a doctor. Calling for professional help is a sign of maturity and sensibility and not a sign of weakness.

## Turnaround Management: After First Aid

What type of restructuring is appropriate for dealing with the specific challenge, problem, or opportunity that the company faces?

You might already know the best course to deal with the situation. It could be a turnaround or it may be an exit. If the company, its products or services are futurable and it were simply operational or economic reasons that led to the crisis, a turnaround might put the organisation back on its feet and ensure it is sustainable.

If there is no future, you might develop an exit strategy. A family owned quilting business in Essex faced dramatically declining business and generated losses. Due to competition from China it was not a feasible option to continue, and several exit scenarios were looked at:

- Closing down and cutting the losses
- Phasing out the business, milking it while reducing capacity and costs
- Asset stripping it

Depending on your strategy you will select the ideal expert. You might need a turnaround expert, a liquidator, an M&A specialist or even an insolvency practitioner.

How should the restructuring process be managed and the many barriers to restructuring overcome so that as much value is created as possible?
Marketing: How should the restructuring be explained and portrayed to investors so that value created inside the company is fully credited to its stock price?


# Case Studies: ICI

Sir John Harvey-Jones of ICI was the surprise choice as chairman in 1981 after the company, a major stock market barometer, had just reported the first deficit in its history, a net loss of £ 20 m on sales of nearly £ 6 bn. This bluest of blue chips was forced to cut its dividend for the first time since its founding in 1926, leaving shareholders and employees shell-shocked.

Harvey-Jones brought a tough nautical discipline and plain speaking frankness to the awesome task of bringing the mighty ICI vessel round. The process imposed severe strains on the structure, leading to the loss of 30,000 jobs in the UK – a third of the domestic workforce – the closure of plants and the withdrawal from whole areas of manufacturing. Even the production of polythene, which ICI scientists had accidentally invented in a laboratory experiment in 1933 and which was, therefore a deep part of the company's history, was abandoned.
The old, bureaucratic management system was flattened out; the old baronial divisions were turned into internally competitive businesses; reporting lines were shortened. Harvey-Jones even revolutionised the way board-meetings were held, preferring shirt-sleeved informality in his office to leading proceedings in the imposing Art Deco boardroom at Milbank with its octagonal table.
After three years, ICI emerged triumphant from its ordeal to become the first British company to announce pre-tax profits (for 1984-85) of over £ 1 bn.

The achievements of the Harvey-Jones turnaround strategy provided a template for others in the 1980s. If imitators failed it was usually because their approach was top-down rather than collectively pursued. ICI had always had a collegiate management culture and its so-called "parliament", dating back to the 1920s, was one of the earliest examples in the UK of workers being empowered to question senior management decisions.

The chairman himself remarked that although there had been a few occasions where he overruled the wishes of the majority, "a company of this size can only be run in a collegiate fashion. Any company that thinks it is a British institution is on the way out."
Exercise:

1. Which role did discipline play in the ICI turnaround?
2. What would have happened if "plain speaking frankness" would not have been introduced?
3. How do you imagine and "old bureaucratic system" and how would you have turned it into "internally competitive businesses"? What KPIs would have used and how would you have motivated staff and management?
4. Why do you think it was important to change towards an informal meeting culture?
5. How would you ensure that board decisions are being challenged and questions by non-board stakeholders?

## Case Studies: Sinclair

Sir Clive Sinclair was a brilliant ideas man but hampered by lack of marketing skills. He invented the pocket calculator in the 1970s, the pocket sized TV, the micro computer and the electric town car but never really made it. Had he employed the skills of business experts and concentrated on what he was good at – inventing, he had made a fortune.

## Case Studies: Rowntree

When, in 1988 Rowntree tried to defend a takeover bid by Nestle, Rowntree's chairman Kenneth Dixon was rarely available to speak to the press and failed to overcome Nestle's arguments about the weaknesses in Rowntree's international business. Short of hard facts, the press began to speculate about boardroom dissension and the battle was lost. A good leader must be instrumental in dealing with the public, the press and other stakeholders. Hiding in an office is no option in a crisis, and neither is being unprepared and unarmed of arguments. Leading means living of words and persuading people, forgetting this fact is lethal.

## Case Studies: Blue Arrow

Another important quality is realism: Tony Berry's strategy at Blue Arrow in trying to acquire such a large target as Manpower was unrealistic, akin to a snake trying to imitate the python by swallowing an animal several the times its size. Even worse when fantasy is paired with dishonesty, as Tony Berry found out after exaggerating statements of the company's assets. The dubious accounting became exposed, Berry ousted and that was the end of it. Beware: Greed eats brain!

> *Richard Branson enjoyed breaking into and shaking up compla-*
> *cent industries, but he never made the mistake of assuming he*
> *had the skills to manage the follow-through himself. "My skills are*
> *finding the right people to run companies and coming up with new*
> *ventures" he said.*

## Case Studies: Guiness

Another classic example of "Greed and Ego eat common sense" was Ernest Saunders. At first things started out the right way. Cutting out the non-core, largely loss-making businesses that have provoked the crisis; second, rationalise the core business; third, rebuild from the new, leaner base. Within two years, 149 Guinness-owned companies had either been shut down or sold. A new, hard-hitting advertisement campaign targeted Guinness at the young 18-35 pub-goer who would normally drink ale. Costs were ruthlessly cut at the company's plants in north-west London and Dublin, involving the loss of 1,000 jobs, and the price to the publican was reduced.

Saunders may have inflated the commercial results of these first two prongs of his strategy, though they were much praised at the time. But it was the third prong – diversification and growth from a newly rationalised base – that led directly to the 1987 catastrophe. Saunders planned to turn Guinness from a UK-oriented brewing company to an international beverage-based conglomerate. But the initiatives he took were risky in both speed and scale.

In 1985, Saunders launched a £ 300 m bid for whisky distillers Arthur Bell. It was a logical choice but the bid was eight times bigger than Saunders had yet tried, and Bell's chairman, Raymond Miquel, was in no mood to accept. A well-publicised and hostile campaign for control of bells was played out all that summer. It ended on 23. August when Guinness won a 70 per cent shareholding following an increase of the bid to £ 370 m.

Now over-ambitioned and dominated by ego rather than prudence, Saunders triumph with Bells prompted him to turn his eye on United Distillers. In the "anything is possible" atmosphere that permeated the investment community at the start of 1986, Distillers was the prize catch for a branded drinks company, owning not only prime whisky brands such as Dewars, Johnnie Walker, Haig and Buchanans but also famous gins such as Booth's and Gordon's and cognacs such as Hine. It also had Cossack vodka and Pimms to its name.

What raised the stakes to dangerous levels was not only that proceedings were highly publicised – speculation about a Guinness bid for Distillers dominated the quality press throughout early January 1986 – but also that they were conducted in the teeth of a bitter counter-bid by James Gulliver, founder of the Argyll Group.

Saunders' opening bid, worth £ 2,2 bn, had the support of the Distillers board, which saw the Argyll bid as hostile and unwanted. But Gulliver, who had long nursed ambitions to acquire the company, immediately launched a bidding war. A vicious battle ensued that involved the referral of Guinness's bid to the Monopolies Commission, not once but three times. There was a row over Distillers' agreement to pay Guinness's bid costs, which forced the Stock Exchange to bar arrangements where a company paid another's bid costs above 25 per cent of the profits, and legal suit was initiated by Guinness for alleged injurious falsehood and defamation in Argyll Group's bid advertising.

In the end, supported by the cream of the City's establishment, Guinness won a majority of the Distillers shares and announced victory on 18. April. But in the process, both before and after the takeover, Saunders had illegally connived in a share-support scheme whereby wealthy investors were persuaded to purchase Guinness shares to keep the company's stock market value artificially high. This was contrary to Section 151 of the Companies Act 1985. There was also enormous share buying from overseas. Between them just two institutions, Schenley Industries and Bank Leu of Switzerland bought almost £ 200 m of Guinness shares. A fifth of the company's entire share capital changed hands in a matter of weeks.

The share ramp only came fully to light when US corporate raider Ivan Boesky confessed in November 1986 to insider trading in the US. Investigators into his case uncovered the fact that Guinness had invested £ 69 m into the Boesky fund. In the fall-out, two British tycoons – one of them creator of the property-based heron Group, Gerald Ronson – admitted they had received over £ 5 m each from Guinness for help with the Distillers bid. And Sir Jack Lyons, a highly respected philanthropist, was found to have accepted £ 2 m. Two members of Guinness's bankers, Morgan Grenfell, were sacked, Saunders himself was fired from Guinness and sentenced to five years imprisonment and Sir Lyons suffered the bitter indignity of having his knighthood removed. All because one man got carried away by greed and ego, ignored that law and seriously though he could get away with it.[1]

Exercise:

1. When should you walk away from a bid?
2. How do you make sure your board is adhering to good corporate governance and abiding the law?
3. What measures can you take to keep your own feet firmly grounded?

1    From Dynasties to Dotcoms, Carol Kennedy

Exercise:

Robert Hortun, who had succesfully turned around BP's Standart Oil business in the US through a ruthless programme of cutbacks and sell-offs, ran into savage resistance when he tried a similar approach as chief executive in London and he, too, was forced out by an alliance of unhappy non-executives and institutional investors. Hortin proved far too pugnacious for the board of one of Britain's industrial icons.

1. How do you make sure you understand the corporate culture you are entering?
2. How can you verify whether the cultural brief you are being given is true, and that you are not tried to be "softened up"?
3. How can you maintain diplomacy while still maintaining the drive and verve you need to enforce tough management?
4. What means do you have at your disposal to bring NEDs and institutional investors to your side?

Exercise:

Allan Leighton who succeeded in 1995 as CEO of the northern supermarket group ASDA, completed a turnaround of this fading business by introducing an Americanised culture, with the CEO wearing a badge proclaiming "I'm Allan, Happy to help". The group got so successful that it was eventually bought up by the US giant discounter Wal-Mart.
The transformation o ASDA owed much to new work practices and innovations such as the "one-team" management style (no surnames, open plan offices, everyone termed a "colleague" regardless of rank). The approach was quickly adopted by the previously hierarchical Sainsbury as the group's old-style management saw how ASDA delivered the goods. An external adviser said about Allan Leighton: "Allan is a back-slapping, brilliant communicator and myth-maker with his staff, he's really brilliant at it".

1. What leadership principle did Leighton demonstrate by wearing a badge?
2. What difference does a "one-team" style make?
3. What benefits do open plan offices have?
4. How do less hierarchical systems improve quality?
5. What makes an outstanding communicator?

# Case Studies: Dyson

1993, when Dyson launched his revolutionary bag-less vacuum cleaner based on dual cyclone technology, was also the year Hoover launched possibly the disastrous sales promotion in history – offering free flights to the US with each cleaner sold, but then retracting the offer when hundreds of thousands of customers claimed tickets. Two years later, Dyson's cleaner overtook sales of the leading Hoover model.

Exercise:

How could this situation been turned around with the greatest possible positive effect while keeping any damage as little as possible?

## Case Studies: Ratner

At the 1991 IoD convention, Gerald Ratner, head of the high-street jewellers, made a now legendary gaffe, describing one of his products as "total crap" – and another as "cheaper than a prawn sandwich". The speech wiped an estimated £ 500 m of the value of the company and was Ratner's personal downfall: He left the company next year.

Exercise:

How could he have more positively promoted the inexpensive prices of his products?

## Case Studies: BP

John Browne, the CEO who transformed BP in seven years from third ranking oil major into the world's seventh largest company who is a finance man to his fingertips who demands accountability from every manager in BP. Often radical in his thinking and a phenomenal appetite for hard work and the ability to excite others with his vision, he demands delivery: "If you cannot keep up and perform, you are dead", says a former BP director.

Exercise:

1. How do you implement an attitude of accountability among your staff?
2. What consequences do you take when staff fails to assume accountability?
3. How do you measure accountability?
4. How do you excite others with your personal vision?

## Case Studies: Marks & Spencer

In May 1998, Marks & Spencer still supplier Britons with a quarter of their suits, almost all of their bras and a third of their sandwiches. It was a British institution and the country's most profitable retailer. In 1998, its annual report showed profits of £ 2 bn and its share price hit a record high of 664p. But in October of that year, it was forced to report the first fall in profits since the start of the decade and, by the end of 1998, its share price had dropped by 32 per cent. Two years later, the share price had fallen to less than 180p.

Bad news kept coming. Long-term chairman Sir Richard Greenbury retired a year early in February 1999 and his successor, Peter Salisbury, lasted only 18 months. Perhaps the lowest point, in PR terms, came when a thousand trade unionists from France, Spain and Belgium demonstrated outside the company's flagship store at London's Marble Arch over the proposed closure of stores on the continent. Worst of all, customers were turning their backs on M&S garments, those classic standbys that had been a byword for value and quality. Some commentators doubted whether the company would survive at all.

The turning point was the appointment of chairman Luc Vandevelde in February 2000, although the bottom-line benefits were not seen for a further 18 months. By that time, the company had an entirely new set of executives up to and including the managing director, Roger Holmes, who came from Kingfisher, the former Woolworths.

As a rise and fall story, the M&S saga has few business equals. So what happened? The answer is that the very strengths on which the company's success was consolidated under the Sieff family in the 1930s – strong central control and top-down attention to detail – had rebounded on it. Centralisation always brings the dangers of complacency – and by the mid-1990s M&S was very vulnerable. Its early lead in pioneering up-market ready-made meals was being eroded by catch-ups Tesco and Sainsbury. Its insistence on buying almost all of its clothes from domestic suppliers, a patriotic asset in Thatcher's 1980s Britain, seemed irrelevant to a more cosmopolitan generation and allowed competitors who imported more cheaply to compete aggressively on price.

In a lecture of innovation in 1997, M&S deputy chairman Keith Oates conceded that the company was almost wholly dependent for new ideas on its suppliers, and by then many of Marks' UK suppliers were out of touch with the new global fashion market. Its centralised buying system also meant that one bad judgement had widespread consequences, as when M&S buyers decided that grey was the colour of the year for female fashion. British women stayed away in droves.

Nor had M&S's ventures abroad delivered on their earlier promises. Clothes sold in its overseas stores were often too expensive because they had details such as buttons finished in Britain. Although the Paris stores had been rip-roaring success, particularly (and ironically) in the food department, growth elsewhere in Europe was slow. Brooks Brothers, the prestige US acquisition, was losing money and attempts to reposition the M&S brand as high-fashion in Asia had not worked at the time when the region was about to belly-up economically.

All of this, reflected in a 23-per-cent fall in half-year profits at the end of 1998 (the first in M&S's 30-year history as a public company), would have been enough to trigger nervousness in the investment community. But that year a lot of the company's scraggy corporate governance chickens also came home to roost. Despite chairing a committee on corporate governance in 1995, Sir Richard Greenbury, chairman and CEO, had been dismissive about the new benchmarks of boardroom probity. Interviewed in 1990, when his assumption of the combined role had provoked widespread criticism in the City, he commented: "The idea that the chairman does the long-term stuff and the Chief Executive does the short-term stuff is rubbish, business school rubbish."

Now, for the first time, the unquestioning loyalty he demanded from the board – stitched into his office cushion were the words "I have many faults, but being wrong isn't one of them" – slipped out of control. Away in India, he was unable to prevent an unseemly power struggle going public over who should succeed him as CEO. Keith Oates even appealed to M&S's NEDs when executive directors indicated they would prefer Peter Salisbury.

The composition of the board at the time was a telling indication of the company's inward-looking character. Sixteen of the 22 directors were insiders. Of the six non-executives, one was a former executive and a member of the founding Sieff family. As the Economist commented in a critical profile of Greenbury in November 1998: "With M&S now selling financial services and going overseas, the narrowness of M&S's senior managers and board directors is a weakness... Taking their lead from Sir Richard himself, M&S executives have failed to understand much of what is happening outside their green and white shop window, let alone outside Britain's boarders."

Not surprisingly, when the first foreign and "outside" chairman in the company's history was appointed, his first priority was not only to bring in the best designers to create a fashion brand beyond St. Michael, but to establish a more balanced board of insiders and outsiders. Vandevelde also ordered a complete overhaul of the parochial, top-down culture. Pivotal in the company's long road to recovery was a two-day workshop in the summer of 2000 by London Business School professor Lynda Gratton. Held at Lord's cricket ground and attended by 500 managers, it threw every previous tenet of M&S management into the dustbin and replaced them with new freedoms of action, using skill tests to find out how comfortable managers would be with the change. It proved the most successful management development event ever run by the company.

In 2003 the company hah hauled itself out of the mire.

Questions:

1.  How can you as a CEO ensure that your strategies and, more particularly, your products are futurable?
2.  How would you prevent union activities when you have to downsize an organisation, hence preventing negative press impacting your share price?
3.  What are the disadvantages of top-down management?
4.  How would you test the most successfully strategies for overseas ventures?

# Case Studies: McDonalds

You can be a turnaround manager even if your remit is just one part of the operation. Jill McDonald, Chief Marketing Officer at McDonald's UK turned around the company's menu, stores and marketing, and was then promoted to CEO.

One of the best stories about Turnaround Management is the one of Lou Gerstner. In his bestseller "Who Says Elephants Can't Dance?" he tells about how he brought IBM back from the brink after he became its CEO in 1993 by shifting its focus from selling hardware to selling software services. However, in an ever changing world, one turnaround sometimes is not enough: Sam Palmisano, Mr. Gerstner's successor, transformed IBM into what he calls the "globally integrated enterprise". In essence, the multinational company of the past was a series of national businesses co-ordinated by a single headquarters. The globally integrated enterprise, by contrast, has swapped national silos for global teams, drawing on the best talent wherever it may be.

1.  What are the charaktersistics of a series of national businesses co-ordinated by a single headquarters?
2.  What are the characteristics of a globally integrated enterprise?
3.  What would be a good strategy to transform the first one to the second?

# Case Studies: Coca Cola

During his tenure at Coke, Goizueta turned around what some business analysts once called an old, conservative company by emphasizing global sales and making moves never seen by the company before.

His motto: return on investment and stock price.

„The curse of all curses is the revenue line," he once said, referring to the need to be profitable.

And fortunate for him and Coke investors, Goizueta's company was just that. Since becoming CEO in 1981, he created more wealth for shareholders than any other CEO in history, largely due to his global marketing skills. Total return on Coke stock was more than 7,100 percent during his tenure, according to analysts. A $1,000 investment in Coca-Cola when Goizueta took the top job would be worth about $71,000 today, including reinvested dividends.

He owned nearly 16 million Coke shares worth roughly $1 billion, making him America's first corporate manager to achieve billionaire status through owning stock in a company he didn't help found or take public, business analysts said.

Goizueta had not cashed in a share of his Coke stock in more than two decades. Close friends said he had not sipped a Pepsi, Coke's No. 1 rival, in more than 10 years.

## Transforming the world of Coke

Goizueta thought Coke had become „too conservative," he said in a 1986 interview. „It took us a little bit longer to change than it should have. The world was changing, and we were not changing with the world."

He arranged a retreat for company executives and presented a „strategy for the ,80s." He promised no cow would be sacred: „We're going to take risks."

The new CEO immersed himself in the company's accounting and economics.

With a new, punchy advertising slogan, „Coke Is It!" he successfully increased domestic sales while continuing to plumb new international markets.

But Goizueta also was responsible for launching New Coke, which he called „the boldest single marketing move in the history of the consumer goods business." The new soda eventually led to protests on city streets as Coke faithful demanded a return of the sweet, caffeinated cola they had come to love.

Coke rebounded by resurrecting the original formula and naming it „Classic" coke.

## Case Studies: CCR

Michael Robb, executive director, Center for Community Resources Inc., turned around CCR by asking the right questions

Michael Robb was prepared to be disliked on his first day.

Tough decisions would need to be made to keep the jobs of his 52 new employees and keep the organization, Center for Community Resources Inc., out of bankruptcy.

"You have to have courage that you're not going to be liked," Robb says about stepping into a leadership role in a turnaround situation. "You have to understand who you can trust, and put your faith and trust in those individuals. You have to know who the players are in the organization and assess that very quickly, because you can't do it alone."

Robb's first days were spent talking to employees on all levels to determine the human services organization's finances and problem areas. Connecting with employees early allowed Robb easier buy-in during the turnaround implementation. That was 2005. Since then, CCR has grown its staff to 89 and has an annual budget of $4.5 million. Seeing the need to help nonprofit organizations, Robb and his team started Alliance for Nonprofit Resources Inc. and Nonprofit Development Corp. As executive director of the organizations, Robb oversees 130 employees and budgets of nearly $8.5 million.

Smart Business spoke with Robb about how to turn around a company.

Q. Where do you start in a turnaround situation?

*What happens is sometimes you go into a situation and people feel like you should have all of the answers because you're hired. You shouldn't ask questions to be able to enact policies. People see asking questions as a sign of weakness or that you don't know what you're doing.*

*I always feel like you have to go into some kind of temporary incompetence. When you walk into a scene, you really need to understand what the culture and the* structure is that you're going to be working in. Those are two critical elements that you need to evaluate: How are things getting done? What is the philosophy behind which those things are done?

Q. To whom do you ask questions?

*No matter where the company is at when you come in, you have to be open to everybody who might provide feedback to you.*

*Some do it willingly; they just come to you. They may come to you for a lot of different reasons and a lot of different motives. Others, you have to seek out. That's where it gets difficult, because who is going to provide you with reliable information and who is going to provide you with information that is not necessarily in the agency's best interest, but it's in that person's best interest, too. You have to evaluate that.*

Q. What questions are you asking?

*There is a double bottom line with nonprofits. The first bottom line that a lot of people focus on is good service provisions: Are we doing it well? The second bottom line is: Are we doing it at an affordable cost?*

*When you look at it that way, I carve out my questions really: What's the finance process? Are we looking at our accounts receivable and our accounts payable? Are we managing our cash flow? Are we looking at a cash basis or an accrual basis? That dictates a lot about how an organization runs and can survive. Who is in charge and who is making the decisions on how money gets released? Who is making the decisions on how money is being sought? Once you find out who is doing those things, then you can start asking the process by how they make their decisions.*

Q. How do you get staff buy-in on ideas and strategy moving forward?

*On two fronts: Is it going to make their jobs better and how they do their work better? Is it going to make their overall experience of being within an organization better? Sometimes people look at coming into a place on two fronts: I like my job, but I hate my employer.*

*What are you trying to do to meet those two things? You have to understand what the employees want.*

*I always found benefit from meeting with staff over those brown-bag-lunch meetings. You sit down at lunchtime. I'd buy pizza. And I'd say, 'Here are some of the things going on. What are your concerns? What are you worried about?'*

*I got a great amount of feedback, which I thought was really relevant. In those meetings, I would say, 'I'm going to take your feedback, and we're going to commu-*

*nicate back. If we can't accomplish those things, here's the consequence.'*

*If you can use not just words, but bring in some handouts to show the staff, 'Here's what it currently is. There's our bottom line.'*

Q. Are there other essential steps that must take place?

*You have to be visible when you're coming in on a turnaround. We had a couple of sites, and I made a point to always be at the other site on a weekly basis. Actually spend time working there. I didn't have a designated office. I would pick a conference room, and sometimes I would get kicked out because there was a meeting.*

*People want to see that you're there rather than behind some closed door. Minds start to race.*

*If you're doing those one-on-ones, if you're meeting with people on a regular basis, it really starts to help ease their concern. They can focus back on what they need to do be doing.*
*You have to give a time frame: 'Within 90 days, we will have structural changes done or some process changes done.' You may not know what those exactly are.*

*You have to understand where things are and pinpoint. Depending on where the cash is for an organization and where they might be in crisis mode will really delineate how quickly you have to react.*

## Case Studies: Ford

Ex-Land Rover, Mazda Chief Says Branding Key to Ford Turnaround

Ford Motor Co. should shed its Lincoln, Mercury, Land Rover, Mazda and Aston Martin marques and concentrate on Ford, Volvo and Jaguar, says former marketing executive Charles R. Hughes.
However, Hughes, a onetime CEO of Mazda North American Operations and president of Land Rover North America, dismisses the notion domestic auto makers can downsize themselves to prosperity, an ongoing strategy at both Ford and General Motors Corp.
Rather, Hughes says, Ford, and to a lesser extent GM, has to reverse years of what he calls "bad branding" in order to be successful.
Good branding, Hughes contends, "gives you recognition with a certain group of customers.
"Branding is a simple business strategy to set yourself apart in the marketplace," he tells Ward's. "Branding is a promise wrapped in an experience. And by promise I mean you have to stand up and make a commitment and stand for something."
Ford overextended itself when it bought Jaguar, Land Rover and Volvo in the late 1980s and 1990s, Hughes says, making it difficult to concentrate on transforming

any one brand into a global powerhouse.

Growing too quickly ultimately led to Ford's current predicament of declining sales and market share in North America, where key leadership positions have changed hands at a frenetic pace, he says.

That means the solution is to shed brands, Hughes says. "Building one world-class brand is sufficiently difficult, and when you (talk about) GM and Ford, you're talking brand portfolios.

"For (Ford) to be successful they have to get down to three brands worldwide, and the three brands should be global and have no overlap," Hughes says. "(Ford) should shut Mercury and Lincoln and sell Aston Martin, Land Rover and Mazda."

Hughes does leave open the possibility Ford could retain its 33.4% ownership of Mazda, or even purchase the remaining shares, as the Japanese auto maker provides Ford with many of its key vehicle platforms.

However, should it decide to part with Mazda, Hughes says, Toyota Motor Corp. would be eager to take Ford's place.

"If I were sitting at Toyota, I would be at Ford asking to buy Mazda," Hughes says. "If you're playing chess, it's like taking a pawn away."

While many pundits say money-losing Jaguar would be the most logical brand for Ford to shed, Hughes says Jaguar remains a valuable brand that has been prevented from realizing its potential by Aston Martin and Land Rover.

"Jaguar has a very bad product lineup," he says. "They can't build the best sports cars because that's Aston Martin's role, and they can't do world-class SUVs because that's what Land Rover does. Having two sister brands is truncating what Jaguar is today."

By trimming its product portfolio to just Ford, Volvo and Jaguar, Ford would have a chance to consolidate its talent and concentrate on strengthening three brands that have virtually no overlap, says Hughes, about to embark on a tour to promote his new book, "Branding Iron," coauthored with longtime auto writer and editor William Jeanes.

He points to Toyota, which despite fielding the Lexus and Scion marques, mostly relies on its Toyota brand for strong worldwide growth and revenues.

Toyota's success can be attributed to a single-minded focus, shared across its entire workforce, Hughes says. "At Toyota, 99% of the people wake up every day to try and make Toyota better. They know what the message is."

Ford could be one of the strongest nameplates in the industry if it intensified its focus on the blue oval brand, Hughes says.

"Ford should clear the decks and get rid of the brands that get in the way and make cars that everyone wants, more so than Toyota," Hughes says.

"We've seen in their past they're capable of doing that. There was a confidence of what they were doing, and they need to get back to that. They need everyone in the company to wake up and think about that."

Suggestions Ford should form a partnership with another auto maker, perhaps the Renault Nissan Alliance, is a "lose-lose" scenario, he says.

"It takes focus and a clear-headed look at the marketplace, and all these arrangements and partnerships take the eye off the ball," Hughes says. "Look at BMW (AG) and Rover (Cars Ltd.). They spent all their time trying to fix Rover. And

DaimlerChrysler (AG), all that effort hurt Mercedes-Benz.

"The companies that are going to win are the ones that look at the marketplace and work hard on revenue and committed brand strategies."

## Case Studies: bmi

When CEO Wolfgang Prock-Schauer took leadership of bmi , he had a Herculean task ahead of him. The airline had made a £181 million ($286 million) loss for 2008 and its 2009 performance turned out to be even worse. He needed to raise £190 million in funding for the period to November 2010, partly at the expense of bmi's crown jewels - its lucrative London Heathrow slot pool.
„It was critical," says Prock-Schauer. „When I arrived there was a lot of uncertainty. The employees were scared about what might happen, whether the airline would be broken up or taken over, so my first job was to reassure them that we had a turnaround plan in place."

For years the question had hung in the air about whether bmi chairman Sir Michael Bishop would exercise his put option, forcing fellow shareholder Lufthansa to buy his stake. As one bmi employee said at the time of the Lufthansa takeover: „Now the ownership speculation is finally over, we can start speculating about our future."

But, in April, Prock-Schauer reassured them that bmi, which comprises bmi mainline, bmi regional and budget arm bmibaby, would stay intact. „We have no plans to divest any of these elements. Every airline has a flow in our set-up, each has a specific role to play. There are no plans [to sell bmi] and no talks with Virgin Atlantic or any other carrier."
Prock-Schauer joined bmi with a firm mandate from Lufthansa is to turn round bmi.
„My job is to create a valuable asset for the Lufthansa Group," he says. „I think bmi's strategic value is understood and acknowledged by our parent company. We have 10% of the slots at London Heathrow, the biggest aviation market in the world. Together with Star Alliance, I think we can really do something. Now it is our job to be profitable as quickly as possible. Luckily, I found a good management team here."

Although the clouds of uncertainty had lifted a little, the hard work was just beginning. The team had to deliver an initial tranche of £100 million in combined cost savings and synergies. This was communicated to bmi's staff in April via a series of briefings. „Some sacrifices needed to be made to turn this company around,".

No restructuring measure is more painful than job losses and cuts formed „an important part" of bmi's turnaround plan. Around 670 positions have been made redundant, against a target for 800. Prock-Schauer says this is a work in progress, but he adds that there will be no more „big bang" cutbacks. The remainder will materialise as bmi streamlines its operation.

On top of the job cuts, bmi has implemented a wage freeze, shifted its network focus, increased its utilisation by 15%, slashed capacity by 20% and axed some of its worst loss-making routes. This means Amsterdam, Brussels, Kiev and Tel Aviv have been abandoned in favour of a new Vienna link and expanded services into Berlin, highlighting bmi's Star Alliance and Lufthansa Group loyalties.

„We are now building a solid base for future expansion," says Prock-Schauer. „The greatest problem bmi had was it had to do everything on its own in order to get economies of scale." A fundamental part of bmi's turnaround plan rests on its carefully managed integration into Lufthansa Group, which will deliver 20% of the £100 million target through back office synergies. But bmi will maintain its independent identity in the areas that matter.

„As much as we talk about the European Union, we are not the ‚United States of Europe'. This becomes clearer every day. The Swiss want a Swiss airline, the Austrians want an Austrian airline. We have to go with what the consumer wants, but we have to act like one airline, getting the economies of scale of a big airline," explains Prock-Schauer.
Leveraging its Lufthansa ties, bmi has already integrated its overseas sales offices and pooled resources for some of its airport activities, such as maintenance. It is also working with the wider group on financing, procurement and hedging, as well as some marketing functions, and bmi is planning to join Lufthansa's Miles & More frequent-flyer scheme, shifting away from its own scheme, Diamond Club. Prock-Schauer is also promoting strong connections and communication between departments at bmi and its parent.

„This is the basis really to get all the synergies we have been talking about. We are a smaller airline, but nevertheless we get the economies of scale of a big group. That's what we're aiming for and we can already see good results coming through," says Prock-Schauer, who is expecting to deliver 60% of the £100 million target in 2010. „The most major benefits will come from having the right network and marketing it in the most efficient way."

On some domestic routes bmi operated seven or eight daily frequencies, but it has cut its Heathrow frequencies to Aberdeen, Belfast, Dublin, Edinburgh, Glasgow and Manchester to maximise its precious slot pool, increase load factors and boost yields. „Our focus will be to further reduce our domestic flights and this capacity will shift to our continental Europe and Middle Eastern routes," says Prock-Schauer. But he insists domestic services will remain part of bmi's core business. „By capping frequencies [on domestic flights], we've already seen improved results because we're using bigger aircraft and keeping prime timings. Even with five flights a day, we can offer perfect timings for connecting traffic."

During its restructuring bmi sold 18 of its Heathrow slot pairs - although they all remained within Lufthansa Group - and leased out a further 10, leaving it with 10% of the total pool. This resolved bmi's liquidity issues and its portfolio, which has shrunk from 87 to 66 slots, is now stable. The leased slots will be returned to bmi over the next one to three years. „This puts us in a unique position because we are possibly the only carrier which can expand at London Heathrow," says Prock-Schauer. „The plan is to stabilise the business, return to profitability, get the slots back and make something meaningful out of it."

With the £100 million plan well on track and already active on an annualised basis, Prock-Schauer is finalising a second £100 million tranche, to be squeezed from bmi's optimised network and its Lufthansa ties reaching maturity. „We need a certain amount of time before we see the full effects," he says. „The first £100 million is clearly quantified, it is coming. The second £100 million is more difficult to achieve, but we are very confident we have identified the majority of measures for the second programme which will take us to breakeven and eventually into a profit scenario."

Prock-Schauer expects bmi to enter the black in the medium term and both £100 million programmes will „definitely" be complete in three years. „When we are profitable, then we will start evaluating aircraft types. This is not my priority. My priority is to return to profitability," he says.

The airline has secured the cash it needed and Prock-Schauer says bmi is now „on track" in terms of liquidity, despite the volcanic ash crisis causing a „big dent" in its recovery. By 2011-12, bmi should be stable and heading for break-even. It will then look to shift its network focus to fully maximise its Heathrow slots, expanding its mid- to long-haul network with new destinations in the Middle East, selected markets in Africa and the CIS. Early signs of this strategy are already emerging with the launch of services between Heathrow and Libya's capital, Tripoli, in December.

In the longer term, Prock-Schauer does not rule out a return to transatlantic flights. „We are evaluating certain projects on the North Atlantic. That could be a complementary offering because of the huge traffic flow from the Middle East, via London, to North America." He says the North Atlantic operation would „not be big scale" and would simply complement Lufthansa's existing network. He adds that no definitive decision has been taken and timelines are entirely dependent on the success of the restructuring plan.

Although bmi only retained one of its three Airbus A330s to serve its three Saudi Arabian routes, a second A330 that it operates for another airline is due to be returned in March 2011. Together with the return of bmi's leased slots, this could be used to support its network redevelopment plans.

In terms of the wider Lufthansa Group, bmi would offer an alternative hub at

Heathrow for onward links. „Lufthansa Group has many different hubs and traffic flows. Eventually the passenger decides," says Prock-Schauer.

But it is still early days. Prock-Schauer's first objective is to consolidate bmi's strongest medium-haul services and maximise their potential, shifting away from its domestic heritage. These medium-haul flights will then provide a feed for its possible re-entry into transatlantic services. Meanwhile, bmi regional will do the legwork of connecting the UK regions to Lufthansa Group's other European hubs. In the shorter term, Prock-Schauer is focusing on rolling out some tangible signs of bmi's new direction, such as a refurbishment of bmi's Airbus A321 fleet, including new business class seats and an in-flight entertainment system upgrade over the next two years. „Especially on our mid-haul services, we want to offer a really competitive product," says Prock-Schauer. „Our goal is to be one of the best in class when we fly these mid-haul routes." The airline has seven A321s in its fleet, configured with two classes, and it is due to take delivery of a further three in 2012.

In the meantime, bmi is rolling out a „quick refurbishment" of its interiors and its lounges, which Prock-Schauer says is in the completion phase. Another immediate measure is harmonising bmi's fleet into its „whale" design livery after the airline ended up with three colour scheme variations - its old colours, the whale livery and an interim scheme from the former BMed fleet. „Now we have the time and are willing to invest more and paint the aircraft properly."

A year after arriving at bmi's headquarters, Prock-Schauer says: „There has never been one day where I thought it [bmi] would collapse. Everybody knows we're still loss-making, but they see that something is happening. We are doing more flying, the aircraft are being repainted into a standardised livery and small investments are coming on line. Naturally, in a loss-making situation, you cannot spend huge amounts of money, but everyone sees that we want to position this company for the future and make something out if it."

## Case Studies: Mulberry

Back in 1999, Mulberry, the traditional British leather accessories company founded in 1971, was sleepwalking its way toward bankruptcy. The minimalist aesthetic of the ‚90s pioneered by designers such as Calvin Klein had all but done for their particular brand of old English craftsmanship. Who wanted a tartan lined oak leather Filofax once the ‚80s were over? No one it seemed.

But Mulberry was one of the lucky few traditional British brands that survived when so many were steamrolled by unbeatable production costs in the Far East. Ironically it was Singaporean businesswoman, Christina Ong - whose distribution and manufacturing conglomerate ‚Club 21' owns all the UK stores for Armani, franchises of Donna Karan and DKNY, Prada and Bulgari and distributes Miu

Miu and Armani underwear - who came to the rescue with a £7.6m cash injection and significant global retail expertise.

Her first appointment was design director Nicholas Knightly whose ,Bayswater', ,Roxanne' and ,Elgin' handbags became instant hits, attracting a lengthy waiting list and celebrity following. The Bayswater is still one of the brand's bestsellers today and is immortalised in the window of their new flagship store in giant, gold, inflatable form.

Knightly was also instrumental in relaunching the dormant womenswear range, starting with a small capsule collection of key items, which later developed into a full catwalk collection under the eye of current creative director Emma Hill, who joined the company in spring 2008.

Perhaps Mulberry's best stroke of marketing genius however, was picking up early on the style icon potential of ex-model and television presenter Alexa Chung. Hill designed the now iconic chic and slouchy satchel for spring 2010, named it the ,Alexa', gave one to Alexa Chung in every size and colour, then sat back and watched the column inches pile up. Gifting bags to celebrities was not a new concept - indeed it has been core to Mulberry's marketing strategy for some time - but this bag was a triple threat: seen endlessly on the arm of the coolest girl on the party circuit, approved by fashion editors and essentially a great design on a practical level that fitted perfectly into wardrobe of real women.

In 2006 Mulberry opened their first stores in New York, and their ongoing expansion into Asia is significant. Hill has also championed entry level price points with trinkets such as cute keyrings, bag charms and bracelets attracting a younger customer.

Finally their opening of their new flagship store on London's New Bond Street, and their prestigious British Fashion Award for best designer brand are the final piece of the jigsaw, affirming Mulberry's rightful position as a leading global fashion brand.

The 5,400sq ft store, which you can see being constructed above, stays true to Mulberry's British heritage and reputation for craftsmanship incorporating an authentic Cotswolds dry stone wall, British oak and leather shelving and sculpted oak timber and textured brass ,follies' that break up the store into a series of mini-boutiques. Light boxes in the ceiling simulate daylight throughout the cavernous space and really blow away any residual cobwebs of old Mulberry once and for all.

As well as being beautifully designed, the store can also boast an impressive carbon footprint, using 50% less energy than any comparable store. „We've taken grandmother's wisdom and added state of the art technology", brand director Georgia Fendley told us, „The dry stone wall for example acts as a ,heat sink', storing heat in the cold and keeping the temperature cool in summer".

Seeing Mulberry's wide assortment of lines, from their highly-covetable bags, to womenswear, menswear, shoes and small leather goods, all displayed on one floor, in such a complimentary environment is the final piece in the jigsaw for the once ailing brand. The giant inflatable gold Bayswater bag and helium balloons that fill the window let you know that Mulberry are in the mood to celebrate, and it's not hard to see why.

Today Mulberry profits tripled on demand for best-selling Alexa handbag, as it struggled to keep up with demand for its Alexa bag and opened new stores in the Middle East and Hong Kong.

The luxury brand now expects profit for the full year to beat analysts' forecasts. Mulberry's pretax profit climbed to £4.7m in the six months to the end of September, up from £1.5m the previous year. Sales rose 38pc to £44.7m. The last ten weeks have also been a success, with like-for-like sales climbing 47pc.
Mulberry said sales at its stores in New York and Paris more than doubled in the first half, as the brand's appeal spreads outside the UK, helped by celebrity endorsement from the likes of Alexa Chung, the TV presenter which Mulberry named the handbag after, and Gossip Girl actress Blake Lively.
In the UK, like-for-like sales rose 36pc in the first half, and full-price sales have increased by 66pc in the last 10 weeks, boosting profit margins. Mulberry said it won't sell anything at a discount in the run up to Christmas.
With VAT in the UK rising to 20pc in January, Mulberry said „some uncertainty exists for the foreseeable future," and said sales over Christmas remain „key" to its full-year performance.
Fashion powerhouse Mulberry is on the brink of becoming a „truly global brand". The quintessentially British fashion house Mulberry is set to have more stores abroad than in the UK by this time next year, according to its chief executive Godfrey Davis.

2010 alone, Mulberry has added new stores in Hong Kong, Malaysia, Doha in the United Arab Emirates and Sydney, and Davis told Reuters today he expected the number of stores and concessions abroad, currently at 38, to overtake the 44 it has in the UK during the next 12 months.

The prospect of international growth would have hardly seemed possible when a young Roger Saul, at 21, founded the company with a £500 loan from his family. It is understood his father suggested he sell Christmas trees or donkeys. Instead he and his mother, Joan, set up a company making leather goods in their garage in Chilcompton, near Bath.

Today the company's headquarters and factory still resides in Somerset, in a building called The Rookery. In the early seventies, local craftsmen helped create Sauls's first collection of leather belts, which were sold to trendy fashion stores such as Biba in London. The following year Saul won a significant order from a Paris department store to make 1,000 belts.

A few years later Saul expanded in Europe and America, selling designs for Kenzo in Paris and a Bloomingdale's range in New York.

The company's growth seemed unstoppable, with Saul striking a licence and partnership agreement in the late 1990s with Kravet and Toray Industries in Japan.

The turn of the century and a new fate awaited Saul, however. In 2000, he sold 42pc of his business to Challice, owned by Singaporean billionaire fashion designer Christina Ong and her husband, an oil and property tycoon Ong Beng Seng.

Just two years later Saul was ousted in a boardroom coup after Davis – Mulberry's current chief executive and Saul's friend of 15 years – sided with Ong in a vote to remove him from the company.
Saul, who is married to former Dior model Monty and collects stylish classic cars, told friends he was shocked and disappointed to lose Davis' support. He owned just 38pc of the company, and Davis' 4.5pc stake was crucial to whether he would survive as chairman.

Before the coup, former advisers described Saul as a designer first, a businessman second. "Going public was a means to an end. It was just a way of raising finance. He always resented the idea that he had to justify his decisions and, more importantly, his designs," said one.

This could go some way to explain how Saul lost control of his own company, a company which has become one of the leading fashion labels of all time and led analysts to predict Mulberry is about to become a "truly global brand".
Mulberry, which employs 740 people in the UK, is firmly sticking to its roots – albeit without the founding ingredient Saul - expanding its factory in Somerset to meet growing demand. The move is expected to create 60 jobs.

Godfrey Davis, chairman and chief executive, said that the expansion will continue and that by the end of next year Mulberry will have more stores overseas than it does in the UK. At present it has 44 shops in the UK and 38 around the world.

During just six months, new Mulberry stores opened in Hong Kong, Korea, Qatar and the UAE. Sales in the US were „significantly ahead" of plan.

Bags and accessories account for more than 90pc of Mulberry's sales. The Alexa handbag sold well and the new Tillie bag is set to become as successful.

## Case Studies: Starbucks

Who would have wanted to be in Starbucks' shoes a year ago? McDonald's had launched low priced alternatives that had huge trial, the economy had stalled and consumers were balking at spending $4 per drink, even at a familiar place.

Howard Schultz announced that the company had „lost its way," becoming too standard and corporate and less entrepreneurial -- less like a local coffee shop. The chain then closed stores on a broad scale for the first time.

Fast forward a year later. Starbucks blows its Q4 numbers out of the water. Get this -- sales were up 4% to $2.7 billion. Comparable store sales were up 4%, which was driven by both increases in store traffic and average ticket price. If that wasn't enough, the company's margins were up by 8.5% to 13%. As a result, the company earned 32 cents in the quarter, up from nine cents in the year-ago quarter. Starbucks now expects to launch 100 new locations in the U.S., and another 200 worldwide.

One of the clues to Starbucks' success lies in a phrase buried in their press release, „Starbucks' consumer research shows higher satisfaction in every major indicator, such as value perception and experience, compared with a year ago." So the results were not driven by price increases alone (even though prices did go up), but by improvements in customer experience as well.

Starbucks customers have noticed a series of improvements at the store from prior years, including reintroduction of the Pikes Peak blend and Via instant coffee, more healthy snacks, improved staff engagement and a new, frequency-based loyalty card.

But I think there is something more. Starbucks two years ago launched My Starbucks Idea, a portal that permits customers to suggest improvements to the store, products, pricing, etc., and for other customers to vote and identify the most popular ideas. Here is the kicker -- real-life Starbucks employees actually respond to the ideas, suggest improvements, identify logistical issues and, when an idea is selected for development and launch (which they actually are!), provide timetables and commentary. Imagine that -- a company that asks customers for ideas, permits them to prioritize the ideas and actually assigns relatively senior people to engage in conversation with their customer community!

The site profiles Starbucks employees that are engaging with customers this week, highlights ideas with the most votes as well as the most recent ideas, and includes a small poll to gain some quick customer insight. The question on Jan. 31 was: „What flavor of bran muffin sounds the most appealing to you?"

Now, My Starbucks Idea is not the sole reason for Starbucks' success. Clean execution, new products and a motivated salesforce all contribute in a big way. The idea of soliciting ideas from customers is not new either. But the execution is so clean, the relationship so transparent and results so clear for mystarbuckidea.com that I believe it helps to motivate Best Customers to return, refer and do all those other things that make Best Customers so important.

"I think My Starbucks is a big part of the turn around but not necessarily because Starbucks heeded useful," said Carol Spieckerman, President, newmarketbuilders. "Simply engaging customers rather than keeping the old „We know what you like" vibe going was a big, positive goodwill step."

"It takes nerves of steel to do this and they did so admirably and in the process, solidified what they stand for," said Doug Stephens, President, Retail Prophet.

"You have to applaud a retailer that asks customers for their input and then directly follows up on their requests," said Max Goldberg, Founding Partner, The Radical Clarity Group. "There is a practical lesson to be learned here: Listen to your customers. How many retailers actually 'get' this simple concept?"

However, in the chapter about the institutional imperative we talked about the lust for activity, and here is a prime example of useless, even dangerous activity just for the sake of it:

When a Turnaround Idea Is Asinine. In January 2011 Starbucks introduced a new cup size larger than human stomach.
Starbucks has garnered some astonished media coverage for a new super-super size drink option the coffee chain is introducing for its US customers. The new „Trenta" cup has a capacity of 916ml - exceeding the capacity of the average human stomach (900ml).

Will the Trenta itself enjoy the same success? I say „No". In a time were moderation is trendy and political correctness and corporate responsibility essential, this move is simply dorky.

Who wants cold coffee? Or does this cup come with an integrated warming plate? Drinking almost a litre of coffee will take you hours.

Too much coffee is bad for you. Has it already been forgotten how „Supersize Me" affected McDonald's, blaming them for damaging the health of the nation? Selling volumes that are bigger than the human stomache inevitable leads to terrible waste. Terrible waste is neither green, not corporationally responsible.

As Starbucks approaches its 40th birthday in 20111, its profits and share price have bounced back. It's a Wall Street darling again, thanks to new products like instant coffee, a new strategy that focuses on international growth, and a quarterly dividend.

| Starbucks at 40 | |
|---|---|
| **Birth date:** | March 30, 1971 |
| **Mission:** | „To inspire and nurture the human spirit — one person, one cup and one neighbourhood at a time." |
| **Size:** | 17,000 shops in 55 countries, including more than 11,000 in the U.S. |
| **Employees:** | About 137,000, down from 176,000 in 2008. About 3,000 work at its Seattle headquarters. |
| **Profit:** | $946 million for the year ended Oct. 2010, up from $316 million two years earlier |

In 2008, Starbucks was in desperate shape.

Profits were falling, and Howard Schultz returned as CEO to save a company he had built from a small chain to a juggernaut with thousands of stores worldwide. He made painful cuts, including closing 900 stores and slashing thousands of jobs.

Now, as Starbucks approaches its 40th birthday in 2011, its profits and share price have bounced back.

The reasons for its return as a Wall Street darling include products like instant coffee, a strategy that focuses on international growth and a willingness to give shareholders a quarterly dividend.

Shortly before unveiling a new logo on Starbucks' headquarters building in Sodo last week, he talked about the challenges of coffee prices, the health-care overhaul and recycling. Here are edited excerpts:

Q: Does climate change present a problem for Starbucks?

*About a year ago, when we solidified the long-term relationship with Conservation International, that gave us more insight and more resources to both understand the challenges of the day and for us to try and participate as much as possible in taking steps to improve the situation. I wouldn't categorize it as a problem but an ongoing challenge and hopefully an opportunity.*

Q: What's the opportunity?

*In many places where coffee is grown, deforestation is a major issue. With Starbucks' position in the marketplace and the respect and relationships we have, we can — and have in some cases — been able to educate and influence people. Something else is important. What we want to do — and our responsibility — is to constantly ask the question, „Are we making our people proud to wear the green apron?" Sometimes, though, I think whenever a company like Starbucks tries to lead with its heart and do the right thing, you have to ask yourself, „Why are we held to a higher standard?" And I think it's because we try and do the right thing, where perhaps other companies are not engaged at the level we are.*

Q: Since you that brought up, why do you publicize your good works?

*We do a partner [employee] survey consistently about the culture issues and the trust issues and how we're doing as a company. And one of the primary things people tell us is, „Why aren't we telling the world all the good things we're doing?" I don't think that we are a marketing-driven organization. Candidly, we try and do the right thing not because of creating press. We try and do the right thing to help the community... . If I look at all the things we do, the things that perhaps we promote are de minimis compared to the works that we do around the world that no one knows about.*

Q: How are you feeling about the economy these days?

*Managing a business, small or large, today requires an extremely disciplined, thoughtful approach with regard to the pressure that people are under.*

*I think one of the ways in which we've tried to overcome that pressure is to provide consistent value for our customers. And the Starbucks gold card and the Starbucks card program really have been a big success in meeting the customer more than halfway and saying, „This is how we can participate with you." I think the economic issues are still fairly fragile. I don't think the recession is over.*

Q: How concerned are you about the high cost of coffee?

*I'm speaking to suppliers and have visited coffee farms, and I cannot uncover this big problem people are talking about in terms of supply issues.*

*I think that is a fictitious component of what has happened this year [to coffee], which has been driven primarily by financial speculation, hedge funds, index funds and people who have decided that the basket of commodities is a place where money can be made.*

*You have to ask yourself, „Why is it that almost every commodity is hovering around record 10-year highs?" It's not an accident. We've seen coffee now — yesterday it was over $2.80. A year ago, it was half that. If this continues, it'll become more challenging for us, as well as every other coffee company.*

*Because of the economy and the fact that we literally want to put our feet in the shoes of our customers, we don't want to — and have refused to — have an across-the-board price increase. It's something we are trying desperately not to do.*

Q: There's a shareholder proposal about recycling again this year. Why don't you have recycling bins in all your stores?

*Starbucks has stores in America in many, many communities that are governed by many, many different municipalities. Starbucks cannot dictate to a municipality in Cincinnati or Kansas City or Sacramento how or why or when there should be a recycling program. That's one of the primary problems.*

*On the other side of the equation, we are a buyer of paper goods from very, very large paper companies who have embedded significant capital costs in legacy factories. So when we go to a paper company and say we want a 100 percent recyclable cup or want to change the material — again, we are a buyer of the product, we can't dictate.*

*We've had two what I would loosely describe as summits in the past couple of years, when we brought all our vendors here to show them the strategic plan that the company has for the near term so they can understand the needs we have to be a very strong corporate citizen in all areas of how we purchase product, food, supplies.*

*We had a summit of paper suppliers this past year to talk specifically about how we can become a leader in this industry. I think we're getting to the point where we have more influence than we had in the past, but we still are dependent on the suppliers to make the sort of investments that are necessary to overcome this problem. And we're asking them to make it at a very challenging time, which is difficult.*

Q: Starbucks was vocal about [wanting] health-care reform. How do you feel about how it worked out?

*We have been a leader for almost 20 years now in demonstrating our heartfelt commitment to making sure that we provide health coverage for the majority of our people.*

*That cost last year was $250 million. We have faced double-digit increases for almost five consecutive years with no end in sight.*

*So, when I was invited to the White House prior to health care being reformed, I was very supportive of the president's plan, primarily because I felt it was literally a fracturing of humanity for almost 50 million Americans not to have health insurance.*

*There's no plan that would be a perfect plan, but the intent of the bill and the heartfelt commitment to insure the uninsured is the right approach. I think as the bill is currently written and if it was going to land in 2014 under the current guidelines, the pressure on small businesses, because of the mandate, is too great.*

Q: Over the years, you've tried to attract more people into your stores in the afternoons. How is that going?

*With fiscal 2010 being the strongest financial year in our history, and the first quarter, which ended in December the strongest in our 40-year history, there are a lot of compelling reasons — that are enduring — that suggest that the company has been transformed in many ways.*

*There are more people going into our stores today at different parts of the day.*

Q: More traffic in the afternoons?

*Yes. But being in any retail business today, we cannot embrace the status quo even though we are now succeeding. We have to keep pushing for reinvention and self-renewal. We must.*

Q: What about selling beer and wine in the afternoon [as Starbucks does in a handful of stores, including on Olive Way in Seattle]?

*We'll continue to test that. Olive Way is without a doubt a success. Our international partners want us to expand that internationally. We've been very careful not to move too fast. I don't think we understand it all yet. There will be more, but it will be modest in terms of numbers [of stores].*

Q: The new food you introduced today is sweets, not the type of health and wellness offerings you've said you're focused on.

*It's not one thing versus the other. We have a significant initiative inside the company around health and wellness. All I have to share with you is, stay tuned on that.*

Q: Your first book [published in 1997] was about building this company almost from scratch. The new book is about a turnaround. Which was more fun to do — build a company or save one?

*The entrepreneurial process of building something I think is much more fun. Transforming a company, though, is more gratifying. Sitting here today having accomplished what we've done in a relatively short period of time, I think the company and our team did our best work. But managing and navigating through a financial crisis is no fun at all.*

Q: Why is it more gratifying?

*If you read the press a couple of years ago, there was a death march about Starbucks.*
*I think people underestimated the resiliency of the brand and particularly the resiliency of our people. So it's quite gratifying to see the company come back so strong and to demonstrate to our people the pride that we all have in what we've built.*

Q: The last time you wrote a book, you retired as CEO about three years later. Does this mean you're headed that way again?

*What I've told the board is I'm here to really see this through. I don't know what that means, but I'm not leaving anytime soon.*

Q: You closed 900 stores and cut thousands of jobs. If you had still been chairman, would you have let [previous CEO] Jim Donald do that?

*I don't think there would have been a change in the decision. The company was in a desperate situation, but it doesn't in any way remove you from the emotional feeling of making those very tough decisions.*

Q: Did Starbucks grow too fast, was it bad real-estate decisions, or the economy, or what?

*There's never one thing that creates a problem like the one we had, and never one thing that's going to solve it. But I think growth in and of itself does cover up mistakes, and success probably creates a fair amount of hubris.*
*When I came back, the first week I publicly apologized to everyone in the company because we had let our people down.*
*Even though I wasn't the CEO, I was the chairman and I was culpable. At the same time, I made a heartfelt promise that day that we would absolutely restore the company back to its glory days, and we have.*

Q: How do you reconcile the need to hold onto Starbucks' roots while also growing and even doing things that aren't coffee, like you've talked about lately?

*There's been a seismic change in consumer behaviour, and it demands innovation*

*and it demands relevancy.*
*The challenge and the art is for us without question to embrace the core values and the core experience while innovating on the edges, and we'll do that and do it well.*

Howard Schultz is a very capable turnaround manager. There is much to learn from him:

- He took the blame. He did not look for a scapegoat but took full accountability and apologised, although he had not even been the CEO when the company went into rough seas. That's real greatness and a very rare quality.
- He made tough decisions, closed 900 unprofitable shops – a job his predecessor would not have done.
- He understands the big picture, the impact of deforestation and world-coffee markets and emphasises the importance of good corporate social responsibility, also reflected in his health care for starbucks' staff.
- He is hands on. He visits suppliers and coffee farmers and hence knows what's going on in his business in great detail. He is not one of those CEOs hovering above the rest in an ivory tower.
- However he is wrong about his assessment of Starbuck's purchasing power when it comes to influencing paper mills so supply recycled paper. In a day and age where global sourcing has become best practice, he surely can find plenty suppliers of recycled paper and cups without any problem.

## Case Studies: The British NHS

The UK has a population of 61 m. Germany has a population of 81 m. The NHS employs over 1,5 m staff. In Germany 4,3 m people work in health care. The NHS' budget is £ 110 bn, Germany's health care budget is £ 150 bn. In 2010 the NHS had a £ 7 bn deficit. In 2011 Germany has a £ 10,3 bn surplus.

|  | United Kingdom | Germany |
|---|---|---|
| Population: | 61 m | 81 m |
| No of staff in NHS / German Health Care: | 1,5 m | 4,3 m |
| Ratio of population per member of staff: | 407 | 19 |
| Health Care Budget: | £ 110 bn | £ 150 bn |
| Ratio £ per head of population: | £ 1803 | £ 1851 |

How come that the UK and Germany have a practically identical budget in perspective to its population (both spend around £ 1800 per head) but Germany manages not only to pay 3 times the number of staff and provide one of the highest health care standards in the world, but also generates a £ 10,3 bn surplus?
If the secret lies not in the numbers, only one other answer is left: Efficiency and management.
Cutting budgets in the NHS will therefore not solve the problem. It will merely condense the same problems onto a somewhat smaller budgetary scale. As long as the same people are responsible and the same ways of working will be applied,

we can only expect the same results. Actually, it is a clinical definition of insanity that continuing to do the same thing and expecting a different result is insane.

The government is not doing anything different when it merely cuts the budget. It would, however, be doing something very different if it would introduce performance related payment to NHS staff, especially to non clinical staff, employ more business managers with experience in running private sector organisations (where they were forced to be profitable) and introduce modern leadership and management principles such as Management by Objectives, lean six sigma, and kaizen.

As of today, no one underperforming in the NHS has to expect any severe consequences. So where is the incentive to improve? Shifting the monkey will not solve problems, and giving GPs control over the budget makes as much sense as putting MBA's in control of brain surgery. Doctors are trained to do surgery and managers are trained to manager budgets. Mixing both leads to disaster.

# Case Studies: Chevrolet

As General Motors emerges from bankruptcy reorganization to launch a new era, it is no exaggeration to say that as goes Chevrolet, so goes General Motors.

The Chevrolet brand has always been central to GM's fortunes. It's the division with the largest sales volume, after all. But at times, Chevy has suffered, along with GM's other brands, from neglect, mismanagement, and the automotive equivalent of malnutrition—a shortage of competitive models, and models sitting without updates in showrooms well past their sell-by date.

To see the results, just look at some market-share numbers. Through the first half of this year, Chevrolet had a 12.3% slice of the U.S. auto market, according to Autodata. GM as a whole had a 19.7% share. GM has agreements in place to sell Saab, Hummer, and Saturn, and it is closing Pontiac. The brands that will remain with the new GM, besides Chevy, are Buick, GMC, and Cadillac. Together, those three accounted for just 4.4% market share.

Suffering from Brand Dilution
Today, Chevrolet markets six passenger cars, eight sport-utility vehicles and vans, and three pickup trucks. That's 17 distinct product lines, adding up to a little more than 12% market share. Toyota, not including Scion and Lexus, has 17 models, and 14.1% share. That doesn't speak well of Chevy's efficiency. And yet, so low are the expectations for GM that many people might think the gap between Chevy and Toyota was even larger.

„If GM had not diluted and shortchanged Chevy over the years to prop up brands like Saturn, Saab, and Hummer, it would be a more powerful brand right now," says Earl Hesterberg, CEO of Group 1 Automotive and former top marketing executive at Ford Motor, Chevy's nemesis. Group 1, a large automotive retailer, has five Chevy dealerships.

Indeed, through the years, billions went into marketing and designing cars and trucks for those ultimately unsuccessful GM brands. Budgets were stretched so tight that GM continued to sell essentially the same vehicles across its hungry brands to fill out their showrooms, with little money to substantially differentiate, say, a Saturn Outlook SUV from a GMC Acadia SUV. And in the case of those SUVs, Chevy didn't even get its version until more than a year after Saturn. The whole system left Chevy dealers scrambling to compete for customers against GM's own Saturn and GMC, instead of focusing on beating Ford and Toyota.

## Japanese Stumble with Trucks

For all its problems, though, Chevy emerges from bankruptcy with strengths that Asian carmakers can't match. „The reaction to the new Camaro has been very strong, and its pickup truck and large SUV remain at the top of those categories,“ says Hesterberg.

Indeed, Toyota, Honda, and Nissan have all stumbled in trying to sell full-size pickup trucks. Toyota sold just over 9,000 Sequoia SUVs in the first half of the year, whereas Chevy sold almost 50,000 Suburbans and Tahoes. Toyota has sold just 36,000 Tundra pickups in the first half, compared with Chevy's 150,000 Silverados. And neither Honda nor Toyota have competed much in the muscle-car category, where the nifty new Camaro plays.

What worries GM, though, is not so much the pickup and SUV business, where it will continue to battle Ford and to a lesser degree, Dodge. „Chevy's, and GM's, worry is how the company will perform in the passenger car and small SUV business, where Toyota has dominated Ford and Chevy,“ says Dan Gorrell of industry consultancy AutoStrategem. „That is where the U.S. market is going—more cars and small crossover SUVs.“

## Greater Focus on Chevy

Consider that in the first half of the year, Chevy sold only 76,000 Malibu sedans—its best reviewed and most acclaimed family car, designed to specifically take on Toyota's Camry—compared with 150,000 Camry/Solara models. And for years, Chevy has been barely competitive in the compact crossover segment with its Equinox SUV, which sold 25,000 in the past six months, compared with

62,000 Toyota RAV4 SUVs and 79,000 Honda CR-Vs. The all-new Equinox, launched earlier this year,
is substantially better than the old model, but it is an example of how Chevy has put up weak entries in important product segments. And it will take time for consumers to even notice some of its latest designs.

To change marketplace perceptions, Chevy may need to overhaul its marketing and advertising. GM's sales and marketing chief, Mark LaNeve, insists a remake is not in order, and that Chevy will benefit from GM's more focused attention. By spreading its dwindling resources the past few years across too many weak brands and dealers, GM shorted Chevy on necessary expenditures to design and sell new cars against Toyota and Ford.

Until the 2007 Malibu launch, for example, Chevy took on Toyota's Camry with only a smallish, generic sedan—the previous Malibu—that was a bigger hit at car-rental lots than dealer showrooms. When the new Malibu arrived, its annual marketing budget trailed Camry's by more than $100 million. Coming out of bankruptcy, LaNeve says, it will take Chevy at least three years to catch up to Toyota's marketing outlays.

## High Quality Marks

Through the years, Chevy has been responsible for some iconic advertising campaigns. It dominated pickup-truck culture during the 1980s and ‚90s with its „Like a Rock" campaign. Its cars were backed for years by „Heartbeat of America." Go back to the 1950s and the brand was easily identified through „Drive the USA in Your Chevrolet." For most of Chevy's history, ad agency Campbell-Ewald, of Warren, Mich., has handled its ads. But the work in recent years hasn't been so memorable. New GM CEO Fritz Henderson says: „There are lots of marketing questions we have to answer, and we will answer them soon." Some of GM's longtime ad agencies will have to fight in the coming months to keep their assignments.

An even more fundamental question needs asking, though: What is Chevy these days? It won't be a discount brand, says LaNeve. „But its chief benefit will be a great car or truck that everyone can afford to own." Put another way, LaNeve says, „Chevy needs to stand for the democratization of greatness in vehicle design, safety, and fuel economy, as well as quality." For a few years now, Chevy has been advertising „An American Revolution." The campaign has had some bright moments, such as John Mellencamp singing to the pickup crowd and Mary J. Blige crooning for cars. But on the whole, it has lacked the iconic quality of past efforts.

Chevy has been making legitimate strides in quality, but that has gone unnoticed by too many car buyers. In the most recent J.D. Power & Associates Initial Quality Study, which measures „things gone wrong" in the first 90 days of ownership, Chevy scored well above the industry average, at 103 problems per 100 vehicles. Toyota scored 101, putting the brands at a virtual tie.

Waiting for the Volt

„That kind of parity in quality is a recent phenomenon," says industry consultant Gorrell. Or, take another area where Detroit has often lagged, vehicle interiors. Only new models such as the Malibu, Equinox, and Tahoe have the kind of upgraded seat designs, instrument panels, and superior-grade plastics that send the right signals of „perceived quality" to the consumer. GM needs to make a habit of that. „It is going to take time and a lot of work to close the perception gap with consumers," Gorrell says.

It's encouraging that Chevy's new Camaro has drawn high praise from reviewers. That shows Detroit, for all its woes, still knows how to engage the public with hot sheet metal. What's unclear is whether GM can make the same connection through fuel economy. Much is riding on the Chevy Volt extended-range electric car, due to hit showrooms at the end of 2010. The car is said to go 40 miles on a battery charge before an onboard gas-powered motor kicks in to power the battery. The electric range alone could give buyers who drive fewer than 40 miles a day an endless number of gas-free driving days, an innovation that GM hopes will catapult the company's reputation, much as the Prius hybrid did for Toyota.

„It will be interesting to see what GM can make of Chevy when it focuses the talent that produces the industry's best pickups, SUVs, and a hot Camaro on turning out equally good small and midsize family cars," says independent marketing and design consultant Dennis Keene. If Chevy doesn't succeed, it's unlikely GM will, either.

# Case Studies: Rodenstock

German spectacles manufacturer Rodenstock is in dept by some € 350 m. Their turnaround strategy is simple, prudent and doable: Selling off licenses for brands not essential for core revenues and reinforcing the sales organization because selling more means more profits. The simple strategy is so convincing that banks have agreed to extend Rodenstock's credit line by another € 40 m. Who says strategies need to be complex and turnarounds need to be difficult?

# Case Studies: Bharti Airtel

Bharti Airtel has started showing early signs of the success of its strategy to tap the global telecom markets for growth. During the December 2010 quarter, its domestic business remained sluggish, but the African subsidiaries reported improved traction with a marginal increase in the revenue market share.

The turnaround in Bharti's operations in the 16 African countries has begun. It reported streamlining of operations and improved volumes in the region during the December quarter. Operating margin before depreciation expanded by over

100 basis points sequentially to 25%, reflecting rationalisation of costs.

This is expected to continue since in the next four quarters, the company will outsource peripheral services such as network management and customer care to other vendors. Bharti also reported a 7% sequential jump in the network minutes per subscriber (MoU) in Africa, which underlines the increasing awareness about the brand. By contrast, its Indian MoU slipped further during the quarter.

While stability is returning to its domestic operations, the growth in total minutes on the network again lagged behind subscriber growth. This means mere subscriber additions will no longer ensure volume growth. Its smaller peer, Idea Cellular , on the contrary, reported an equal growth in the two parameters.

It also shows that Bharti will have to keep a tight lid on operating costs to maintain margins in an environment of slow volume growth, which it has managed to do so far. Its margin on earnings before interest, depreciation, and tax sans one-time branding costs was stable at 33.8% on a sequential basis. The downward pressure on margins from hereon looks limited given the tapering decline in the domestic per minute revenue and rising profitability of its African venture.

In the near term, the scheduled launch of 3G services and mobile number portability, which became active since January, will decide the course for domestic telecom operators. To begin with, mobile operators have reported higher subscriber churn in the December quarter.

Both Bharti and Idea lost more subscribers on an average during the quarter than in any of the six previous quarters. This may further exacerbate once the number portability mechanism stabilises.

On the positive side, operators have reported gradual increase in the share of non-voice or value-added services (VAS). These account for more than 13% of the revenue for Bharti and Idea, higher than 11% a year ago. These services face lesser tariff pressure and, hence, cushion overall profitability. The upward trend in the share of these services in the total revenue pie is likely to continue after the advent of 3G services.

Analysts have maintained a ‚buy‘ call on Bharti. The company is likely to benefit from tapering competitive pressure on the domestic front and improving prospects overseas.

## Case Studies: Burger Edge

It has shades of Victor Kiam from the old Remington shaver advertisements.

„I liked it so much, I bought the company.“

But that's exactly what happened to Australians Issam and Enza Soubjaki.

And now they stand in the middle of an ambitious national expansion, while the rules governing the industry are in flux.

The Melbourne couple went to eat at a Burger Edge store in 2005, and liked it enough to throw in their corporate careers and become franchisees, and state master franchisee a year later.
But the franchise was struggling, despite the popularity of the gourmet burger concept.

„The other franchisees were saying to us ‚you guys need to take it (the entire company) over, otherwise we're out of here‚,“ Issam Soubjaki said.

After three attempts, and in the early days of the global financial crisis, they secured funding from three private investors.

They were then faced with the problem of how to turn the business around. Not an easy task in the fraught world of franchising.

„Sometimes you've got to cut off the arm to save the body,“ Mr Soubjaki said.

They closed three underperforming stores, rewrote the operations manual, and began the turnaround.

„They were tough decisions but in the end there was nothing we could do. We basically started again.“

The remaining franchisees were invited to dinner, during which the Soubjakis outlined their plans for the future.
That enabled them to sell the  concept of a new operations manual - the key document in a franchise which outlines procedures - as well as a redesign of the brand.

The strategy slowly but surely paid off, with an interstate expansion. From about 12 stores in Victoria, Queensland, and Sydney when they took over, Burger Edge now has 17, expanding into WA, and possibly in the near future South Australia.

Both the latter states have proposals before parliament to introduce franchising laws, which have been the source of much debate. But it does not put off the Soubjakis.

„The move into WA has been fantastic for us,“ he said.

„While Australian laws are probably amongst the toughest in the Western world, I'm all for (the state laws). They only serve to better the industry.

„The only reason a lot of this new legislation comes up is because franchisors have not treated franchising as a partnership.

„The franchisor must be prepared to put the franchisee ahead of themselves, becuase if the franchisee isn't making any money, the franchisor isn't making any money, whereas it doesn't work the other way around."

While the gourmet burger concept has gained popularity, it is also fiercely competitive. However, Enza Soubjaki said that was good for the industry.

„People are more aware of what's out there now, it's almost a staple like pasta and pizza and people expect more from their food," she said.

And not only Australian competition. Multinationals also have their eye on the country but the Soubjakis said they were prepared.

„At the end of the day it's welcome competition whether they're niche players, burger bars selling $50 burgers or whatever," Mr Soubjaki said.

„We're not growing too fast, we want to make sure our growth and development is sustainable. Financially we're debt free, cashflow positive, and we've got some provision for some acquisitions."

## Case Studies: AACo

AUSTRALIA'S largest beef cattle operation, Australian Agricultural Company Limited, is on the road to recovery, banking a modest net profit of $900,000 last year.

The profit is the result of a $54.6 million turnaround in net profit after tax, following losses of $53.7 million in 2009.
Chief executive David Farley put the progress down to improved productivity and efficiency on-farm and greater margins from the company's international meat business.
Lifting fertility, pregnancy rates, brandings and weight gain as well as improving management practices had been central to turning the company around, he said.
„It's step one of a three-year turnaround...and while modest, it is a profit of or above our expectations in a number of areas,'" Mr Farley said.
„Yes, we've delivered black ink, but more importantly, we've put the company in a good position for the years ahead."
AACo's herd increased 13 per cent to 577,144 and total production (due to weight gain and natural increases) lifted 26per cent to 64.2 million kilograms.
The Wagyu component of the business increased 30 per cent, making AACo one of the world's largest Wagyu fattening businesses.

„We're focused on growing and marketing animals where the best margins are. Wagyu is a substantial enterprise for AAco and for the Australian beef industry," Mr Farley said.

Adjusting the age and composition of the herd meant the company had the right mix to make the most of an excellent pasture base in 2011 and meet growing global demand, he added.

Key export destinations for boxed beef, namely Korea and the US, were showing positive signs while emerging markets across Asia continued to strengthen.

And, although weight restrictions on live export to Indonesia had forced the company to market cattle elsewhere, the impact on the bottom line had been minimal.

„The price per kilo from Darwin has actually been higher; the controlled weights have tightened supply to Indonesia and so the price has come up," Mr Farley said.

Vertical integration into processing - this year the company hopes to kill three in four of its own cattle, up from one in four last year is also high on the agenda with plans for an abattoir in Darwin underway.

## Case Studies: Reddit

Of all the storied properties owned by Condé Nast, which one is generating the most pageviews?

It's not Vanity Fair, it's not Vogue, and it's not GQ. It's none of the usual suspects. The answer is Reddit, the popular news aggregation/community, which is drumming up the most pageviews for Condé, with one billion served last month.

That's an incredible achievement for a site started by two guys in 2005. It's even more impressive when you consider it did it under the thumb of what could be considered a stodgy old-media company like Condé Nast.

Reddit is not just a successful website, it's also an example of how big companies can win in the tricky M&A game.

It would have been easy for Condé to crush Reddit, or starve it. And, truth be told, it almost did starve it. Reddit was complaining about being thin on resources because revenue was light last summer. But, Reddit was given room to figure out its own solutions, and it has grown from 280 million pageviews in July to 1 billion last month.

While Reddit revenue generation doesn't dwarf its corporate siblings like its pageviews do, it has started to figure out a business models that works. Yesterday it announced its generating enough revenue to hire four new hires new employees, with more to come. (For what it's worth, we recently heard Reddit ads are outperforming a number of its competitors.)

We asked Reddit's cofounder Alexis Ohanian how he felt about Conde. He left the site in late 2009, but says Reddit was „rather autonomous" under Condé. Ohanian says the Condé folks basically said, „You've done a good enough job in the last year and change to make us want to acquire you, just keep doing what you're doing to grow the site & community and we'll support you."

That sounds exactly right to us. Here's some lessons we take away from Reddit's success:

Buy early. Buying early is scary, because it's more risky. But what often happens is that if you wait too long, a site will grow so big that it really doesn't want to be bought anymore. A classic example is Yahoo, which had the opportunity to buy Google several times, but never did.

Leave them alone! The best acquisitions are often the ones that are supported by the acquiring company, but left mostly autonomous. A great example of that is YouTube, which has thrived under Google, but the best one is Amazon, which typically leaves the companies it acquires alone, like Zappos, Diapers.com, Woot and even IMDB.
Acquire founders with vision. Reddit's founders Steve Huffman and Alexis Ohanian stuck around working on Reddit until 2009. Most founders don't wait that long, and earnouts often don't mean much. What matters is founders who really really want to do something big, and are given the means to carry out that vision. Huffman and Ohanian kept working on Reddit because they clearly love Reddit. Another example is Andy Rubin at Google, who founded Android. Rubin clearly believes in the vision of the mobile ecosystem Android has created, and Google gave him the means to do just that.

What does this all mean? It means that big companies should really think of themselves as venture capitalists, because not all acquisitions will pay off, and you have to trust people. But Reddit-style acquisitions have the best potential for a big payoff.

## Case Studies: Garuda Airline - Turnaround By Customer Service

Garuda is a turnaround case but despite its challenges has gone public and managed to raise $ 350 m in a single day. How? Because the market and investors are fully confident that the airline will for some time to come completely outperform its competitors. How?
International travellers who dread standing in long lines at passport control may be interested in one innovative service Garuda offers: immigration staff on some of its flight routes. Does this mean passengers can bypass those lines? Yes.
„I have to say that this immigration onboard service that we give, I think it's the only service of any airline in the world in terms of giving full immigration onboard in the aircraft. So, passengers flying Garuda from Japan, Korea, Australia, and also from Europe, we're going to do the immigration on board," he said.
"For foreigners who would like to go for visa on arrival, we'll give you the visa in the plane itself and therefore once you arrived in Jakarta or Bali you don't have to queue anymore in immigration," he added.
As I said several times: There is always a better mousetrap to be built and there are

always new and better ways to improve on customer service. With better customer service you still can blow your competitors right out of the water. This story is the proof of the pudding.

## Case Studies: Auto Windscreens – A Textbook Example of Management Mistakes

On February 2011 Auto Windscreen went into administration. The firm collapsed on Monday leaving 1,100 staff fearing for their jobs.

 The administrator said: „As of today there is no money to pay staff for the 14 days' work they have done this month, nor is there money to pay them for their employment ongoing.

Apparently, there was neither a cash flow forecast or cash flow management in place nor any honest communication with the firm's stakeholders. But without recognizing and addressing the problem, it is impossible to develop a solution. The management of Auto Windscreens has done what countless managers of failing business do: Denying and ignoring the problem, putting off uncomfortable discussions and decisions and hoping that a miracle would make all the problems go away.
A business with a short term cycles such a the replacement of auto-windscreens where purchases are made quickly and payment is made rapidly cannot always predict the long term cash flow, but independent for any economic swings it seems that the number of cracking windscreens must still be a rather static and predicable number. Windscreens do not crack in higher or lower numbers because of the economy being up, down or sideward. So if the need for replacement widescreens hasn't declined, why went the organisation in trouble?

A statement from Deloitte suggested the company was in the midst of a turnaround plan, but that delays in implementing a new IT system and a surprise drop in revenue towards the end of last year had created a cash flow crisis.

Here you have it! It has been said a million times that in a turnaround situation time is f the essence and delays are not acceptable. A sudden drop in revenues can only have one out of two possible rot causes: Either costs could not cut down fast enough, which is likely and probably been worsened by the delay of a IT system providing management with financial information, or revenues haven't been developed fast enough, in which case management had omitted to develop and implement a strategic plan and it omitted to put in place any contingency plans for the case of a crisis, both fundamental jobs of the management.

„The company had been in extensive discussions with a large number of interested parties to provide the funding required recapitalising the business. However, before a recapitalisation could be agreed, the company received a winding up

petition from a large creditor and had notice from one of its major customers that it was terminating the contract," the statement from Deloitte said.
The large creditor was HM Revenue & Customs.

Again, if the worst case happened before a refinancing agreement could be found, the only logical conclusion is that such negotiations have started much too late and that communication was poor, because it is rare that creditors submit a winding up petition if they know that the company is about to close a deal on getting funded, enabling it to fully repay its debts. The fact that HMRC was a credit points to bad financial management as no provisions had been made to pay VAT or corporate taxes. Money owed to HMRC has been spent on other things.

The company has been heavily loss-making in recent years. Accounts for the year to the end of December 2009 showed pre-tax losses of £5m, an improvement on 2008's pre-tax loss of £18.6m. It recorded revenues of £99m in 2008 and £77m in 2009.

Again, this shows hat the problems were not new and there was time enough to do something, but management failed to take timely and radical action.

Its fate has proved strikingly similar to that of the British School of Motoring. Both were owned by Aviva, then sold to German firm Arques Industries. Arques sold both to its former executives, and both have now gone into administration.

This shows another classic: Employed managers are rarely successful entrepreneurs; otherwise they would not be employees in the first place. The fact that one has worked in a company does not constitute competence to run it succesfully when buying it. That's why so many management-buy-outs fail.

All these sad scenarios could have been avoided if managers had recognized where they lack of experience, had removed ego from the equation and called in the help of turnaround experts when it was still time.


## Case Studies: Harry & David

After years of slowing sales, missed opportunities and most recently, corporate implosions and finger-pointing, one of Oregon's most drooled-over brands appears headed toward bankruptcy.

The undoing of Harry & David Holdings Inc. has played out painfully over the past year at its headquarters in Medford, where the 101-year-old gourmet gift basket company is one of the region's top employers.

Two rounds of layoffs stripped away 200 jobs across its operations. A shake-up in the corporate office liquidated nearly two dozen of its top leaders, including long-time executive Bill Williams and, on Friday, it's CEO. Net income dropped over the past four years, dragged down in part by the millions in interest due on debt its parent company piled on after its 2004 purchase.

After a sluggish holiday season -- on which Harry & David heavily relies -- the company reported that net income in its second quarter ended Dec. 25 tanked 57 percent, to $13.8 million, compared with the same period the previous year. That left it short of promises made to lenders.

It never ceases to amaze me how the bleeding obvious is still ignored by so many companies who so easily could get out of trouble. Take this wonderful company with its great products for example. After 4 consecutive years of decreasing profits and a product that is predestined for international online sales, Harry & David still blame a sluggish holiday season. Why for crying out loud does the company not use its website to exploit the global gift market? There is more than one country that has a holiday season and last time I checked not all 189 export markets went through a sluggish holiday season simultaneously. Yet, out side the US, even outside Oregon Harry & David is barely visible. The only modest investment is to pimp up the website and Bob's your uncle. Not even the huge US Mexican community seems to be catered for: No Spanish page, no reference to Piñata, nada. I suggest they get themselves some marketing directors from Amazon and Ebay and learn how it's done.

„There can be no assurance that our efforts to obtain capital and restructure our obligations will be successful," the company said in the filing earlier this month, adding it had begun conversations with other creditors. „There are substantial doubts as to the Company's ability to continue as a going concern."

At least they are honest. But a company with a strong brand and a market that has a future will always attract some interest from investors. It can be sorted out by rightsizing, driving efficiency and lean production and improving marketing and sales, mainly into the international arena. If all fails, perhaps management should take to staff and offer them a buy-out, it would not be the first time and not the worst strategy for a viable business to be taken over by those with a key interest to keep it alive and with enough expertise, experience and motivation to make it work.

The company announced Friday that it had replaced Steven J. Heyer, brought on a year ago, with restructuring specialist Kay Hong who also will serve as interim chief executive.

I wonder why they brought in someone just a year ago when they replace him already. Either management exercises a poor selection process and poor judgement or they haven't been aware of the problems and brought in the wrong person as a result of ignorance – both is very bad.

Although Harry & David is a direct-marketer, selling its products through catalogues and online, it also has 122 retail and outlet stores, including this one in Woodburn. It's also a manufacturing company and a farming operation that owns thousands of orchard acres.

For a direct marketer, executing on global penetration sucks. But this can easily be rectified. As the most successful companies demonstrate, there is neither a reason nor benefit in owning retail stores. These overheads have to go. If it doesn't make enough profit, sell it of franchise it out. Manufacturing is a toxic asset in itself. In order to succesfully sell branded products, you don't need to manufacture them; if you are smart you outsource manufacturing, thus becoming flexible and more competitive.
Though it has deep roots in southern Oregon, the company named after its founder's sons has had three out-of-state owners since 1986.
New York buyout firm Wasserstein & Co. bought the Harry & David seven years ago for an estimated $260 million from Yamanouchi Pharmaceutical Co.

Soon after Wasserstein's purchase, Harry & David began filing its financial reports with the Securities and Exchange Commission in preparation for an initial public offering. Sales picked up, peaking at close to $600 million in 2007. And Harry & David's long-term debt grew from zero to around $200 million, an amount, Wasserstein's CEO Ellis Jones has said seemed appropriate for its performance.

Then, of course, the economy began to rot.

Harry & David's pear-stuffed gift baskets, Moose Munch, and spendy fruit-of-the-month clubs were seen as splurges and started getting crossed off cash-strapped consumers' gift lists. The public offering was postponed.
„Perishable foods and flower gifts goes straight to the heart of discretionary spending," said Mark Brohan, director of research for the trade magazine Internet Retailer. „Harry & David is not the only Web retailer that's either had problems or continues to have problems in terms of gaining back a solid base of e-commerce sales."
Of course – if you put all eggs in one basket (the US market) and something happens to this market, naturally you are stuffed.
Intelligent management would have diversified and spread risks and opportunities across international markets timely and answered a time of crisis with a range of new products exploiting the budget buyer. But resting on ones laurels and hoping the problem will go away and waiting for things to go back to normal was rarely a successful strategy.

## Beyond the catalogue

And though Harry & David is a direct-marketer, selling its goodies through catalogues and the Web, it's also a retailer with 122 full-price and outlet stores scattered across the country. Upping the ante, it's also a manufacturing company and a farming operation that owns thousands of orchard acres.

Several former employees pointed to those varied -- and at times conflicting -- missions that distracted the company from its goals and drained away its coffers.

Surprise surprise. And yet again an ignorant and egomaniac management ignores the advice of those who must know, even it is the bleeding obvious.

Looking for a quick fix to boost sales, the company bought Wolferman's, another direct-marketing company that sold English muffins and breakfast treats, for $22.8 million in January 2008. Later that summer, it bought Cushman's Fruit Co., a direct-marketer of citrus products, for $8.5 million.

Another nonsense classic gambit of textbook management mistakes: What on earth is the fix in buying additional products to sell, as long as you struggle to sell the ones you already have on your plate? How would more of the same solve your problem? When you can't get a business going, what makes you think you get the same business going when you add another $ 23 to your problem? The problem doesn't change, it simply becomes bigger. But greed and ego never fails to eat common sense.

„Frankly, I wonder how many people are buying English muffins online," said Renee Fellman, a Portland-based turnaround executive.

Dead right she is.

An ailing company may attempt an acquisition to survive, she said, or it may roll out a price increase or hire of a new leader.

„In the case of Harry & David," she said, „They have done all of those things."

Wasserstein fired Williams a year ago and brought in Heyer, a former CEO of Starwood Hotels & Resorts Worldwide Inc., and president and chief operating officer of Turner Broadcasting System Inc.

In a video filmed at a private equity conference last November, Heyer joins Wasserstein's Jones as he described one of the main issues Harry & David had faced.

People only think of the company for gifts and, in particular, at the holidays. The job, Jones said, is to push customers to buy Harry & David's products year-round and ultimately, for themselves.

„We just did not have in place the team with the creativity and imagination to execute it," Jones said.

Dead right he was.

## Failed effort

One of Heyer's first initiatives was to roll out holiday pop-up stores.

„Before I even arrived, I knew we had to do pop-up stores," he said in the video, „we needed to reintroduce the company to America. ... We have taken the heritage of the company and contemporized it."

Not everyone was impressed

In late January, several analysts told the industry publication Multichannel Merchant that Harry & David's redesign lacked, well, creativity.
„It looks like management there was looking at the numbers, and no one was plugged into the merchandising," Tony Cox, president of the 5th Food Group consulting firm, told the trade publication. „They threw the baby out with bath water, and I'll bet its core customers didn't respond."
In a recent financial filing, Heyer said this year's holiday season fell „well below expectations," even though his company had been able to attract new customers, re-engage old ones and grow its Web traffic.
The criticism even piled up on Harry & David's own Facebook page, just below the pictures of its perfectly ripened pears and treat-stuffed baskets.
Last weekend, customer Kellie Kirk wrote, „Never got my replacement pears as promised. Done with Harry and David." A few hours earlier, Lisa N. Horace Jung had written, „... half our order came bruised, discoloured, and some were mouldy.... there was enough mould there that we could started our own pharmacy!"

There is simply no excuse for bad customer service. A company who is not able to treat it's customer in a professional way can as well shoot itself. At least that way death comes faster and more painless.


# Case Studies: Tin Star

Like a lot of great ideas, the concept of Tin Star Sizzle, Smoke and Salsa was great, but not perfect, out of the box. Founder Rich Hicks' goal started out simple in 1999: elevate tacos, quesadillas, soups and salads from the uninspiring taqueria to an attractive fast casual platform that would appeal to mainstream audiences.
To grow his concept, he drew the adoration and investment dollars of multiple franchisees, who signed on to scatter Tin Stars across the American landscape. But, that growth strategy was not only short-lived, but nearly tragic for the small chain.
From its Plano, Texas, base of five stores, it couldn't adequately support far-flung units in Colorado, Florida, Indiana, Nebraska, Nevada and South Carolina, and simply lacked the manpower to really help franchisees, said Greg Cutchall. Cutchall is the owner of Cutchall Management, a multi-concept franchisee of Sonic, Paradise Bakery, Famous Dave's, Rock Bottom Restaurant and Tin Star units.
"That was a big stumble for Tin Star," he said. Challenging store-level execution complicated things as well. "As fabulous as the food is, it's not your typical fast-casual easy execution. And that made things worse.
By 2006, Hicks had created a second concept called Mooyah Burgers, and began seeking a buyer for Tin Star. He found one in Mike Rangel, a senior vice president and chief operations officer for the parent company of Lone Star Steakhouse and Texas Land and Cattle Steakhouse. A Dallas resident and fan of Tin Star, Rangel wanted to acquire a restaurant company and go out on his own, and he discussed

a buyout with Hicks.

The deal was consummated for an unreported sum in 2008—just as the American economy was hitting the skids. At the time, there were three corporate stores and five franchises, about half the unit count at the company's peak.

"I definitely wouldn't say I didn't have some buyer's remorse," Rangel said, laughing. The industry veteran knew there were tough times ahead, but he believed he was well-enough capitalized to push Tin Star forward, albeit in small steps. "We went pretty slow at first to make sure we understood exactly what we bought and what needed to be changed. The concept and the food were right, but we had to focus on operations and create some brand awareness."

## A reorganization

Rangel decided to stop franchising Tin Star until a solid strategy was developed to do so.

"Every location outside of Texas except for one closed within 18 months of opening. We knew that part of the problem was in how spread out the earlier restaurants and we weren't repeating that," he said.

Rangel's team focused first on the basics of food consistency, restaurant cleanliness and retraining employees. Then came a name change. Tin Star Sizzle, Smoke and Salsa didn't describe the concept's core attributes on its own, he said, and so the new moniker of Tin Star Taco Bar soon followed.

Like nearly every other restaurant concept, Tin Star's flagging sales in the recession forced Rangel's team to be creative with marketing. New efforts using Twitter, Facebook and Foursquare began, and fans and followers were encouraged to post pictures on Tin Star's Taco Blog.

"We now do a quarterly food program where we roll out new tacos, enchiladas and salads, and we've had guests help us name them," he said. "Social media has become a great way to engage with our fans and brand advocates."

Newly named items include the Brisky Business and The Commander tacos.

Cutchall is pleased with Rangel's leadership and the direction Tin Star is headed. As of last year, Tin Star returned to franchising and added two units. An 11th store is slated to open in February, and a few others could follow this year.

"I believe they've got the right guys at the helm now, and they've been very supportive to franchisees when we needed them," Cutchall said. "They're very hands-on. The previous owners were great visionaries, but not maybe as operationally focused as the new group."

Unlike Hicks, Rangel is determined to grow the company from Dallas outward first, then to neighboring Texas cities followed by moves to neighboring states. Developing greater market concentration will boost brand recognition and make advertising buys more affordable. Plus, with a host of similar concepts just starting up in existing Tin Star markets, Rangel knows he needs to win the fan battle quickly.

"We've had six competitors open up around us within the last 15 months," Rangel said. "But I believe that if we stay true to our values and the integrity of the brand, we can do very well."

Cutchall believes Tin Star's unique market position on the upper end of the fast casual range (check average is $9.40, and each outlet serves margaritas and beer) will help it succeed against even better-known burrito concepts. The menu also features a diversified offering of cheeseburger tacos, quesadillas, gourmet tacos and entrees such as the Fire Grilled Salmon.

## Case Studies: Toll Road Trucking[1]

On a recent weekday afternoon in Bridgewater, Mass., USA, business is bust-ling at Toll Road Trucking. Bus drivers pull off North Bedford Road and into the company's lot with their vehicles. Inside the offices, phones are ringing, and owner Scott Burgess is writing checks to contract workers.
In the back shops, workers are welding, doing brake work and performing other maintenance on clients' trucks.
It's hard to imagine that just three years ago, this business was struggling to stay afloat.
Under Burgess' watch, the company has come back from the brink, building from one employee in 2008 to 16 now and annual revenue of about $2 million, accor-ding to Burgess. Now Toll Road has customers that include Horizon Beverages, National Grid, two state colleges and several towns' departments of public works. Toll Road Truck and Trailer Corp. was founded in 1964 by Robin „Red" Brittain, an ex-Marine and dedicated Rotary Club member. Brittain manufactured and sold truck parts and performed maintenance on trucks as well, growing Toll Road into a mammoth company with two Massachusetts locations and one in Pennsyl-vania. At its peak in the 1980s, Toll Road was a $7 million business, Burgess said. But when Brittain's health started deteriorating in the 1990s, the company deteri-orated as well. The 10-foot by 10-foot shack where he kept his office was disorga-nized and unwelcoming to clients, Burgess said. In addition, Red did not change his business practices with the times. Often, he would give his clients a verbal estimate of the price, and work would not be completed on any agreed-upon timetable.
„Cities and towns can't work that way," Burgess said. „They need written quotes and they need to know when things will get done.
„The business dwindled down to virtually nothing in 2008," Burgess added.
At that point, Burgess, who had previously owned and operated a construction company, purchased Toll Road for $100,000 and the 4.5 acres of land Brittain was renting for $1 million.
„We started to reconstruct the business," Burgess said. He was determined to re-turn the company to its heyday.
Burgess updated the computer system to automate more of the business. He clea-ned up the yard and office space, adding heat and electricity to make it more welcoming. He also turned the tiny work shack into a 16,000-square-foot facility for manufacturing and repairs. The company gained clients, hired workers and started making money.

„I think it was pretty much proving ourselves," Burgess said.

Rocky DeSimone III, who does sales for the business, has another take on their success, saying that Burgess brought a construction company outlook to trucking. „He's here at six in the morning, nine at night. It's kind of the ‚get it done at any cost' mentality," he said.

The long hours are attractive to landscapers and other businesses that work nontraditional hours, because Toll Road is available to work on their equipment when it won't interfere with getting their job done.

Burgess bought up an additional 6.5 acres adjacent to the business and has visions for putting a 30,000-square-foot facility on the premises. He is also considering doing component manufacturing to return the company to its roots.

Interestingly enough in this economy, one of Toll Road's biggest challenges is finding sufficient employees.

„One of the toughest things we're finding is trying to get the right help," Burgess said. They are looking for welders and people who can do sheet metal work, wiring and other trades. These skills are hard to come by these days, he said.

„Immediately we have at least three openings — for the right person," Burgess said. „If and when the expansion comes through it could be upwards of 25 people."

DeSimone said that truck repair and manufacturing is a subset of automotive jobs, which can be more dangerous and less glamorous. In addition, it is an industry in which workers often learn on the job in an apprentice-type arrangement, but it can take years before they have the knowledge to be profitable for a business.

„There's no school to go to and learn what we do," DeSimone said.

Still, needing to add personnel faster than Burgess can find them is not the worst problem a business can have. It is a sign of a company well on its way to regaining its glory days.

„We took it from the ashes and brought it back," Burgess said.

## Case Studies: Lyrtech Inc.

MONTREAL – Quebec City's Lyrtech Inc., which specializes in digital signal processing technology, said it gained sharply from 2010 year's turnaround.

"The recovery translated into high-margin development contracts for Lyrtech, including many with associated production orders," CEO Louis Bélanger said. "The strong demand for our products and the recent streamlining of activities have helped us to improve our operating performance."

Sales of equipment to network and wireless communications, audio and video processing firms worldwide, especially China, India and Japan, were up 19 per cent, to $8.6 million, in 2010. The net loss was reduced to $900,000 in 2010 from $1.9 million in 2009.

Selling and marketing expense dropped 15 per cent as the company switched to dealing with distributors from agents, but financial expense increased because of the higher turnover financed mostly through factoring. Research spending (net of tax credits) was $1.3 million, up from $1.1 million in 2009.

There is a great deal of sound turnaround expertise contained in this short article, let's analyse it:

1. The company pursued high-margin contracts rather than pushing mere volume. This is a great strategy as so many turnaround managers focus purely onto bringing costs down but neglect tod rive sales – high profit sales that is.
2. "Strong demand" for its products suggests that the company kept developing and improving it's products, it's services and it's value proposition, corner stones without there would be no demand, and without demand there can be no sales.
3. "Streamlining" activities is another classic "Do". The smart application of Lean Six Sigma leads to reduced waste and reduce costs and improved performance, which in turn often leads to improved revenues – and so it did in this textbook example.
4. While so many companies seem to complacently remain within their traditional but fading markets, Lyrtech is selling exactly where it should be selling to: To the vast emerging markets of China, India and Japan, and their clever strategy is mirrored by its well deserved revenue growth.
5. Last but not least it achieved higher sales with less sales and marketing expense, so one can only applaud to Mr. Bélanger for doing a first-class turnaround management job.

# Turnaround: How Long Does It Take?

Sainsbury has overtaken Asda as Britain's second-largest supermarket, seven years after it lost the position. Sainsbury's share of customer grocery spending rose from 16.3 % to 16.6 % during the four weeks to December 26 2010, Asda's share dipped from 16.6 % to 16.5 %. Not much you might say, but just like in a 100 meter race, it's about being first, second and third, not about the distance between the competitors.

The pivotal movement comes 15 years after Sainsbury's lost its position as Britain's biggest grocer to Tesco, as it failed to match its arch-rival in opening out-of-town space and moving into non-food categories during the late Nineties and early Noughties.

Justin King, Sainsbury's CEO, who was appointed to turn around the company in 2004. Asda consistently lost market share to its competitors last year. In an effort to jolt its performance, it bought Netto's British stores in a deal that is expected to be formally approved soon. However, growing or even turning around a company by acquisition is not the best strategy: More than half of all M&A's eventually fail, so it's a big risk, and if a company needs' to buy another company because it cannot grow or sustain its profit on its own, it means that something is fundamentally wrong with it, and that problem won't go away by acquiring more of the same: When you can't sort out the problems of your existing organisation, what makes you believe that piling more on the same heap will somehow solve your management problem?

Last week Asda it embarked on an aggressive guarantee to be 10 % cheaper than its four largest rivals, another ill strategy, because against the believe of CEO's, it is never about price. If it was about price only, why is Tesco the largest supermarket and not Aldi? If it price only, why was it Woolworth that became the first victim in the recession? Why are internet sales up? It costs more to have your supermarket deliver the goods into your home than going shopping there. Why do people top-up at their local "convenience" store? Observe the name – big hint! Consumers don't go shopping in Pound-stores usually; they go shopping where it is convenient and pleasurable.

It would be a far more profitable strategy to drive customer service and outperform competitors by blowing away consumers. Why not have bagging and carrying services at the check outs as standard? Why not simply manning all the check outs instead setting up a big number of them to pretend speed of check-out, and then deliberately manning 50 % of them to artificially increase dwell time so consumer buy more? Why not following US examples and offer complimentary water and coffee? More service stations such as shoe-shine, dry cleaning, key cutting, better quality products and shopping experience, THAT would attract more customers, drive spending and outperform competitors. If you don't believe it, check out the world's largest superstore Stew Leonard's, it is one single store with 2.000 staff and $ 300 million turnover, mind you one store that is, not a chain. Then let's talk again about the alleged importance of "price is everything".

So, back to our question "How long does a turnaround take?" In the case of

Sainsbury's it took 7 years but of course that's a period of time companies in financial dire straights cannot afford. The larger the organisation the longer it takes but a real fire fighting turnaround manager usually needs to demonstrate tangible results in less than 9 months.

# Turnaround Communication: The Turnaround of Compaq

‚It's been a learning experience for me', says Ben Rosen. ‚The difference one person can make to a large organisation.' He's referring to Eckhard Pfeiffer, the chief executive of Compaq Computer - and the tribute is especially remarkable, coming from a man of Rosen's immense experience as a venture capitalist. Pfeiffer proved himself the ‚right leader' for a company in deep trouble by overcoming deep corporate resistance to a sea-change in policy: and Rosen has no doubt about the key to this success.

‚The more you go down the organisation', says Rosen, ‚the more of a job it is to get people to change. You really have to communicate'. A top executive, Gian Carlo Bisone, echoes this view. ‚Eckhard really shared with us. There were a lot of sceptics'.

Today a management communication group of 150-200 people from all over Compaq's world meet monthly to hear Pfeiffer explain his strategy in ‚very clear terms', to question him, and to carry the message back home. During Compaq's crisis, these meetings were weekly.
The gravity of that crisis in 1991 can't be exaggerated. Passing through general recession is testing enough. But having its own private recession in the midst of general gloom gave Compaq one of the sharpest falls from grace of any major company. Its first-ever quarterly loss in April-June 1991, however, has been followed by recovery and resurgence swifter and fuller than has ever been made in any industry. Cutting jobs and costs was ‚necessary, but not sufficient' to achieve this, says Rosen. The real driving force behind an astounding turnaround was a complete remaking of strategy.

The previous strategy had achieved equally extraordinary success. Compaq had passed $2 billion of world-wide sales faster than any company in history by concentrating on the higher-priced end of the personal computer market. By end-1990 there were one or two unfavourable trends - ‚particularly the increase in market share of companies selling PCs on price'. But any fears expressed in the boardroom were ‚allayed by management'. Any business always has problems at any time - and at first nobody suspected that the rise of the cut-price clones heralded fundamental change.

The first Compaq officer to spot that sea-change was Rosen himself. His special position as non-executive chairman, which derives from the role of his venture capital firm, Sevin Rosen, in Compaq's genesis, played a crucial part in its rebirth. Unusually, the small board (eight members) includes only one executive: the CEO. The board's ability to take an independent view is far stronger than in the typical company, where executives in general, and the CEO in particular, dominate the board.

In what he saw as Compaq's looming crisis, Rosen felt free to circumvent the CEO (and principal founder), Rod Canion, by sponsoring an independent, two-man mission to discover how quickly and cheaply the company could produce a counter to the clones. The time and cost were both much lower than planned by Canion (who knew nothing about the mission). Though ,brilliant and extremely competent', the CEO was unwilling to change the strategy and systems that had served Compaq and himself so well. Canion had to leave - and four other corporate officers went too.

Before Canion's fall, Pfeiffer, a German by nationality, had been transferred from Europe, where his build-up of Compaq had contributed vitally to group growth. Born in 1941, Pfeiffer spent 20 years with Texas Instruments, ending in top jobs in corporate marketing and marketing strategy. He masterminded Compaq's international expansion after joining the original executive team in 1983. Remarkably, he is the only member of that 13-man group who is still with the company.

That fact is evidence in itself of the unprecedented volatility of this industry. The timing of Pfeiffer's move to Houston from Munich was fortuitous: the head of North American operations had retired young to breed horses. Pfeiffer (who has an American MBA) was thus on the spot, serving as chief operating officer, when the need arrived to replace Canion - ousted, at a now-famous, 14-hour board meeting, on 24 October 1991. The day before, the first-ever redundancies had been announced, and a meeting with Wall Street investment analysts was scheduled for two weeks later.

There wasn't ,much time to provide the answer' to Wall Street's legitimate questioning: in Pfeiffer's words, ,Would Compaq go down the tube or would he bring about change?' The pressure of external communication, though, enforced a key element in tackling any crisis: speed of decision. The two weeks was all it took for Pfeiffer and Co. to redesign Compaq from top to bottom. Their aim wasn't short-term salvation, however, but long-term success.
Like speed, opting for a growth strategy was crucial. Cut costs when sales are static or falling, and you may eliminate losses. Cut costs when sales are rising, though, and you get a double-whammy: in two years, sales per employee doubled to 1993's huge $716,000. That year's profit levels (narrowly a record at $462 million) were left far behind in the next nine months; net income doubled on a 52% sales increase. Pfeiffer was as surprised as anybody by the turnaround's speed and scale: but both flowed directly from that fortnight of compressed, total rethinking.

What he communicated to the analysts ,was exactly what was implemented all the way through today'. Crisis had come about because Compaq, blinded by vast success, was locked into its ‚financial model'. That was based on lowering prices by somewhat less than rapidly falling unit costs and thus maintaining nice, fat gross margins: 45%. Its chosen criteria showed well in the six months to March 1991; so Compaq was ‚not attentive enough to other signals' - notably that rising market share of rivals like Dell and the myriad smaller IBM clones.

Concentrating on the high end, Compaq insouciantly became the high-cost producer. The consequent crisis was fully shared by the dealers on whom it depended. They, too, badly needed communication and reassurance. At the nadir, ‚the world around us', says Pfeiffer, ‚was so confused, in doubt, lost'. The dealers, unable to sell the over-priced Compaq lines, asked, ‚what do you want us to do?'. The only answer was to slash prices on ‚high-cost products to keep our customers' while forcing through the foundation of Pfeiffer's new Compaq: an entry-level, low-margin line, designed to sell profitably at prices that matched the low-cost competitors, and acting as the base of a vastly extended range.

Pfeiffer told the analysts that, in addition to its traditional high-end products, Compaq ‚would meet all other product requirements'. That positioning and the creation of ‚low cost capability' would ‚expand our reach into all sectors', and enable Compaq to be ‚fiercely competitive'. That ‚fiercely' gave the rethinkers some pause, but Pfeiffer used it all the same. True, it was the antithesis of Compaq's previous comfortable stance. But Pfeiffer's top team had exposed that stance's weakness by ‚a very comprehensive analysis of what went wrong, putting aside all denials and all excuses'.

That's a third key to the perfect turnaround: (1) speed, (2) growth strategy (3) soul-searching, or ‚interior communication', which, like all communication, depends on absolute honesty. Pfeiffer's group didn't look at the obvious symptoms of failure, but at ‚the root causes' of weakness: and strength. The question ‚What are our strengths?' came up with some encouraging answers. They included ‚all that product and engineering capability, global manufacturing and presence, brand recognition and loyalty', plus a strong cultural base - a ‚can-do attitude'.

Pfeiffer's task was to ‚build on and leverage' these strengths. Here he faced an immediate, urgent and searching test in the new, low-priced line. Ben Rosen wanted the life-saver before the first quarter-end of 1992. That urgency left Pfeiffer with no option but to break with Compaq's past: an independent business unit (Project Ruby) was set up, well away from other activities on Compaq's glass and steel campus in Houston. ‚One champion, completely tuned in' was given a free hand to pick his own team.

Richard Swingle was told to ‚show the way to the lowest cost in the industry, whatever it takes'. As Pfeiffer says, the rush to end-March shipment ‚almost precluded the obvious step of putting engineers to work' and thus getting imprisoned in the company's old mind-set. So ‚we pursued OEM sourcing', buying-in all components. Only five or six weeks into the crash project, though, a fundamental conundrum appeared. Could the far cheaper PC still be called a Compaq?

The team, which didn't think so, adopted a brightly coloured design that looked neither like a Compaq nor anything else on the market: but Pfeiffer was deeply concerned about the customers. A fundamental difference between the old and new Compaq, according to Rosen, is another vital aspect of communication: ‚we changed the whole customer satisfaction approach. Before, we never talked to customers.‘ When Pfeiffer initiated this dialogue, major buyers told him what they wanted: ‚Do what you're doing, only competitively, and give us what we've been asking for‘.

They didn't expect a clone from Compaq; and how could a non-Compaq Compaq fit the strategy of building on the corporate strengths? Shortly before Christmas, Pfeiffer was presented with a batch of component purchase orders to sign: but ‚I just couldn't do it‘. On the flight back home to Munich, intuition and analysis alike convinced Pfeiffer that the planned product ‚wouldn't save our factories and our employment base‘. At the risk of de-motivating the team, he ‚switched gears‘. The object was still a low-cost, low-price PC, but within a range covering all performance points all the way to the top, where Compaq had pioneered client-servers for networks.

Pfeiffer had to disappoint Rosen on time: the new PCs couldn't appear until 15 June. Before that, though, main dealer reaction, especially to a vague price of ‚under $1000‘, was ecstatic. When the ProLinea finally appeared, at $900, it was Pfeiffer's turn for ecstacy. A flood of orders ushered in ‚a new era‘ and in many ways a new Compaq. The cost base tumbled down as output shot up: the company was on its way to producing at five times the 1991 rate in the same square footage with the same number of people, at costs down amazingly from 31% of revenues to 13.5%.

Achievement of this order, visible to everybody, is powerful communication in and of itself. The scepticism mentioned by Gian Carlo Bisone could hardly survive this explosion of efficiency. Anyway, it was effectively lanced by the extension of Compaq's severance programme (needed initially to reduce labour costs) to volunteers. Those uncomfortable with the new era departed - and ‚within six to eight weeks the number of sceptics fell pretty much to zero‘. That echoes the famous Montgomery communication exercise on taking over the Eighth Army: ‚If anyone thinks it [beating Rommel] can't be done, let him go at once.‘

Those who stayed had the excitement of ‚almost impossible‘ goals - and often exceeded them. One member of Project Ruby, Bill Ramsey, was told to drive down material costs by no less than 30%: and to prove that what became the ProLinea could be made in-house, rather than the Far East. That was ‚very important‘. Had the team not proved ‚that we could build at a competitive price internally‘, the work would have gone off-shore, and the new Compaq might have been still-born. As it was, ‚what we learnt ran across the company‘ - another exercise in practical communication.

So was Pfeiffer's choice of goal. Often vision and mission statements are inspiring, but insufficient - not precise enough to act as target and spur. That didn't apply to Pfeiffer's commitment to become world leader in personal computers in 1996. His ambition once sounded wildly optimistic for a company which, at its previous peak of profits, trailed IBM by three-to-one. The trebling of market share since then, though, took Compaq into the lead, at least temporarily, in 1994 - two years ahead of a schedule that now looks highly conservative.

Britain was first to meet the original turnaround target. The whole of Europe followed, then America. Whether or not this lead holds in 1995, beyond primacy lies the aim of building what Pfeiffer calls ‚a significant leadership position‘ - much larger than the odd percentage point. A business, says Rosen, that ‚was a portable company, then a PC company‘ has plainly moved into a new zone; it ‚is now a computer company‘, capable of meeting any needs from the fast-growing home market to the corporate territory once occupied exclusively by mainframes - mostly from IBM.

Thse aren't opportunities that could have been taken with equal speed and success under a founding regime which, in only ten years, had become more conservative, ‚less experimental‘. But despite Pfeiffer's remarkable success, the crisis that might have laid Compaq low leaves a crucial question. Could it recur? Rosen's answer is an unequivocal Yes. He adds, however, that ‚having been through it once, we're less likely to get complacent. We're much more on guard, much more willing to make changes‘.

The dangers of getting smug, arrogant and complacent must increase when a company is ‚riding high, as we are now‘. But Rosen points to a difference which could well prove to be a saving grace. What happens if performance - in the market place, say - diverges from plan? In the past, dishonest interior communication held sway: ‚If we saw differentials we didn't like, we would explain them away‘. Two little words almost always betray this common and pernicious failure of inner strength: ‚yes, but.‘

For instance, Canion explained away (‚yes, but‘) IBM's success in beating Compaq to the punch with a PC using Intel's 486 microprocessor: yes, IBM announced first, but when the chip came into full production, Compaq quickly took the market lead. ‚Now‘, says Rosen, ‚we try to avoid denials‘ - and to act swiftly to remove differentials and their root causes. IBM played a more general role in Compaq's old culture of denial: ‚We denied that we had any other competitor‘.

That's utterly changed since 1992, when Compaq removed the price umbrella that used to protect the clones. They have been left with ‚little to sell on‘, which explains much of Compaq's sales surge. Stealing from the clones has helped make Compaq easily the ‚fastest-growing computer company‘. As Rosen wryly points out, expanding sales in 1993 by 75% from a $4 billion base was ‚non-trivial‘. The ‚most formidable competitor prospectively‘, though, remains the old enemy: IBM.

The latter's ‚costs are still high‘, however, ‚which will limit what they can do‘. Compaq's sales per employee are approaching four times those of IBM. The giant is struggling with a culture change that has already taken several years, compared to the nine months or so which remade Compaq. The IBM PC Company has been striving through technological and management upheavals to make a profit from an allegedly ‚unmanageable‘ proliferation of models. Pfeiffer's range is just as broad, though with more commonality. ‚It is manageable‘, he says unemotionally. ‚But you need a whole new set of tools and processes‘.

That's the ‚can-do‘ culture at work. Provided that it keeps low-cost, low-price leadership, Compaq looks more vulnerable to industrial and economic downturn than any competitive threat - though, as Pfeiffer says, you can't exclude wrong products (as Compaq found recently with a line of laser printers that was rapidly axed). The most serious threat, though, lies within. ‚You always run the risk of „we have it made - we're unbeatable"‘, says Pfeiffer.

That complacency was at the root of the crisis. To prevent a recurrence, the five pillars of the turnaround triumph will be required continuously: speed, a strategy of growth, focus, the decisive ‚can-do culture‘ (even Pfeiffer hadn't thought Compaq could ‚execute so well, with so broad and enthusiastic an acceptance‘) - and ‚intense communication‘, in Pfeiffer's own phrase. Much of the excellence in execution and acceptance, along with the stunning speed and smashing success of the turnaround, can be attributed to that intensity. The ace communicator adds a powerful thought about communication: ‚In hindsight, it's never enough.‘

Key learning points about information and communication in a turnaround:

- Tell the staff the reasons why the decision has been made. If you didn't make the decision, say so. Also, if you don't know who did it, find out whose direction it was and make sure your information is correct. Doubts and ambiguities make matters worse.
- Remind your team / department what the goals and objectives are and reassure them that these can still be met. If for some reason (such as the decision that has just been taken) these objectives can't be met, re-adjust the targets so that they are achievable.
- Let them know how sorry you are about how things have worked out. If compensation is an option, tell them what it is. Maybe you won't be increasing their salaries this year but you can allow them to go home an hour earlier on Friday afternoons.
- For a morale boost, try to give them something they can put their energy in to. If they are good at organising events, offer them the opportunity to raise funds for their pet charity – doing a fun run or similar.
- If the bad news you have to communicate is that you have had to sack one of their colleagues, you must do so immediately after the dismissed person has left the building.

# Turnaround Performance Management: Why Turnaround Always Means Change

Who can handle the crisis management role? This is a predicament. Clear thinking must prevail and a special set of skills must be applied.

If there is a qualified leader within the company, then delegate the job of turnaround to that person—and provide proper support. If there is not a qualified leader in the company, and there usually isn't, don't hesitate to go outside to locate a professional at this type of work. The answer often resides outside the company in the form of a turnaround specialist.

But what guides the decision?

Different companies need different kinds of leaders. The CEO that managed the company while it got into trouble probably doesn't have the skills to doctor it back to health. And conversely, the CEO that can bring a troubled company from the brink of failure may not have the skills to manage long-term, day-to-day operations.

Let's put the leadership role into proper perspective. Leadership requirements differ between those for healthy, growing companies and for those in a troubled situation. Compare the differences in our chart.

| SKILL | STABLE OR GROWTH SCENARIO | TROUBLED OR TURNAROUND SITUATION |
|---|---|---|
| Focus | On Objectives | On Survival, Action On Problem Solving |
| Decision Making | Deliberate | Decisive, Immediate |
| Authority | Delegate | Direct Involvement |
| People | Develop | Recruit Talent Communications |
| Respected For: | Management Reputation | Financial Credibility |
| Known For: | Consistency | Ability to shift gears |

Differences in style are a key to success, in either situation. In the stable or growth scenario, team building and coaching are the buzzwords. But in the initial crisis and subsequent turnaround situation, time is an enemy. Decisive action is required.

The focus is dramatically different. This is one reason why the troubled environment is so foreign to many managers, and hence, the difficulty finding qualified talent from within the company. The stable environment allows for mistakes and longer lead cycles to achieve goals. Troubled companies have primarily one goal—to survive and get well. If the symptoms persist with no cure, the patient can die.

Just as with a critical patient, the immediate focus at a troubled company should be on action—make something happen. The first goal in an absolute crisis is to stabilize and buy time. After calming the waters, take a reading on where things stand—which is normally still. Look for changes in ratios and trends to determine what is, or more importantly, what is not going on in the business.

Following this diagnostic stage, the transition can begin towards a turnaround. Most importantly, the leader needs to get things moving again. Movement must occur in two areas—On the Volume In (revenue/sales) side, look at where and how revenue is generated. Is it from existing customers and contracts or new business? Most importantly, keep it coming in. On the Volume Out (throughput/production) side, look at getting the product or service 'out the door'. How else can you bill for it?

Companies often get into trouble because management procrastinates when it comes to making decisions. If the decision is made by default, it is akin to making no decision at all. Much of that early, and overall, survival also depends upon being immediate—upon making decisions in a timely manner. Even a wrong decision means movement and direction. If a decision turns out to be wrong, change it, but keep things moving.

Time is also an important dimension when it comes to authority. In a stable company, there is time to delegate and nurture the growth of the management team; time to work on long-term issues and projects. In the troubled situation delegating takes on a different role. Managers must be held accountable not only for performance, but for timely results.

In a troubled situation, the decision-maker must get directly involved. It is hard to worry about the long-term future when there may not be one. The leader is pressed closer to the immediacy of the day-to-day operations. If you want action, request a decision ... or make one.

In a stable situation there is time to develop talent. But at a troubled firm, you must exploit the talents of those who can perform and recruit the talent that is lacking. It means building a permanent management team that can bring the company back to health—and add value to the company.

Communication is critical—with everyone who has a stake in the company's success. Talk to employees, but more importantly, listen to what they have to say. Be assured, they know when problems exist.

What message are you sending? Remember, what is not said is often more destructive than what is. Unnatural actions or behavior, such as 'closed door meetings,' will most certainly set off the rumor mill. People need to know or they're left to their own imaginations—and that is always worse.

Equally important, level with people—then get the stay versus go decision. To address the issues in a forthright manner is no guarantee that you will keep everyone, or that everyone will believe what has been said. But to not communicate what is going on is a lack of leadership, so don't be surprised when employees don't do what you want them to.

Turnaround leaders didn't start out as such—they were often managers that worked their way up the corporate ladder through hard work and (hopefully) fair play to build a solid management reputation.

They have also developed a set of skills to handle problem solving, with minimal resources, (tight) cash flow management, negotiating and dealing with bankers,

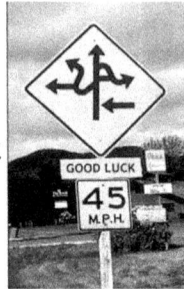

# Change Management

GOOD LUCK
45 M.P.H.

investors and creditors. The stakeholders will usually work with a turnaround leader—if he or she is credible.

A key initial element to a successful turnaround is to establish a good relationship with your bank. Capital is always required in tough times, not to mention that it's desired in good times as well. If the leaders who were in power while the company's position was allowed to deteriorate are still there, why should the lender believe that they will now be instrumental in correcting the situation? With all the suspicion that can surround a troubled company, it is important that trust be re-established with the bank. Credibility with the lender(s) is mandatory to success—and most likely to keeping that cash flow at the bank. And with the bank holding the trump card, the institution must feel comfortable working with the turnaround leader. It means laying everything out on the table to keep the situation honest—and honoring commitments made to the lender.

Where consistency is important in a stable environment the name of the game in a turnaround situation is uncertainty. You can absolutely, positively count on surprises. "When it rains, it pours" may be clichéd, but when applied to a troubled company, one can be sure that 'Murphy is shaking the clouds.'

The ability to deal with change at a rapid pace is essential. This is why a seasoned practitioner can be the answer to a successful turnaround plan.

The existing leadership is often 'out of its element' as it enters this untrodden ground of trouble. And when people haven't had to manage in this environment before, the odds are that they will at the very least, have a difficult time.

One alternative is to work with consultants. They can't be leaders because they can't make decisions for the company. They can make recommendations, but often to the same leader who failed to make a decision in the first place.

The practitioner, on the other hand, is a hands-on decision maker who actually takes control of the company—often as CEO—for a period of time. He is in control of the company's destiny. He must know how to be decisive, know how to isolate the problems and find solutions.

Affecting a turnaround takes an array of skills. When in crisis there is no time for a warm up. Just as with that patient in intensive care, the longer a company is on the critical list, the harder it is to nurse it back to health. To affect a rehabilitation, the right leader will know how to make the quick and proper decisions, put a plan into action and keep a talented team moving towards a healthy and more valuable end.

Building Trust

In times of great change within a company or organization, people are more apt to feel insecure. Feelings of distrust—not only between employees and management, but among employees themselves—can mount.
The following tips may help maintain calm and encourage trust in such times of uncertainty:

- Share information. Mistrust stems as much from what employees aren't told as from what they are. Misperceptions can build up as they move along the grapevine. By announcing the facts about a change openly, you help put the information in proper perspective.
- Admit it when there are things you don't understand. When you lack information, go to the source and ask for clarification. Subordinates will wait for more information if confident you have their interests in mind and will seek answers for them.
- Don't neglect horizontal communication with peers. The information loop does not just encircle those above you and below. Keep the entire team informed.

# Turnaround Performance Management: Why Firing Beats Training

In a turnaround situation the one thing you don't have is time. The other thing you can't afford is trial and error. Training people takes time and is a long term strategy that may or may not work out. Furthermore, you might be able to teach skills, but you never can train attitude.

That's why professional turnaround leaders during a crisis do not waste any time on trying to teach new tricks to old dogs but rather fire the old non performing dogs and get a new puppy they can train.

You may not agree and you don't have to, but remember: Just like a surgeon sometimes needs to amputate a limb in order to save the patient's life, a turnaround manager sometime needs to fire a few non-valors in order to save the company and through that to save the jobs for many.

Is has long been proven, for example, that happy sales people outsell their pessimistic counterparts by 56%. Imagine being able to grow your organisation by 56% with no additional investment or increased effort, but simply by replacing those with a negative attitude by ones with a positive attitude.

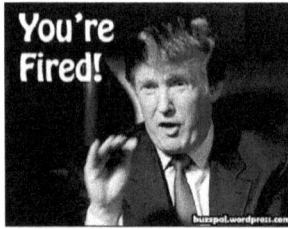

## Turnaround Performance Management: Why Poor Performance in YOUR Company Is Not Being Addressed, Putting Your Business At Risk, And You Even Know About It And Yet Do Nothing About It

Imagine: One of your staff is performing under par. This might be anything from not hitting sales targets to poor attendance; the details are unimportant. One thing is clear – it demands action and the rewards that follow are obvious. Dealing with it might produce more sales or higher productivity, say, depending on the precise details. Yet…with such things there can seem to be many reasons for delay. You think (or rather hope) that it will get better. You wait for other things: The end of the month (bringing further figures or evidence) or a forthcoming appraisal (which you know means you cannot put it off later than that). More than anything you blame other things. You are busy, you have greater priorities, or, even less convincingly, you are sorting other problems – fire fighting.

The truth his you do not want to deal with it. You may be unsure how to do so, and that can be awkward. More likely you do know what to do, but know it will be awkward or embarrassing to do so. Addressing it will take you into the discomfort zone, and you would rather distance yourself busying yourself elsewhere (with something you designate "more important"!) and remaining safely outside the zone of personal difficulty.

The facts of the matter are usually clear. It is not rocket science and you can usually deal with it if you address it. A poor performer is a good example. It is important, yet it is not complicated. Essentially only three options are possible. You can:

1.  Put up with the poor performance, and allow it to continue (which is surely something no one would defend or recommend).
2.  Address the problem with a determination to cure it, persuading or motivating someone to perform better; or training or developing the person to do whatever it is better, if their poor performance is due to a lack of some skill or competence.
3.  Conclude, perhaps after option two has failed, that they will never get better and fire them (or otherwise move them to other areas of responsibility).

Both options two and three may be awkward. It is embarrassing to have to tell someone his or her performance is unacceptable, and most of you would find firing someone worse. So, action is delayed.

Get real. The situation here needs to be addressed head-on. Such a situation is not a failing of logic, not a deficit of information or understanding, or anything else that mistakenly leads you away from the sensible and necessary course – it is a personal decision: You put avoiding personal discomfort above sorting the problem out, and very likely, delay makes the problem worse.

If you are a business owner, this is foolish. It you are an employed manager, it is criminal, because you are damaging the company you are paid to protect because of your personal incompetence to overcome your personal discomfort.

Before you say "But I would never make that kind of decision", consider further. If thinking is partly subconscious, then that is likely so because you push it into the back of your mind, refusing to really analyse what is occurring, or simply allowing other activity to create a blinding smokescreen. Now let us think more constructively. Which elements of your work are likely to run foul of this kind of avoidance technique? Dealing with poor performance has already been cited as an example. Others include:

- Speaking to your bank about your pending or approaching cash flow problems
- Raising a difficult issue at a meeting (it gets put off rather than risking controversy or argument)
- Cold calling (you should do more but it is not your favourite thing)
- Networking (sounds good: You hope to meet people at that conference you attend who will do the selling for you by recommending you (because selling sucks and you are afraid of it or bad at it) then come out with one business card because you are not quite sure how to approach people (I said "you are bad at it" – approaching people IS selling)
- Chasing poor debtors (you hate it, avoid it or do it half heartedly and so cash flow suffers; yet you recognize that it is not an order until the money is in the bank)
- Follow up (when the customer said "I'll think about it", how many times do you make one perfunctory phone call to be told they are in a meeting, then leave it so long that the moment passes because you are not quite sure what to say next time?)

Such things are, to an extend, routine. Others may be more personal, linking to a particular skill or activity. For instance:

- Avoiding presentations, even when they offer promotional opportunity, because "It's not really my thing"
- Avoiding sitting on a committee where you might make valuable contacts

because meetings are in the evening and "It's not fair on the family"

You may well be able to extend the list in both categories (be honest, as I said at the beginning).

So, what do we conclude from this? There is a significant opportunity here. You need to resolve actively seek out uncomfortable situations. Real leaders and turnaround managers do that. You need to see the discomfort zone as an attractive place to go to. Somewhere where you can achieve action and influence results, and often do so quickly and easily. That's the attitude and the approach business recovery specialists take.

## Turnaround Performance Management: How To Be Efficient And Effective

You could take a whole morning phoning people who really aren't interested in talking to you or listening to what you say – some people call this networking. Others spend the hours between 9 am and 5 pm walking around with a handful of papers. They are off to see someone, going to a meeting, just popping upstairs to accounts, heading towards the photocopier to duplicate documents they don't need. Perhaps it's time to check the BlackBerry again – after all, it's at least two minutes since you last looked to see what is, or isn't happening on your mobile technology.

Don't be confused by the difference between effectiveness and efficiency. Efficiency is performing a given task (whether important or not) in the most economical manner possible (stuffing envelopes can be done efficiently – if you have all the inserts laid out in the table and the envelopes are self-seal and you have a franking machine). But it's probably a required task rather than an important one.

Effectiveness is doing the things that get you closer to achieving your goals. What's the point of being efficient in checking your emails twenty times a day? You may have developed an elaborate system of folders for storing them, with sophisticated retrieval techniques to locate these irrelevant communications once you've filed them. But why? What does this activity achieve?

Remember the golden rule: Doing something unimportant well does not make it important. If a task requires a lot of time to accomplish this does not make it important either. What you do is infinitely more important than how you do it. Efficiency does matter, of course, but it is useless unless it is applied to the right things.

## Hierarchy in a Turnaround Situation – The More, The Better - Honest

Turnaround situations are different indeed. Usual wisdom and usual practice do not apply in a crisis. When the house is burning it is not the time for democratic brainstorming sessions about 40 ways to fight a fire or lengthy training. Instead, the leader needs to regain the reigns, shout the orders and the crew has to jump – or else. "Else" in a crisis usually means "bust".

That's why in a turnaround situation more hierarchy is better. Let me explain: The skilled CRO organises his organisation into several hierarchical levels. This is not only done because it always was this way, but because it is important for the canalisation of the flow of information (D.S. ALBERTS/ R.E. HAYES, Power to the Edge).

The situation is shown on the picture below: If a team of four persons is organised in 3 levels (left: red = turnaround manager) then there are 3 lines of communication. Contrarily, if a team of four persons is organised in a network with 4 equal members (right: blue = member) then there are 6 lines of communication, twice the number of the hierarchical organisation.

The ratio grows even worse if you add one more turnaround member to the structure: In the hierarchical
structure one more (green) member is one more LOC (line of communication), in the network structure one more member adds as many LOCs as there are members already in the network.

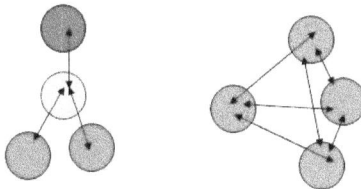

How can both requirements be fulfilled?

The decision is made by a group (to have the diffusion of responsibility), and 2. The turnaround manager remains in control (because only the manager knows what is best for the turnaround). The procedure to come to the wanted result is known in the psychological sciences as „groupthink" (E. ARONSON, ET AL., Social Psychology). To invoke groupthink there are only a handful of prerequisites:

1.  The turnaround manager makes clear what the result of the discussion should be at the beginning of the turnaround group meeting.
2.  The turnaround manager in person stays with the turnaround group as long as the discussion takes place and makes sure point no. 1 is satisfied.
3.  The turnaround members who are erroneously not supporting the wanted result should feel uncomfortable. This normally is necessary only during the

first two or three arguments in a discussion. From then on other members will automatically switch their opinion to feel comfortable and group cohesion is assured.

4. Any piece of information that runs against the predefined decision should be ignored or played

5. down. External opinions only count if they support the group opinion. With just these four points the turnaround manager creates the best of all worlds and if a decision in the future will turn out to be inappropriate, well, diffusion is a fine thing.

Documentation – vast amounts of

Recently there are tendencies to reduce the amount of turnaround documentation to a minimum. Especially agile procedures aim at this goal (culminating in absurd statements like: the code is the documentation) Such approaches are for all practical purposes rubbish. The saying goes: „If it is not in written form it does not exist." A manager should insist on vast amounts of documentation. A documentation only is good if really everything and the opposite of everything can be found in it. So if something goes wrong (and most probably in a turnaround things will go wrong) the skilled manager can point to one part of the documentation or the other (by this definition the Soviet legal and governmental system most likely was the best practiced documentation ever). Human resources in a turnaround will change, only paperwork will definitely endure. And only paperwork is the real indicator for progress in a turnaround.

The interested reader may already have witnessed the practices described above in his/ her turnaround.

Not only because they are so widespread in use but also because they are so successful and substantially facilitate the turnaround manager's work. Therefore it is justified to call them best practices. To achieve good turnaround results, of course, other best practices should be followed.

# Energizing Employees in Recessionary Times - Try Motivating, Not Mandating

Cost-cutting efforts could be a reality for some time to come. One dimension of cost-cutting is often disregarded—the critical need to ensure cost cuts occur in ways that obtain positive emotional commitment within the context of the culture. Employees need to somehow feel positively motivated to support decisions and to commit to behavioural change that reduces costs.

This is a "tall order," especially when layoffs are at the centre of the cuts. However, in our experience, cost-cutting and layoffs fail when executives simply try to mandate attitudes and behaviours. These efforts will more likely succeed when companies make positive employee motivation an integral part of the process. The first step is for executives to take on the responsibility of ensuring that front-line leaders' actions appeal to employees' hearts and minds.

*Positive motivation cannot be delegated or mandated.*

## Why Most Cost Reductions Fail

Under tremendous recessionary pressures, executives in a range of industries are currently considering, launching, or already grappling with cost reduction programs. Unfortunately, many of these efforts will be disappointing, to say the least. In 2005, a McKinsey[1] study reported that only ten percent of companies sustain cost reduction benefits after three years. A 2008 Archstone Consulting survey of 350 companies[2] highlights several reasons why cost reduction efforts fail. In the most frequent reason given—by 44% of respondents—executives indicated that "implementation
was not well managed." In other words, people did not do what they were supposed to do. Why does this happen?

## "Phantom Savings" Prevail

A common problem is that companies unwittingly put themselves into a suboptimal cycle of cost reduction that is both short-term and short-sighted. The cycle begins when managers launch an initiative to identify and implement cost reductions in different functions. The first problem is that many of these cost savings are "phantom"—the organization does not sustain the savings once the initiative goes away and many of the savings are nothing more than deferred expenditures.

## Fundamentals Are Not Addressed

The second problem is that the initiative does not address fundamentals. Productivity does not improve, leadership systems are unchanged, and "cost-accommodating" behaviours persist. As a result, headcount savings in functions creep back in the form of higher expenditures with vendors,
potentially impacting SG&A or cost of goods sold. Moreover, additional hiring occurs (often at higher cost) as "new" needs emerge.

## "Mandating" vs. "Motivating" Cost Reduction

So what should companies embarking on cost reduction do? They should probably start by asking themselves if "quick and dirty" costs reductions are all they want or need. If not, they should look honestly at the ultimate impact of any earlier cost reduction efforts. Important savings commitments may not have been implemented. Examples include purchasing commitments not followed, or new departments put in place to replace others that were downsized. Pull out the PowerPoint presentations from several years before and ask what happened, separating justified and unacceptable reasons for deviations. Avoid the natural human tendency to justify past decisions. In short, learn from the last effort before launching a new cost reduction initiative.

## The "Mandating" Approach – Firmness, Discipline, And Often Fear

If companies are going to approach cost reduction better than they did in the last recession, they have two very different approaches to consider: they can simply rely on mandating or they can emphasize motivating. While there is an unavoidable overlap, the primary emphasis is what matters most.

Top-down mandating is the classic way to launch a cost-cutting effort. "Mandaters" believe that the cycle of suboptimal cost reduction can be broken through more firm resolve, discipline, and fear. It will not be surprising to see the rendition of Al Dunlap and his provocative style (approach restructurings under the principle of "do it once, do it severe, get it over with"). Targets are set, the axe falls, and everyone from the CEO downwards does their best to follow through on the cost cuts.

In many cases, executives call upon experts from headquarters or outside consultants to quantify opportunities for cost reductions and to complete the effort quickly. These initiatives frequently use methods and analytics that are unfamiliar to the organization and are hard for many people to understand and learn. Consequently, many of these efforts remain focused on the project and its science, rather than on the real needs of the company and its people. Despite well intended top-down communications, employees suspect they are not getting the whole story. Firmness and discipline start to feel more like shouting selective messages and bullying as leaders push managers to "try harder" to enforce the cost reduction effort. Negative rumours circulate, insecurities build, and water cooler scepticism persists. Senior leaders and line managers tend to rely too heavily on human resource departments to find ways to reduce anxieties, clarify top-down directives, and help displaced employees find new jobs.

Despite these efforts, the cumulative impact is a set of employee anxieties that often generate "deer in the headlights" reactions. Some of the deer hope the lights will just go away and do not move; others try to hide in the bushes and convince themselves that they are exceptions who will be spared.

Of course, the human resource department works hard to ameliorate the anxiety that people feel. They put proven programs and processes in place to manage the cost reduction effort, and they launch broad-based engagement efforts. Unfortunately, these efforts seldom address the disruption to a company's culture that the mandated approach brings. Nor do they obtain the help of front-line supervisors, who are the critical link to motivating employee behaviours. A major part of the problem lies in lack of integration between senior leadership actions, front-line supervisory efforts, and formal HR programs. As a result, the informal elements of the organization become confused, resentful, and counter-productive.

## When Agent Orange Turned Sour

The Home Depot co-founder Bernie Marcus believed that if you motivate employees to empathize with their customers, you ensure both low cost operations and high-quality service—a belief that became known as "Agent Orange" and which defined The Home Depot's unique culture.

When we researched The Home Depot in the nineties, one employee confided that she would rather spend her Saturday working than relaxing at home. A store manager proudly revealed he measured each day's performance simply by counting the smiles on the faces of customers leaving his store.

When Robert Nardelli imposed more rigorous management disciplines, important elements of Agent Orange rebelled. Many executives and managers left, and others resisted or simply hunkered down behind the counters waiting for the storm to pass. And pass it did, as the Board replaced the CEO yet again at the beginning of 2007. According to the company's financial reports, operating expenses as a percentage of sales rose from 20.7% of sales in 2000, just before Nardelli's tenure, to 22.4% of sales for 2006, just before he departed. Operating costs per square foot, using year-end square foot data, rose from around $77 to $79 in the same period. The culture rebelled, even though this operating cost story is hardly harsh. Emotional commitment did not accompany rational compliance.

In its latest year-end financial filing, The Home Depot notes that payroll costs increased by 76 basis points due to a number of factors, some of which reflect investments in store labour and bonus plans. After the trauma of prior years, The Home Depot ended up having to re-invest in employees and their motivation. In fact, associate engagement is now listed as The Home Depot's first key strategic priority. Unfortunately, employee "engagement" on its own will be of limited motivational value unless it connects directly and emotionally to the work itself (and you really need the help of frontline motivators to make that connection). Nardelli's approach had only limited success in cost containment—not because he was a poor choice as CEO, but because there are no short-cuts around employee commitment. The Home Depot learned the importance of working with the Agent Orange
culture.

## The Positive Motivational Approach – A "Proud To Be Thrifty" Mindset

Fortunately, companies have a more effective alternative to top-down, negative mandating, as well as to trying to engage employees superficially while the cost-cutting effort runs rough-shod over the positive elements of the culture. They can adopt the "positive motivational" approach. At first glance, executives might dispute that they can motivate employees and managers in positive ways around cost-cutting. Indeed, no one should pretend that headcount reduction can be as intrinsically motivating as other business experiences, and managers at all levels will still have difficult decisions to make.

But the motivational approach to cost reduction involves employees committing emotionally to the cost challenge. "Motivators" look for ways to secure positive employee commitment—emotional as well as rational—to company decisions and behaviour change. A few companies are able to do this systematically because they have built a culture that is "proud to be thrifty." They communicate a noble purpose or positive theme that focuses their people on cost and value, such as the commitment by Southwest Airlines to making safe, comfortable air travel available to the average American. At Southwest, employees have been known to pay for energizing events, such as holiday celebrations, out of their own pockets.

Some companies also use formal processes to support motivation. For example, hourly employees at Nucor have lower per-hour compensation, and yet they earn more than their counterparts since Nucor uses an incentive structure that encourages low-cost behaviour. These companies also generate informal momentum to encourage frugality. Thrifty companies draw on stories to celebrate the frugality of leaders, like Ingvar Kamprad, the founder of IKEA, who said "waste of resources is a mortal sin." Marshalling these different approaches can help people across an organization take pride in keeping costs low at all times, thus creating a sustained cost reduction program that continues as an integral part of the culture.

## But Can the Motivating Approach Work In The Short Term?

Unfortunately, companies facing an urgent need to cut costs seldom have a "proud to be thrifty" culture and cannot create one overnight.

Hence, executives might be tempted to say: "I know positive motivation is important, but we don't have time to worry about that right now. I can't see anyone feeling very positive about what we have to do in any case. So let's go with mandating." In fact, employee engagement is always critical in peak performing cultures—particularly when it connects directly and emotionally to the work itself.

A 2006 study from Towers Perrin-ISR4 showed that over a period of one year, companies with highly engaged employees increased net income by thirteen percent, while those with less engaged employees showed a four percent decline. In recessionary times, this employee engagement can be harnessed to speed cost reduction—because lots of people energize one another around specific tasks that move towards the same goal. Executives who are tempted to ignore employee motivation and alignment in their cost reduction efforts should ask themselves the following questions:

- Are we sure we have all the solutions needed for cost reduction (e.g., outsourcing, discarding a business, headcount reduction, bonus cuts), or does the complexity of our problem require individual responsiveness and on-site problem-solving from our employees?
- Will mandated cost reductions be undermined without positive support from employees?
- Will rational compliance be enough to sustain the behaviours we need, or do we also need emotional commitment?
- Will cost reductions damage our value proposition to employees, relative to our competitors?
- Are we in danger of forcing short-term actions that we will regret when our company is growing again?
- Are innovation, collaboration, and customer empathy critical in our business, at the level of requiring the energy and enthusiasm of our employees?

In most cost reduction efforts, employee motivation will be a critical business objective that executives, as well as front-line managers, must personally lead in consistent ways.

## Motivating – Getting People To Do More Than What You Ask

Positive motivation is not about engaging people broadly at a company-wide level while compelling them at their work stations to do what you prescribe from the top. It is about energizing employees to work with you on reducing costs, encouraging individual employee actions that cannot be prescribed, and recognizing employees with more than money when they take these actions.

For example, Amazon.com perpetuates a "door desk" award that is given on a monthly basis to an employee who achieves significant savings. The door is not worth much money and it symbolizes the makeshift desk that Jeff Bezos used as a thrifty measure in the early days.

Generating positive motivation is seldom easy to and it rarely depends on money alone. People have to feel good about tasks that are not financially rewarding or intrinsically motivating. This requires developing emotional commitment to support painful decisions, applying self-disciplined behaviours beyond mandatory processes, building peer respect and support for reducing any and all costs employees can control, and making sure the informal organization supports the formal.

## Motivating Cost Discipline

Reliant Energy, a Texas-based electricity provider, significantly reduced its cost base by integrating critical leadership objectives with a positive motivating approach to get the best of both the mandating and motivating approaches.

In October 2002, Reliant's stock was trading at less than a dollar, compared to $30 at the time of its IPO in May 2001. The company grappled with debt from major acquisitions and the uncertainties of a deregulated Texas energy market, was rapidly losing the confidence of Wall Street, and faced bankruptcy.

But in two years, Reliant turned itself around by cutting $340 million in operating costs out of a base of approximately $1.3 billion. The urgency of Reliant's situation certainly made these changes mandatory.

At the same time, Reliant saw a twenty percent lift in measures of both employee satisfaction and pride. What is it that Reliant and other successful cost-cutting "motivators" do that allows positive feelings to counter-balance negative fears?

## Leadership Cohesion & Commitment

"Motivators" establish leadership cohesion and commitment at all levels, conducting a fair process for cost reductions. Reliant leaders were aligned and united in the task of significantly reducing the company's cost base and were highly visible in communicating both formally and informally after
committing to a thirty-five percent reduction in costs. Senior executives recognized that motivation was a critical issue from the start.

For instance, their "brown bag" lunches with employees became known as venues for candid discussion and underscored what leaders and employees were trying to do: talking and acting together—with integrity—to achieve what needed to be done.

## Importance of Fairness

"Motivators" recognize that employees care deeply about fairness—which means making the cost reduction process transparent, timely, and effective. Reliant balanced a central mandate with a significant amount of local autonomy. Different groups were allowed to pursue savings on their own
schedules, subject to an overall corporate timeframe. Similarly, BMC, a leading software company, developed a turnaround plan with milestones and a scorecard on its top five priorities, including cost reduction and a monthly report out to the whole company.

## The Emotional Case and Role of Frontline Motivators

"Motivators" create a positive emotional case in addition to a rational business case. Both need to be clear and well reasoned. Companies need to develop an emotionally appealing theme as well as deciding on the primary carrier or carriers of that emotion through facts, not guesswork. Reliant conducted a survey of its employees in 2002 and learned that the two most important potential sources of pride were the company's reputation and the quality of its people. That became the basis of a well-organized change plan. The most effective cost-cutters also enlist the best frontline motivators, collectively as well as individually, to connect sources of pride to the work itself in ways that mobilize the organization. Reliant established "Motivation Governance," including a Motivation Champion, a Motivation Squad, and most critically, Local Connectors. These Local Connectors were selected from interviews and peer nominations and were responsible for carrying out motivation activities locally (e.g., celebration events for achieving company objectives), as well as providing frontline perspective and upward feedback to the Motivation Champion.

## More Than One Hammer

Executives require objective data to make critical decisions around where and how to cut costs. Multiple approaches are required to get everyone onboard. Too often, companies adopt one method (e.g., benchmarking) and impose it on the organization, ignoring the complexity of what might be driving costs.

As one executive said, "You need more than one hammer." For instance, costs are often driven by organizational inefficiencies, such as too many layers or too many hand-offs. Employees know this, and want these issues examined. Employees also want to be involved in the problem solving. In 1993, Texas Commerce Bank hosted hundreds of focus groups that involved almost half of its 9,000 employees in a major improvement initiative that replaced its monetary target with an aspiration of "eliminating what annoys our bankers and customers."

The initiative eventually exceeded the initial target of $50 million in reduced costs, achieving savings that were around three times the target. It is critical to do the analysis to shed light on a broad set of opportunities and to use the findings to design organizational solutions that create lasting behaviour change. At Scholastic, there was a need to create a shared services organization to better manage and leverage spend across several business units. Rather than creating an expensive new organization with the associated hand-offs, the company created a council with clear authority and the right balance of membership.

## Getting Through a Recession Requires "The Best of Both"

Mandates have their place in serious cost reduction efforts, but you also need "a little help from your friends" down the line. Cost-cutting has never been easy but companies will increase their chances of success by involving their employees in ways that obtain positive emotional commitment to decisions and behaviour change. You may be able to mandate your way to an immediately lower cost structure, but if you also motivate people in positive ways that produce emotional as well as rational commitment, we believe strongly that you will get more costs out sooner, and the benefits will be more lasting.

# Remuneration Strategies in a Turnaround Situation

When you are in a turnaround situation, you often need to replace staff quickly and get world class talent into the organisation, and at the same moment you need to turn existing staff in highly motivated, high performance teams.

This often entails a review and possibly restructure of the company's salary system.

Get your remuneration packages right and you will attract reliable employees with the skills your business needs. Get them wrong and you will be unable to recruit or retain these people.

Since the remuneration package is the most visible part of any job offer, you must pitch it right to interest the right people. But even that can be easy, compared with fine-tuning the rewards to keep good people with you.

This briefing covers:

- Deciding how much to pay.
- Complying with statutory obligations on minimum wage.
- Structuring pay and benefit packages.
- Using non-financial rewards.
- Handling pay reviews.

## 1 The market rate

Establish the market rate, as a starting point.

Paying the market rate involves careful job evaluation (so you know what's being compared) and external research (word-of-mouth, advertisements, published surveys).

1.1 The skills needed may be widely available.
- Compare rates at local employment agencies and Jobcentre Plus.

1.2 The job may demand specialised skills.
- National newspapers focus on specific skills areas on different days of the week.
- Refer to published pay reports by Brook Street, Hay, Monks Partnership and others.

1.3 You may require highly specialised skills.
- Going rates are usually easy to check in professional journals.
- Job advertisements in the specialist press often inform candidate's expectations.
- It may be worth commissioning a bespoke salary survey, if it helps you get the right person for a specialised role.

## 2 More or less?

Whatever your research tells you about the market rate, you will probably want to adjust your offer to reflect the job and circumstances.

2.1 Are you looking for a higher-than-averagecalibre of employee?
- Do you need trained people or are you prepared to offer training?

2.2 What are the particular problems you face in recruiting the right people?
- Are there geographical factors (eg travel to central London, or a remote location)?
- Are the skills you need wanted urgently or in especially short supply?

2.3 Must you offer relocation allowances to attract good people from outside the area?

## 3 Basic pay

The most basic level of pay is set by law, with the national minimum wage (NMW). The NMW is currently fixed at £5.93 an hour for employees aged 21 or over, £4.92 for those aged 18 to 20 and £3.64 for workers aged 16 and 17. Apprentices under the age of 19 or over 19 and in the first year of the apprenticeship are entitled to a minimum hourly rate of £2.50. Above that, you can decide what and how you pay your employees.

3.1 Will you pay by time or performance? There are several possible approaches.
- The choice between wages and salaries is often a matter of tradition or expectations.
  Weekly wages suit companies with a fixed working day, short working hours or irregular patterns of work.
- Hourly pay may lead to high overtime costs if demand is irregular.
- Annual hours contracts can offer flexibility for both you and your employees, while avoiding premium payments for overtime.
- Piece rates link pay directly to productivity.
- Commission can range from the icing on the cake to the main element in the pay packet.

3.2 Your pay structure may be simple, but there should be some logic to it. It should be clear and fair.
- The aim is to create a situation where employees can feel their pay is reasonable, compared with each other.
- Part-timers and full-timers should be able to see how their pay is related.
- You must meet your legal obligations (eg to give equal pay for work of equal value).
  Make sure all decisions are free from discrimination.
- Equal pay questionnaires allow employees to ask specific questions

about pay levels, so you need to make sure you go by the book. Record all decisions and make sure they are supported by a robust process.

- Consider undertaking an equal pay review to identify any problematic areas and potential corrective measures.

3.3 Decide what part overtime is going to play — and how you are going to value it.

3.4 Be aware of tax and National Insurance (NI) thresholds. Do not pay people amounts that will put them just above a threshold.

- It may be possible to use tax-efficient incentives, rather than raising pay (see 5).

3.5 Paying out cash as share dividends, rather than income, is still a tax-efficient way of remunerating shareholders — usually directors, investors and senior employees.

- If you and your partner are employed in the same business, make sure you have good evidence of what each does. HM Revenue & Customs (HMRC) has recently been targetting spouses paid through dividends.
- Dividends attract income tax, but no NI.

4 Bonuses and commission

Bonuses and commission payments need to be seen by employees as extras, or there will be no incentive effect.

4.1 Incentives work, if the targets are right.

- Incentive pay is only effective when it relates to specific achievements.
- It needs to be closely matched to the business and to the people involved.
- Incentives based on competition backfire if the same people always win.

4.2 To get the desired results, you need to decide whose performance an incentive scheme should be based on.

- Incentives may be linked to performance at the company, team or individual level.

The right linkage will depend on factors such as how much one person or group's success depends on the efforts of others.

- Research shows many performance-related pay schemes give disapointing results, though this may often be due to poor targeting and unrealistic expectations.
- Profit-related pay is a type of performance-related pay that automatically reflects a whole company's achievements. Even without tax breaks, profit-related pay (paid to everyone at, say, ten per cent of salary) can be a powerful, non-divisive incentive.

4.3 Performance bonuses need to be large enough to be significant to the individual.

- You will usually need to make bonuses between ten per cent and 25 per cent of salary to motivate employees effectively.

4.4 Other bonuses can be used to focus attention on areas that affect the success of your business (eg a weekly productivity bonus or a 13th month's pay to boost staff retention).

4.5 Commission is the usual basis of pay for sales operations.

- But low-basic, high-commission pay structures may not be the best way to motivate and retain people, as commission will be seen as income, not as incentive.

## 5 Using shares and options

Share schemes and share option plans allow you to link long-term incentives to long-term goals. They give employees a stake in the company's growth, making them hard to poach.

5.1 Shares and options granted under HMRC-approved employee share schemes are free of income tax and NI, as long as they are held for the specified period.

- You may be able to offset the costs of setting up and funding such schemes against corporation tax.
- Approved schemes include Share Incentive Plans (formerly All-Employee Share Ownership Plans) and Enterprise Management Incentive schemes.

5.2 Shares held by employees in the companies they work for now count as business assets for capital gains tax (CGT) purposes.

5.3 Unapproved schemes bring fewer tax breaks, but can be set up on a larger scale.

5.4 One brake on the progress of share plans in smaller companies is often the original owners' concern about diluting their equity.

- You also have to negotiate a market value of the shares with HMRC. There was a significant change to the way CGT is calculated in 2008. It is advisable to seek professional advice on the impact these changes may have on any share scheme you offer.

## 6 Benefits

NI is payable on all taxable benefits-in-kind. If there is tax on a benefit, the employer has to pay NI at 12.8 per cent.

6.1 Pensions are usually the first benefit provided for employees.
Contributions are treated favourably, with no tax or NI to pay on HMRC-approved schemes.

6.2 Cars and car parking are still high on the list of benefits that employees find attractive.
- Though the tax advantages of a company car have been reduced, most employees still accept a car, if offered as they can avoid the hassle and costs of running their own car.
  A parking space at or near the place of work can be a valuable tax-free benefit.

6.3 There is no tax to pay on mobile phones provided by an employer, but this exemption only applies to one mobile phone per employee. Second and subsequent phones provided to an employee or members of his or her family will be liable to tax. (Note that a Blackberry is not regarded as a mobile phone by HMRC so does not attract the same tax exemption.)
- If employees have part of their home phone bills reimbursed, including some private call costs, they will have to pay tax. It may be better to provide mobiles.

6.4 Childcare vouchers up to £55 per week per employee can be provided on a tax and NI free basis.

6.5 Living accommodation can be tax free for those who have to live in a certain place to do the job (eg caretakers and oil rig crews).
Elsewhere, it is taxed as a benefit. But even with the tax charge, potential recruits may find the offer of accommodation attractive.

6.6 There are several minor benefits that cost little to provide, are valued highly by employees and get favourable tax treatment.
- Staff discounts (on your products) are not taxed and can be an attractive perk (eg in retailing, transport and travel).
- Personal loans of up to £5,000 are not taxable and do not attract NI. Offering season ticket loans or interest-free loans to clear credit card debts can build loyalty.
- Long-service awards do not attract tax, providing the employee has worked for the business for 20 years. The value can be up to £50 for each year of service.
- Annual parties (or similar celebrations) paid for by the employer are tax free, up to a cost of £150 a head.
- Bicycles made available by an employer to employees are not liable to tax or NI contributions.
  Analyse the full costs and benefits of all the perks you offer.

## 7 Non-financial extras

Money is not the only thing people want from their jobs — and not the only motivator.

7.1 Use holidays creatively, as part of the employment package.
- Agreeing to extra unpaid leave may provide a trade-off if you cannot afford full market rates for specialist skills.

7.2 Flexitime working can be a powerful attraction for potential recruits.

7.3 Job content and fulfilment are what many people want most from their work.
- Most employees want to be extended ('stretched'), but not stressed.
- Use appraisals to fine-tune the role and get the best out of the person.
- The feeling of doing something worthwhile, for a worthwhile organisation, is a strong motivator for many people.

7.4 Training is particularly attractive to young, ambitious employees.
- Experience in a new role enhances a person's CV and earning potential.
- Training makes the person more valuable to you, but also to any other employer.

## 8 Pay reviews

Pay reviews need to be regular and should be kept separate from performance reviews.

8.1 Aim for a steady increase in real earnings, over the months and years, for employees whose performance is satisfactory.

8.2 Build in a performance-related element for every employee, including juniors.

8.3 Ask people what their needs are.
- A dissatisfied employee will not always be won over by a pay rise, even a large one.

8.4 Make a clear distinction between promotion and increases in pay for the job.

8.5 If there are trade unions in the workplace, involve them in reviewing the operation of your pay structure.

8.6 Pay must be based on the principle of equal pay for work of equal value; this applies to bonuses and commissions as well as basic rates of pay and salary.

*"Overwhelmingly, exit interviews show that most employees only join another company 'for more money' if they are unhappy in their existing job in the first place."*

-Bob Havard, Havard Consulting

*"The cafeteria system, where employees are given a menu of benefits and allowed to choose their own, up to a certain value, is finally catching on in the UK. There is a price to pay, in terms of admin costs, but employees love it, so it is a great recruiting magnet."*

-Kenny Gibson, Business Link West Yorkshire

*"Recruiting people is relatively easy. The hard part is judging the whole remuneration package so that you are able to keep the good people with the skills and experience the company needs."*

-Lesley Stalker,Robert James Partnership

*"If you can't afford to incentivise your key staff by paying them in cash bonuses, then using employee share schemes — by awarding them shares or share options, subject to performance — may be your best response to potential staff retention problems."*

-Fred Hackworth, Employee Share Ownership Centre

# Remuneration Strategies in a Turnaround Situation: Incentive Pay

Productivity and high standards are important to you. Recognition and encouragement are important to employees. Incentive pay is a way for you and your employees to achieve results.

A good incentive pay scheme can motivate employees to work better for your business. A badly thought-out scheme, on the other hand, can be divisive and demoralising.

This briefing explains:
• How to set objectives.
• The types of scheme to consider.
• How to ensure your scheme works.

## 1 Setting objectives

Design your incentive pay scheme to achieve specific objectives.
Your targets should be 'SMART' (specific, measurable, achievable, realistic, time-limited).

1.1 Decide what business results you want to achieve. For example:
      • Hitting a certain sales target during a sales campaign for a new product.
      • Specific improvements in customer service.

Targets should be challenging — but not impossible — to achieve. Aim for a marked improvement in performance. You need to be confident that the benefits of the scheme will outweigh its costs.

1.2 Decide which employees should take part.

A specific group of employees, such as the sales team, whose work directly influences the result you are aiming for.

- The management team, so you can retain the key individuals your business needs.
- All employees, to raise general productivity and morale in the business.

If you only reward one group of employees, there is a danger of alienating the rest, or being accused of discrimination.

1.3 Decide how long the scheme should run.

- If you want to concentrate on one particular result, limit the time. For example, until a backlog of orders is cleared.
- Consider adopting a scheme as a permanent part of your business' culture.

Incentives will often become less effective as employees get used to them. Change the scheme according to circumstances.

## 2 Using cash

Cash is always popular with employees. It is the most widely used form of incentive payment. But it has some disadvantages, too.

2.1 Incentives to increase sales almost always take the form of commission.

- Commission is generally set as a flat percentage of sales.
  It is self-limiting. If the goods are not sold, the payment is not made.
- The rate of commission depends on the selling price and the degree of effort involved in making the sale.

It could range from five per cent, where the item sells readily, to 30 per cent or more where the effort required is substantial.

- High-performing sales people may be able to earn huge amounts under this system.
- Guard against sales people cutting corners to clinch sales.
- Time the payments to ensure that staff can always see another big payout coming.
- Very high earnings may cause resentment if the sales depend on a team effort.
- It is difficult to curb an over-generous commission agreement later, without upsetting and demoralising the sales team.

Start by offering basic pay plus a moderate rate of commission. If business justifies it, you can raise the rate later.

2.2 For production employees, an element of piece work pay is the equivalent.
- Payment is directly related to production. If nothing is produced, nothing is paid.
- Pressure to produce and earn more may lead to a decline in standards. Link quality standards to the production targets.

2.3 One-off improvements in non-sales areas — for example, production or support — can be encouraged with bonuses.
- Bonuses can be offered on either a team or an individual basis.
- Unless there is a clear-cut benefit to the company, the bonus is just another cost.
- Bonuses are often paid out of 'gainsharing' cost savings. With gainsharing, any gains made from cost reductions — for example, a cut in hours worked for the same level of production — are shared with employees.
- Audit improvements in productivity carefully. Things may not be as they seem.
- With team bonuses, make sure that all team members are contributing. One freeloading individual can demoralise the whole team.

2.4 Continuous improvement can be encouraged by instituting a system of performance-related pay.
- You must set demanding but realistic goals for each employee or team.
- Provide feedback on progress towards these goals at intervals during the year.
- Determine the pay increases by the progress made.
- Use objective measurements, or you risk accusations of favouritism.

Tax and National Insurance contributions (NICs) have to be paid on any cash payments to employees.

For the incentive to work, the after-tax amount must be significant. Employees are unlikely to respond positively to anything less than an extra ten per cent in their take-home pay.

## 3 Using shares

Offering shares in your business is more complicated than offering cash. But share schemes can be much more effective in linking the interests of the business and the employees, as well as encouraging long-term commitment. Grants of shares through approved Employee Share Schemes will generally be free of tax and NICs (see below).

Any gains will be subject to capital gains tax (CGT), if they exceed the individual's annual exempt amount (£10,100 in 2010/11). There are two rates of CGT, 28 per cent for higher-rate income tax payers and 18 per cent for those paying the lower tax rate.

3.1 Offer senior executives or key employees the chance to participate in an approved share option scheme, for example the Company Share Option Plan (or CSOP).

- You give selected employees the right to buy shares at their current price, at a later date.

If the shares increase in value in the meantime, they will make an immediate profit when they exercise their options.

- Each employee may hold options on shares worth up to £30,000.
- The option can be exercised after three years, but not later than ten years.
- Employees who own ten per cent or more of the company's shares cannot participate.

No income tax will have to be paid when the option is granted or exercised.

3.2 Small companies (gross assets not exceeding £30 million) can offer share options to employees through the enterprise management incentive scheme.

Companies can seek 'advance assurance' from HM Revenue & Customs (HMRC) that they meet the scheme's requirements.

- All employees can take part in this scheme, if the employer so chooses.

  The total value of shares under option must not exceed £3 million.
- The employees must spend substantial time working for the company. This means at least 25 hours a week or 75 per cent of working time.
- Provided the options are exercised within ten years, and at the market price when they were granted, employees do not pay income tax or NICs.
- The value of the shares under option must be agreed with HMRC when the grant is made.

3.3 Consider setting up a Sharesave scheme.

- All employees must be able to take part on similar terms.
- All members get the right — but not the obligation — to buy a number of shares, normally at a discount to their current price, after three, five or seven years.
- They save a regular amount with a bank or building society in the meantime, to pay for the shares.

  They can save £5 to £250 per month.
- If the shares rise in value, employees have a profit when they buy shares.

If the shares fall in value, they ignore the option and take the savings instead.

No income tax is payable on the grant or exercise of the option, or on the interest.

3.4 Many companies set up non-approved share schemes, which are usually reserved for executives, senior managers and other key employees.
- There are no limits on the amounts that can be granted under such schemes.
- The shares count as business assets and currently qualify to be charged to CGT (see 3.5). But employees who receive benefits have to pay income tax on the full amount.
- Conditions are normally imposed. The idea is to ensure that the rest of the shareholders benefit as well.

In the longer term, shares have been a much better investment than cash. But they can fall as well as rise, for reasons outside your control.

3.5 There was a significant reform to the way CGT is calculated in 6 April 2008, and again in June 2010.
- Higher-rate income tax payers are liable to pay CGT at 28 per cent. For those paying the lower income tax rate, CGT is charged at a flat rate of 18 per cent.
- Taper relief and indexation allowance was withdrawn.
- Entrepreneurs' Relief was introduced, which reduces CGT on the first £5 million of qualifying gains.

In some circumstances, gains arising on the sale of shares will be qualifying gains. Consider taking professional advice on the impact these changes may have on any share scheme you offer.

## 4 Other incentives

Incentives other than cash and shares can give your employees more fun and cause less hassle.

4.1 A company car may be necessary to the job, and a top-of-the-range model is certainly an incentive to some employees.
- Company cars can be a big overhead.
- Be aware that the employee will have 'benefit in kind' charge if they use the car for private use.

4.2 An all-expenses-paid foreign trip can be an effective incentive.
- Set minimum performance requirements that will comfortably pay for it.

- It can bring some fun into the workplace.

It will be discussed by other employees, but is unlikely to be resented — as an equivalent grant of money might be.

4.3 Incentive award vouchers are becoming increasingly popular.
- Whereas cash payments tend to be spent on an employee's monthly outgoings, vouchers are spent on something specific.

This visible reward usually acts as a more effective incentive than cash. NICs are payable on non-cash vouchers.

## 5 Implementing a scheme

In order for an incentive pay scheme to work, your employees must be fully committed to it.

5.1 Explain the reasoning. A written explanation will answer most questions.
- Agree a strategy and list of objectives.
- Agree the way to measure improvements and calculate incentive pay.
- Discuss specific responsibilities and goals with each employee. Employees should feel that they own the scheme.

Act quickly to defuse any conflicts between different objectives or between employees.

5.2 Continue to manage your employees.
- Provide regular feedback to help employees achieve their goals.
- Listen to their suggestions.
- Agree targets at a regular review.

5.3 Analyse the success of your incentive pay scheme regularly.
- Amend the scheme if it does not work.

## 6 Finding help

6.1 The Institute of Actuaries and the Faculty of Actuaries list members in your area, many of them specialising in employee benefit consultation. (www.actuaries.org.uk)

## Valuing unquoted shares

Employees who hold shares could make big gains if an unquoted company floats on the stock market, or gets taken over. They are therefore likely to be more committed.
But putting a fair value on unquoted shares is difficult.

Different methods will be fair for different types of business. You should consider:

A Valuing your business at a multiple of after-tax earnings.
  - Select the multiple by reference to the ratio of price to earnings on quoted companies in the same business, allowing a discount to this ratio if your company is unquoted.

B Valuing your business at a percentage of gross profits.
  - Particularly in a cyclical business, this could produce big swings in value.

C Valuing your business by reference to the asset value.
  - This is difficult to apply to a business where the assets are largely intangible.

Whichever method you choose, you will have to clear it with HMRC first, if you want to offer your employees one of the tax-favoured schemes (see 3).
Share Incentive Plans

The Share Incentive Plan (SIP) is a tax-advantaged plan which encourages employees to buy shares in their company from pre-tax pay.
  - The costs of setting up a SIP and any money you pay into it can be set against your company's taxable profits.
  - You can give your employees shares worth up to £3,000 a year. The amount can be linked to performance.
  - Employees can allocate up to ten per cent of pre-tax salary (up to £1,500 a year) to buy shares through the trust tax free.
  - You can provide up to two matching shares for each share bought by the employee, up to a maximum of £3,000 a year.
  - Shares are free of tax and NI as long as they are held for a minimum of five years.
  - You can require your employees to give up free or matching shares, if they leave within three years.
  - SIPs can create a market for the shares in private companies.
  - You may receive capital gains tax relief if you sell shares in your own business through a SIP.

For a small company setting up a Share Incentive Plan, HMRC suggests set-up costs of £5,000 to £15,000, as well as compliance costs.

What are bonuses, cash incentives and non-cash incentives?

Bonuses and cash incentives are a form of variable pay based on the use of cash lump-sum payments – that is, they are not consolidated into basic pay – linked to individual, collective or organisational performance (or some combination of these factors).

Non-cash incentives are a means of incentivising higher performance among employees by the awarding of prizes or 'gifts', such as merchandise, travel or retail vouchers, associated with some performance measure (such as volume of sales).

It is important to draw a clear distinction between the concepts of cash incentives and bonuses, although the two terms are interlinked, and sometimes used interchangeably.

Incentives aim to directly affect future employee behaviour or performance, usually via the setting of targets: if a specific target is met, the employee will receive a particular mandatory cash payment.

Bonuses encompass a wider range of purposes and could be discretionary or non-discretionary. Like incentives, they may be used in an attempt to directly influence employee performance or behaviour to meet pre-set objectives – but they could also be used on a more ad hoc or retrospective basis to reward past performance.

It is similarly helpful to differentiate between the following:

Non-cash incentives (sometimes known performance improvement plans) which are forward-looking, formal schemes that aim to affect directly employees' future performance.

Employee recognition schemes which are retrospective (as they recognise past performance rather than aiming to directly incentivise future efforts) and may be informal and discretionary. Although not directly covered by this factsheet, such schemes may be inter-linked with non-cash incentive arrangements.

## Background and rationale for bonuses and cash incentives

The increasing trend to incorporate bonus and incentive plans into reward packages has been driven in part by the influence of the 'new pay' philosophy – which advocates that 'guaranteed' basic pay should comprise only a relatively small element of the overall reward package – and shift towards strategic reward linking employee performance and pay to the wider business strategy.

In addition, there has been a move in certain sectors towards market-based pay, whereby an employee might only receive a pay increase if the market rate for the role (for example, management accountant) had increased: in this scenario, individual contribution could be recognised via a bonus instead of a pay rise.

For the employer, the advantages of bonuses/cash incentives when compared to consolidated salary increases include:

- ongoing motivation effect as bonuses have to be re-earned
- lack of impact on certain employer on-costs that are linked to basic salary

levels

- capacity for maintaining market pay competitiveness without necessarily inflating the annual paybill
- flexibility through, for example, the ability to reduce or even halt payments during economic downturns.

For the employee, the main benefits are:

- greater control over own levels of remuneration
- higher payments are potentially possible.
- But the downside for employees includes:
- in effect, the flip side to certain advantages for the employer, for example, that non-consolidated payments must be re-earned or may not currently count towards pensionable pay
- payments may be unpredictable or lower than expected if targets cannot be met.

## Types and coverage of bonuses and cash incentives

The payment of bonuses and cash incentives is generally linked either to the quality and/or quantity of work, on an individual or collective basis, or to some measure of company performance such as profit levels (or both).

Schemes may be broadly divided into the following categories, although definitions vary and may overlap or be linked.

Individual-based. Under these schemes, payment of the bonus/incentive is determined by some measure of individual performance, hence there should be a considerable incentivisation effect. Sales commission could be included within this category (although this might be regarded as a distinct form of remuneration in its own right).

Schemes driven by business results. These schemes often use company profit levels as a measure to help determine bonuses.

Team-based. Such schemes link the bonus with some measure of team performance, often with the aim of fostering effective teamworking.
Ad hoc/project based. This arrangement might be used when a particular deadline is imperative, for example to reward construction workers for completing a building project on time – although such schemes may be open to manipulation.

Department/site-based. A variation on the collective bonus theme, payments could be pitched to reward, for instance, production workers who attain productivity improvements in one particular plant in a manufacturing firm.

Gainsharing. An approach based on the idea that employees should be able to share in financial gains achieved through improved performance (particularly enhanced productivity).

Combination. Bonus or incentive payments can be based on a combination of two or more of the above programmes.

There are also a number of more specialised bonuses that are beyond the scope of this factsheet, for example the Christmas bonus, the attendance bonus and the retention bonus.

According to our 2010 Reward management survey, the majority of employers overall operate some form of cash-based bonus or incentive plans. However, such schemes are far more common in private services and manufacturing than in the public or voluntary sectors.

The most popular arrangements include individually based plans (for example, personal performance or commission), plans driven by business results (such as revenue) and combination schemes.

There is more detailed information on how to design and implement bonus plans in our guide.
Payment levels and recent developments in the use of bonuses

## Levels of payments

If they are to impact on employee behaviour or performance, bonus or incentive payments need to be 'worth having', that is, set at a sufficiently high level to have an effect. By contrast, caution needs to be taken in setting bonuses at very high levels to avoid driving undesired behaviours or outcomes. Market practice may also need to be taken into account.

An important factor in the calculation of any bonus is that it is kept as simple as possible. Ideally participants should be able to measure progress against targets and carry out the calculation themselves so that they know how they are progressing and what payment level might be achieved.

Employers need to decide the means to be used for determining bonus payments, including whether to make use of a formula and how to express payments (for example as a percentage of salary or as a flat rate payment).

Our 2010 reward management survey includes a detailed examination of both target and maximum bonus/incentive potential broken down by sector and occupation. More detailed information tracking specific breakdowns of bonus payments over time (by gender, for instance) can be found in the government-sponsored Annual Survey of Hours and Earnings1.

## Recent developments

In the wake of the global banking crisis and structural upheaval in the financial services sector, the use of bonuses has become a highly contentious issue with the whole nature and mode of operation of bonuses called into question. Remuneration practices were deemed to be a 'contributory factor to the market crisis' in a report from the Financial Services Authority (FSA)2. Practices in investment banking in particular tended 'to reward short term revenue and profit targets' and, in so doing, 'gave staff incentives to pursue unduly risky practices'.

A range of measures has been introduced, with further proposals anticipated, in respect of the regulation of remuneration in the finance sector, particularly affecting senior pay. These include the bestowing of a duty on the FSA to ensure remuneration policies are 'consistent with effective risk management'3.

Essentially, many reward specialists belive, there is a need for a continuing clear link between high levels of performance and the payment of bonuses, but with a need to avoid the problems that may arise if a lack of rigour in the application of this principle means that bonuses are in practice rewarding less-than-robust performance.

## Background and rationale for non-cash incentives

Cash may not be the most effective means of motivating employees, it is sometimes argued, as it does not necessarily motivate them to 'go the extra mile' in their current role. The use of non-cash incentive schemes, based on the receipt of a gift or prize, is arguably more memorable and exciting – hence the greater incentivisation impact.

Typically found in customer-facing industries, non-cash incentive schemes may be based on the use of a single prize to be won by the highest-performing individual employee or encompass a range of awards recognising different levels of achievement.

The benefits of using non-cash incentives include:

*Affordability:* Non-cash incentivisation programmes may be more affordable than alternatives such as cash bonuses.

*Simplicity:* It is very easy for a sales employee to understand that, say, selling so many insurance policies will result in the receipt of a new flat-screen television. Psychological impact: it is acceptable for employees to speak openly with pride about the winning of gifts in a way that would be considered by many to be socially unacceptable it they were seen to be 'bragging' about cash bonuses.

On the downside, drawbacks may include:

*Lack of credibility:* Such prizes may not be taken as seriously as cash.

*Lack of employee awareness:* Employees may be less conscious of the value of non-cash incentives over 'hard cash'.

While the incentivisation industry is more highly developed in the USA, it is also growing in popularity in the UK. According to our 2010 Reward management survey (see link above), however, non-cash incentive schemes are currently operated by only a minority of employers – and are most commonly found among private sector and larger organisations.

## Designing and operating non-cash incentive schemes

### Types of non-cash incentives

The main types of non-cash incentives may be broadly divided into the following categories:

- merchandise, such as ipods, mobile phones or watches
- activities/special events such as meals out, hotel spa accommodation/treatments or hot air ballooning trips
- travel, for example an all-expenses paid trip to Australia
- retail vouchers, which are often obtainable at a discount to 'face value'

the awarding of points under a points-based systems that may be converted into a range of awards.
It is worth noting that under some stricter definitions, the latter two categories might not be regarded as 'non-cash' items.

### Selecting a supplier

Numerous suppliers of non-cash incentives are in operation. Such organisations often provide a wide-ranging service encompassing not only employee non-cash incentive programmes but also other employee schemes such as recognition and team-building activities. More information on suppliers can be found in the journal Incentive and motivation4.

### Tax implications

Employers need to consider the tax implications of implementing a non-cash incentive scheme as awards over a certain level are subject to income tax. It may be possible for employers to arrange payment of any tax or national insurance owing on behalf of employees. Detailed information on the tax implications of non-cash awards can be found in guidance from HM Revenue and Customs.

# Remuneration Strategies in a Turnaround Situation: Incentive Schemes for Individuals

Key Points:

- Individual payment schemes include payment by results, piecework and bonuses, work measurement (including measured day work) and appraisal and performance related pay
- Other individual types of scheme include market-based pay, which links pay to what is available outside the organisation, and competency/skills based pay, which offers the opportunity for higher reward based on the acquisition and utilisation of additional skills and competencies

Many sectors of employment use pay systems that contain direct links to individual performance and results. On an individual basis this may be via:

- payment by results (PBR) eg bonus, piecework, commission
- work-measured schemes and pre-determined motion time systems
- measured day work (MDW)
- appraisal/performance related pay
- market-based pay
- competency and skills based pay.

## Individual payment by results (PBR)

The aim of any PBR scheme is to provide a direct link between pay and output: the more effectively the worker works, the higher their pay. This direct relationship means that incentives are stronger than in other schemes. However, traditional bonus, piecework and work-measured schemes have declined in recent years, as many employers have moved to all-round performance rather than simple results/output based pay. Many bonus schemes incorporate quality measurements or customer service indicators in the assessment to avoid the likelihood of workers cutting corners or compromising safe working methods in order to increase output.

Earnings may fluctuate through no fault of the individual. Supervisors and managers may fail in their responsibilities towards workers by inconsiderate allocation of work or using the incentive scheme to control output. Targets may not be accurate enough resulting in the perception of easy or difficult jobs. Material shortages or delays can affect production. Individual skills are not rewarded and indeed the most skilled may be put onto more difficult and potentially less rewarding work.

In instances where workers regulate their own output to satisfy their individual needs production can be affected and forward planning made more difficult.

## Piecework, bonus schemes and homeworkers

Piecework is the simplest method of PBR - workers are paid at a specific rate for each ‚piece' of output. This means the system is straightforward to operate and understand, although open to the disadvantages that quality and safety may be compromised to achieve a higher output. Pieceworkers must be paid at least the national minimum wage and there are special rules for working this out(4).
Other individual PBR schemes include incentive bonus schemes where for instance an additional payment is paid when volume of output exceeds the established threshold, or where there is an increase in sales which exceeds given targets. Variable bonuses can also be paid in relation to performances achieved against pre-determined standards so that the higher the performance achieved, the greater the level of bonus generated.

Homeworkers must also be paid at least the national minimum wage, with employers being able to demonstrate that they have worked out rates paid to homeworkers to ensure compliance.

## Work measured schemes

Work measurement is often used to determine target performances and provides the basis for many PBR schemes for shop-floor workers. In these systems, a ‚standard time' or ‚standard output level' is set by rate-fixers, or by work study, for particular tasks. Work study calculates a basic time for a task by using laid down methods, observing workers performing the operation and taking into account their rate of working.

Incentive payments are then linked to performance or to the output achieved relative to the standard, or to the time saved in performing the task. British Standard Institution (BSI) formulas are frequently used to calculate the incentive payment and examples of these are in the

As the setting of standard times usually includes an assessment of how the individual being studied is performing, which can have a significant impact on bonus earnings, such judgements often result in disputes. Organisations using this system often train trade union representatives in the technique to promote understanding of the way judgements are made.
An alternative is to use ‚pre-determined motion time systems (PMTS)'. In these systems a synthetic time for a job is built up from a database of standard times for each basic physical movement. A common form of this system is Methods Time Measurement (MTM). Allowances for relaxation and contingencies are then added to the basic time to form the standard time for the task. Such systems are arguably less open to dispute than work-measured schemes as long as the synthetic times upon which the standards are based are acceptable to the workers and their representatives.

When the organisation is considering the relationship of performance to reward there will generally be a starting point from which additional pay is attracted - performance at or below the starting point attracts no additional payment, but performance above the starting point attracts additional payment at a proportion of the basic wage or bonus calculator. Most schemes are ‚straight proportional‘, which allow the reward to rise in direct proportion to the rise in performance.

Schemes should include provisions covering the effects of downtime or other non-productive time on pay. Schemes should be controlled fairly and regularly reviewed to ensure there is no degeneration of work-measured standards. The operation of the scheme should be audited regularly. Arrangements need to be in place to accommodate changes in product, material, specifications and methods - remeasurement of the job may be necessary.

Work-measured schemes may be appropriate in organisations that work on short-cycle repetitive work, where changes in methods are infrequent, where shop-floor hold ups or downtime are rare and where management should be capable of successfully managing the scheme to increase productivity. Procedures should be in place to deal with any grievances or issues that might arise. Even the simplest systems require a set of rules or guidelines to ensure fairness and equal earning opportunity for equal effort.

## Measured day work

Measured day work (MDW) is a hybrid between individual PBR and a basic wage rate scheme. Pay is fixed and does not fluctuate in the short term providing that the agreed level of performance is maintained. MDW systems require performance standards to be set through some form of work measurement and undergo revisions as necessary. Motivation comes from good supervision, goal setting and fair monitoring of the worker's performance.

MDW is difficult and costly to set up and maintain. It requires total commitment of management, workers and trade unions. There must be effective work measurement and efficient planning, control and inventory control systems. The pay structure is often developed by job evaluation and with full worker consultation.

A version of MDW is ‚stepped‘ MDW. Under this scheme the worker agrees to maintain one of a series of performance levels and different levels of pay apply to each one. Movement between levels is possible, usually after a sustained change in performance.

MDW is now relatively rare. It suits organisations where a high, steady, predictable level of performance is sought, rather than highest possible individual performance. MDW may be worth considering where stability of earnings is important, or where the manufacturing cycle is lengthy.

## Appraisal/performance related pay

Appraisal/performance related pay is generally used to link progression through a pay band to an assessment of an individual's work performance during a particular reference period, often a year. Alternatively, the reward may be an additional sum of money paid in the form of a bonus.

Assessments usually relate to an individual's achievements against agreed objectives relating to output and quality of work but may also include an element of evaluation of personal characteristics, such as adaptability, initiative and so on.

Advantages of appraisal-related pay:

- it may provide a ‚felt fair' system of rewarding people according to their contribution
- higher performance within the organisation may result
- it provides a tangible means of recognising achievements
- people understand the performance imperatives of the organisation
- the link between extra pay and extra performance is clear.

Disadvantages:

- appraisal-related pay can prove difficult because measurements of individual performance may be broad and lack objectivity and may be inconsistent
- as noted, such schemes also usually involve only an annual assessment and payout, which may weaken any incentive effect
- many appraisal-related or performance pay schemes pay quite small sums in terms of performance pay progression or annual ‚bonus'. While any such scheme may encourage workers to focus on organisational objectives, they are unlikely to provide a great deal of individual motivation and may even demotivate.

Linking pay to appraisal can also have the disadvantage of turning the appraisal into a backward looking event where assessments are made and where workers may become defensive, as opposed to using the appraisal to look forward and agree new objectives, discuss development and any training needs. Where pay is at stake the individual may be less receptive to work counselling and may seek to negotiate softer objectives at the outset.

If a worker rated ‚less than satisfactory' receives no increase at all under an appraisal pay scheme their motivation and morale may be adversely affected. It is important therefore to focus appraisals on the assessment of performance, the identification of training needs and the setting of objectives, not on any dependent pay.

Any organisation that chooses appraisal related pay should have good industrial relations and good communications systems in place. It is also important that the finance necessary to operate the scheme is available. Appraisal related pay is most successfully introduced when it is linked to an existing appraisal scheme that is working well, rather than a simultaneous introduction of appraisal and appraisal-related pay.

It is important to monitor the appraisals, to pick up any drift from the overall distribution of ratings and to check the fairness, equity and consistency of the ratings.

Recent surveys have shown that individual performance related pay schemes maintain popularity, particularly for senior managers in the private sector. They have also been introduced in the public sector, and lower level jobs in both sectors.

Managers need to be trained to operate individual performance related pay schemes and should be aware that team-working may be adversely affected - such schemes may prove divisive as workers seek their own performance improvements without consideration of any effect on the work-team and perhaps withhold help and information from co-workers.

Individual performance related pay needs to be carefully considered in the light of any organisational move towards teamwork and worker involvement. Such schemes also tend to lack the transparency sought by workers to properly understand how their pay is decided.

## Market-based pay

Market-based pay links salary levels, and progression through the scales, to those available in the market. It is often used in conjunction with a performance pay matrix, which allows faster progression from the bottom of the scale to the market rate, which will be the mid-point. Progression then slows, regardless of the performance of the worker, as they are deemed to be earning above the market rate for their job. It is rarely used as a scheme in isolation, but may be part of a reward strategy incorporating several performance elements.

## Competency and skills-based pay

Competency and skills-based pay schemes have increased in popularity in recent years. A direct link is created between the acquisition, improvement and effective use of skills and competencies and the individual's pay.

Competency and skills-based schemes measure inputs, ie what the individual is bringing to the job, unlike traditional performance based schemes which measure outputs.

Competency may be generally defined as the ability of an individual to apply knowledge and skills and the behaviours necessary to perform the job well.

Competency based systems have become more wide-spread because many organisations already use competencies in recruitment and in performance appraisal for non-pay purposes, such as development and training. It goes along with the increasing tendency for pay to be linked to the abilities of the individual rather than a single set rate for the job.

Competency based pay is often used in conjunction with an existing individual performance related pay scheme and will reward on the basis of not only what the individual has done, but how they have achieved their targets. Examples of competencies may include leadership skill, or team-working ability. Competency-related pay fits well with an overall organisational philosophy of continuous improvement.

Difficulties may arise in defining the competencies valued by the organisation. There are differences between behaviours that are in-built and those that can be developed. Problems may also arise because of the complex nature of what is being measured and the relevance of the results to the organisation. Judgements about people's behaviour may be less than objective.

Competency assessment rests on several factors - identifying the correct competencies, choosing the right form of assessment and crucially, training the assessors to make accurate, objective judgements.

Skills-based pay also rests on workers gaining new and improved skills - often in a manufacturing environment. Reward is given for skills that can be used in other jobs in the same job band, encouraging multi-skilling and increased flexibility. Workers may also be allowed to develop the skills of a higher job band. Skills may be based on National Vocational Qualifications or internal evaluation and accreditation.

Both competency-based and skills-based pay have similar advantages and disadvantages:

Advantages:

- increased skill and flexibility in the workforce
- reduction in traditional demarcations
- increased efficiency
- tangible benefits for workers in return for changes in working practice.

Disadvantages:

- payroll costs will increase as workers gain higher rewards for increased skills
- increased training costs (time and expenses)
- employers may be paying for skills/competencies rarely used
- queuing for training - if people cannot be released, then there might be re-

sentment and questions of fairness
- can de-motivate once workers reach a ceiling of their training opportunities or there are no higher grade positions available when they have completed their training
- highly trained workers will be more marketable and may be ‚poached' or tempted to leave.

# Remuneration Strategies in a Turnaround Situation: Incentive Schemes for Groups

Key Points:

- Group pay schemes include those based on the performance of the team, plant or company. They also include ‚gainsharing', which is a form of added-value scheme which links pay to the achievement of organisational goals. Share incentive plans involve the provision of shares to employees - either by giving them direct or allowing them to be bought - and can be related to performance.

Some organisations utilise pay systems based on the performance of the team, or group. Sometimes it may be the performance of the whole plant or enterprise that is the trigger for the performance elements of pay.

## Team-based pay

While team-based pay has been around for some time - in the shape of departmental or group bonus systems - it has taken on more importance with the increased interest in teamworking.
In team-based pay systems the payments reflect the measurable goals of the team. Teamworking may be most effective in situations involving high task interdependence and creativity, although it can be difficult to define the team, the goals, and the appropriate reward. Schemes can be divisive if they are not open and transparent. Goals should not be shifted once agreed - they need to be achievable. The aim of team-based pay is to strengthen the team through incentives - building a coherent, mutually supportive group of people with a high level of involvement. The team achievements are recognised and rewarded. Peer group pressure can also be helpful in raising the performance of the whole team.
As with any other pay system, involvement of the workers who will be affected is crucial in the design of the scheme. They must be involved particularly in the way objectives are set, how performance is measured, and the basis on which team rewards are distributed.

Team-based pay has both advantages and disadvantages:

Advantages:

- it can encourage teamworking and co-operation between workers
- team goals can clearly be integrated with organisational objectives
- it encourages less effective performers and acts as an incentive for the whole team to improve
- it may help in developing self-management within the team
- it enhances flexibility of working and encourages multi-skilling.

Disadvantages:

- difficulty in defining the team
- it can take time for teams to become well-defined and work together effectively
- individuals may feel their personal self-worth is diminished
- peer pressure could be oppressive and lead to conformity rather than creativity. Pressure on individuals perceived to be under-contributing or not ‚fitting in‘ can degenerate into bullying and/or harassment
- inter-team competition may become dysfunctional for the organisation as a whole
- once effective the team could prove difficult to change or break-up in response to changing processes, markets or competitive pressures
- each team should have equality of earnings opportunity or inter-team movement will be restricted
- introducing a new member to a team may be problematic, if the team perceive that their earnings could be affected by a less skilled operator
- reduced flexibility because individuals in high performing teams are often reluctant to move to other teams

## Plant or company based pay

Plant or company based performance pay schemes are based on larger groups than teams, for instance, divisional, plant or the whole organisation. They may well use the same factors as team-based or individual performance schemes, or perhaps total sales within a set period, or comparative reductions in labour costs. The most common forms of plant or company based payment systems tend to be based on overall profits (profit sharing), or alternatively on schemes that owe more to the improvements within the direct control of the workforce, such as added value or similar types of gainsharing systems. Overall profitability in an organisation is subject to factors outside the workforce's control, such as depreciation, economic changes, taxation, as well as the productivity improvements of individuals and therefore may not reflect real efficiency gains by the workforce. Plant/company based pay schemes are generally most effective in organisations where the workforce can clearly see the results of their efforts. They are successful where communications and employment relations are good and where the performance measurement is not subject to major changes arising from external causes.

There are advantages and disadvantages to plant and company based pay schemes:

Advantages:

- they can encourage wider co-operation within the plant, with workers being more aware of their contribution to the total effort of the organisation
- they provide a more obvious and direct link with the organisation and its ability to pay
- they may encourage greater flexibility in ways of working to increase efficiency and productivity.
- Disadvantages:
- the direct incentive value of such schemes tends to be relatively weak, as the link between daily work and bonus may seem quite remote, especially if the payments are quarterly or annually
- bonus payments may come to be seen as part of normal pay
- added-value schemes may involve complex financial information and may be difficult to understand.

## Gainsharing

Gainsharing is a form of added-value pay scheme linking workers' pay to the achievement of organisational goals by rewarding performance above a pre-determined target. This may be in the form of a share in the profits generated by sales, or on measures of customer satisfaction, but is almost always led by measures of productivity, performance and quality.

Gainsharing schemes have to be based on factors that are in the workers' control. Gainsharing should be part of a long-term strategy to improve communications, staff involvement and teamwork. The goal is not  to work harder, but more effectively. It may be used as a replacement for bonus/piecework schemes, where quality is sometimes lost to quantity.

All workers and management who have any involvement in the product of the organisation should be included in any gainshare plan. In this way their support is encouraged so that they can feel a direct responsibility for the plan's success. Performance measures and results should be made available and everyone encouraged to offer suggestions for improvements. Open communications and exchange of information are crucial.

Common types of gainsharing schemes include:

Scanlon plan

- this formula measures labour costs as a proportion of total sales and sets a standard ratio which will trigger some distribution of savings to a pre-established formula.
- Rucker plan
- this is a refinement of the Scanlon plan which measures labour costs against sales less the cost of materials and supplies and provides a simple added-value calculation.
- Other gainsharing / value-added schemes
- there are several forms which further refine the calculations and link bonus payments to the increase in added value, above a given norm. Value-added deducts wages and salaries, administration expenses, services and materials from income derived, and thus represents the value added by the production or other process within the organisation. The level of added value of an enterprise is an indicator of its efficiency.

Some examples of the above gainsharing schemes are included in the Share incentive schemes.
Share incentive schemes involve the provision of shares to employees - either by giving them direct or allowing them to be bought. The aim is to encourage staff involvement in the company's performance and therefore improve motivation and commitment.
The Share Incentive Plan (previously the All-employee share ownership plan (AESOP)).
The share incentive plan („SIP") was introduced by the government as part of the 2000 Finance Act. SIPs can include four types of shares:

Free shares - companies can give up to £3,000 worth of shares a year to each employee
Partnership shares - employees can buy up to £1,500 worth of shares a year
Matching shares - companies can reward this commitment by giving up to 2 matching shares for each partnership share an employee buys
Dividend shares - companies can provide for dividends paid on free shares, partnership shares and matching shares to be reinvested in further shares
Companies can award some or all of their free shares on the basis of performance - so long as they satisfy certain criteria laid down by HM Revenue & Customs.

Other schemes

Examples of other share incentive schemes include:

- Savings Related Share Option Schemes (SAYE) - tax advantaged share option scheme for all employees and directors. Participants save up to £250 per month and use the savings and tax-free bonus to exercise their options and acquire shares at the end of a 3, 5 or 7 year period.

- Enterprise Management Incentives (EMI) - companies with gross assets not exceeding £30 million can grant tax and NIC advantaged share options worth up to £100,000 each to any number of employees, subject to total share value of £3 million under EMI.

- Company Share Option Plans (CSOP) - up to £30,000 worth of share options each can be granted to any number of employees with tax and NIC advantages provided the options are not exercised within three years of grant.

- Although share-owning schemes can appear attractive to employers it is not always helpful to a company's finances to have a constant turnover of shareholders. Companies therefore need to be clear about how much of the equity can be held in this way and how to create ways to get workers to keep their shares long-term.

# Remuneration Strategies in a Turnaround Situation: Defining Performance-Related Pay

Performance-related pay (PRP) is a method of remuneration that links pay progression to an assessment of individual performance, usually measured against pre-agreed objectives ('classic' PRP also known as individual PRP or merit pay). Pay increases awarded through PRP are normally consolidated into basic pay although sometimes they involve the payment of non-consolidated cash lump sums.

While the focus of this factsheet is individual, consolidated PRP as a means of pay progression, PRP can be defined more broadly to include many differing systems that link individual and group performance to pay, for example bonus schemes. CIPD members can use our tool on developing bonus and incentive plans.

### How PRP has developed

PRP was the 'big idea' of the1980s, embraced enthusiastically by many employers as the holy grail of driving high performance. Increasingly, there was a desire to move away from service-related pay progression increments (for 'just being there') towards an ethos where individual or group employee performance goals, often linked to pay, were used to support business performance objectives.

However, PRP has proved in some circumstances a rather crude instrument and the 1990s and beyond witnessed a number of challenges to the theory. As some of the earlier schemes failed to deliver the promised results, some employers brought in new or revised PRP schemes or moved to new approaches altogether (for example, skills-based pay) while others have developed hybrid schemes.

Today, the notion of linking pay to a wider definition of employees' 'contribution' rather than simple 'performance' is gaining ground. This emphasises not only performance in the sense of the output (the end result that is achieved) but also the input (what the employee has contributed in a more holistic sense).

Under a new merit pay scheme at Kent County Council, for example, the review process assesses four elements including behaviours (inputs) as well as the delivery of personal objectives linked to business requirements (output).

## PRP rationale

The objectives of PRP systems may be grouped under three main headings:

1. Encouraging high performance levels by linking performance to pay

Arguably, however, PRP is not actually a good motivator – although it may be that even where the direct incentivisation impact is limited, the use of PRP can act as an important lever for wider organisational change. It is often the underlying improvements in performance management that have the greatest impact on bringing about positive developments, rather than the associated pay enhancement. For more information on performance management generally, see our factsheet on that topic.

2. Embedding an entrepreneurial or high-performance culture across an organisation

While PRP can help to send out a message in this respect, there are other (non-monetary) ways of communicating the need for high performance.

3. The notion of equity or fairness

There is more widespread acceptance of the effectiveness of PRP in this respect – that it is right and proper that employees who perform better at work should be rewarded more highly. Our latest employee pay attitudes survey finds that 60% of private sector workers would ideally like their rewards to reflect their performance. By contrast, just 36% of public sector workers would like their pay to reflect their performance.

## Measuring performance

PRP typically uses a system based on consolidated pay progression within pay brackets attached to each grade, level or zone in a structure.

However, in order for performance to be rewarded, it is first necessary to have an effective means of measuring that performance – most commonly via a performance appraisal or review system. See our factsheet on this topic for more information.

Using this approach, each employee's performance is ranked on a scale – typically incorporating three to six categories – ranging, for example, from 'unsatisfactory' to 'superior'. Some systems allow for management discretion in translating these scores into levels of pay rise. However, it is more usual for the performance element of the pay rise to be determined by the use of a formula or a matrix system linking each grade, level or zone to each of the performance categories. This may involve the use of a comparison ratio, or 'compa ratio' – the term given to the relationship between each employee's current salary and the mid-point of their grade. Thus for an employee at the mid-point of their pay range, the compa ratio would be 100%.

It is often felt appropriate for the pay rises associated with each performance category to be higher for employees at lower points within the pay brackets, given the presumed existence of a learning curve for new entrants to a grade. However, more senior employees who are performing very highly may resent the award of comparatively low percentage pay rises.

# Who gets PRP?

Various estimates exist of the coverage of PRP, partly as a result of differing definitions of PRP adopted by researchers. However, some broad themes and trends may be identified:
Individual PRP is far more prevalent in the private than in other sectors – and indeed is virtually the norm' in some parts of the sector such as financial services.

In the public sector, by contrast, the vast majority provide for a basic percentage increase, with a small proportion including a performance-related element.

The use of PRP remains relatively rare in the voluntary sector.

Merit pay most commonly covers managerial and other white-collar staff – and despite a growing interest in the idea of extending coverage to manual workers, few schemes do so.

Our recent employee pay attitude survey (see link above) finds that of those workers who asked their employer about its pay decision, 34% said the increase was linked to their individual performance.

There are of course major differences in coverage of PRP internationally – for example, employers in France make greater use of merit pay than occurs in Great Britain2. Ironically, this is partly attributable to the much more highly regulated employment background in France that leaves individual managers keen to exert some control over the improvement of performance via pay.

## PRP in the public sector

Despite considerable interest in linking pay to performance in the public sector dating back many years, this has proved harder to translate into practice. Where performance pay does occur, it often takes the form of non-consolidated bonuses and/or team-based incentives – an approach recommended by the 2000 Makinson report on performance pay in central government3 – rather than 'classic' individual merit pay.

Nevertheless, there have in recent years been a number of high-profile initiatives such as the introduction of a PRP scheme for teachers, which some researchers argue has resulted in some discernible performance improvements.

A number of distinct issues arise when introducing PRP into a public sector setting, including the potential difficulty of measuring individual effort in certain roles. Moreover, public sector workers such as nurses are arguably motivated by a public service ethos which could actually be undermined by some forms of PRP. One theory though is that PRP in a public service setting can help employees to work more effectively rather than to work harder, by encouraging employees to focus on key objectives.

As concluded by a study covering various forms of incentive pay and bonuses in the public sector:
Public sector workers do respond to financial incentives – and, while responses are sometimes small, this reflects the fact that the incentives are also small.

There is, however, also evidence of 'gaming' – defined as 'manipulation of behaviour that uses resources and does not increase productivity' in response to schemes.

Any overall benefits to society in respect of higher levels of public service are harder to assess.
Current trends in merit awards

Under PRP arrangements, the pay review process may provide for either:

- pay progression entirely on the basis of individual performance appraisal ratings (known as 'all-merit' awards), or
- a general pay rise for employees in addition to an element that is linked to individual performance ('basic-plus-merit' awards).

Trends in performance pay are commonly measured via the pay bill budget allocated for the merit element of awards. Key developments in the most recent pay round as monitored by IRS6 include:
83% of the survey sample reported that the recession was having an impact on the operation of their organisation's PRP scheme. More than half said the budget al-

located to fund performance-related awards had been cut and anecdotal evidence showed that some employers had abandoned PRP, at least temporarily, preferring to give all employees an across-the-board increase, even if just a modest one. However, a small number had gone the other way with 13% abandoning across-the-broad pay awards in favour of merit-based increases.

The median value of the percentage increase in paybill allocated to fund merit awards was 3%.
PRP budgets were highest in manufacturing and production.

## Implementing PRP schemes

For PRP to be effective, employees need to perceive a clear and prompt link between the effort expended and the reward that will be obtained, and also to feel that the level of reward on offer is worth the effort.

The key issues for employers implementing PRP include the following.

Objectivity/consistency of line managers

The role of the line manager is key to the effective implementation of PRP, and steps should be taken to involve this group at an early stage in designing systems, and to ensure consistency and transparency when assessing performance. Some schemes insist that all managers band a certain proportion of staff in each performance pay grouping (for example, 10% 'poor' and 10% 'superior'). Ensuring objectivity is also important to avoid the 'blue-eyed boy' syndrome. Particularly serious is the potential for unlawful discrimination such as sex or race discrimination. It is important for appraising managers to have training/awareness of these issues and for monitoring of merit pay awards to take place (for example by gender, ethnicity and so on).

Distribution of pay awards

As noted by many HR commentators, pay may not be the only motivating factor – or even the most important one – for some employees. Moreover, the performance element of pay is often relatively small, particularly for those relatively middling performers who will by definition form the bulk of the workforce. The problem is accentuated during times of low inflation when the pay bill increase is usually limited to relatively small percentage figures. Even where PRP may have a motivational impact for high performers, the unfortunate corollary can be the demotivation of the bottom performers. As well as careful consideration of pay distribution, the use of performance management techniques in support of PRP can help to tackle such issues.

Identification of development needs

A major concern for HR practitioners is that the linking of pay awards to the performance review process may inhibit an open and honest discussion of an individual's training and development needs. One solution is to separate the pay review aspect of performance measurement from the broader performance/development review, for instance by holding separate meetings some weeks or months apart.

Time-consuming nature

The processes associated with PRP can be very time-consuming. In general, it is important to allow sufficient time away from day-to-day duties for managers and employees to be able to engage in the PRP process effectively.

Undesired impacts on employee behaviour

Poor objective setting can lead to undesired behaviour changes – for example a focus on short-termism or unwillingness to engage in teamworking – as employees try to achieve their individual PRP awards for the year. The aim should be to design objectives carefully to avoid such effects, for example by ensuring that they encourage high performance in the long term.

PRP is not a silver bullet – for this approach to succeed, effective arrangements must be in place to define, measure, appraise and manage performance. The focus should be on encouraging high performance first – underpinned by effective performance management and appraisal systems – and only then on pay as an incentive to help achieve that goal. To create a sustainable high-performing workplace, the whole range of financial and non-financial rewards must be carefully designed to ensure that they support and are supported by PRP.

# Managing Performance in a Turnaround

What is performance management?
In their definitive text upon which this factsheet is based, Armstrong and Baron define performance management as ,a process which contributes to the effective management of individuals and teams in order to achieve high levels of organisational performance. As such, it establishes shared understanding about what is to be achieved and an approach to leading and developing people which will ensure that it is achieved'. They go on to stress that it is ,a strategy which relates to every activity of the organisation set in the context of its human resource policies, culture, style and communications systems. The nature of the strategy depends on the organisational context and can vary from organisation to organisation.'

In other words performance management should be:

- Strategic - it is about broader issues and longer-term goals
- Integrated - it should link various aspects of the business, people management, and individuals and teams.

It should incorporate:

- Performance improvement - throughout the organisation, for individual, team and organisational effectiveness
- Development - unless there is continuous development of individuals and teams, performance will not improve
- Managing behaviour - ensuring that individuals are encouraged to behave in a way that allows and fosters better working relationships.

Armstrong and Baron stress that at its best performance management is a tool to ensure that managers manage effectively; that they ensure the people or teams they manage:

- know and understand what is expected of them
- have the skills and ability to deliver on these expectations
- are supported by the organisation to develop the capacity to meet these expectations are given feedback on their performance
- have the opportunity to discuss and contribute to individual and team aims and objectives.

It is also about ensuring that managers themselves are aware of the impact of their own behaviour on the people they manage and are encouraged to identify and exhibit positive behaviours.

So performance management is about establishing a culture in which individuals and groups take responsibility for the continuous improvement of business processes and of their own skills, behaviour and contributions. It is about sharing expectations. Managers can clarify what they expect individual and teams to do; likewise individuals and teams can communicate their expectations of how they should be managed and what they need to do their jobs. It follows that performance management is about interrelationships and about improving the quality of relationships - between managers and individuals, between managers and teams, between members of teams and so on, and is therefore a joint process. It is also about planning - defining expectations expressed as objectives and in business plans - and about measurement; the old dictum is ‚If you can't measure it, you can't manage it‘. It should apply to all employees, not just managers, and to teams as much as individuals. It is a continuous process, not a one-off event. Last but not least, it is holistic and should pervade every aspect of running an organisation.

Over time, the focus and emphasis of performance has shifted away from individual output to inform development or pay decisions, to individual contribution to organisational objectives through output, behaviour and capability. As such, performance management is now as much about driving engagement and collecting information and data to provide better insight into the drivers of performance as it is about providing information about individuals.

See our recent publications which review how the practice of performance management has evolved since the early '90s and look at the current trends and practice.

## How does performance management work?

Because performance management is (or should be) so all-pervasive, it needs structures to support it. These should provide a framework to help people operate, and to help them to help others to operate. But it should not be a rigid system; there needs to be a reasonable degree of flexibility to allow people freedom to operate.

Performance management is a process, not an event. It operates as a continuous cycle.
Corporate strategic goals provide the starting point for business and departmental goals, followed by agreement on performance and development, leading to the drawing up of plans between individuals and managers, with continuous monitoring and feedback supported by formal reviews.
CIPD members can use our practical tool which sets out the five stages of a development programme to help organisations improve performance management.

## Tools of performance management

It is impossible to go into details of each of the tools used by performance management, so the following paragraphs simply provide an outline.

## Performance and development reviews

Many organisations without performance management systems operate ‚appraisals‘ in which an individual's manager regularly (usually annually) records performance, potential and development needs in a top-down process - see our factsheet on performance appraisal for more information on this topic.

It can be argued that the perceived defects of appraisal systems (that line managers regarded them as irrelevant, involving form-filling to keep the personnel department happy, and not as a normal process of management) led to the development of more rounded concepts of performance management. Nevertheless, organisations with performance management systems need to provide those involved with the opportunity to reflect on past performance as a basis for making development and improvement plans, and the performance and development review meeting (note the terminology; it is not appraisal) provides this chance. The meeting must be constructive, and various techniques can be used to conduct the sort of open, free-flowing and honest meeting needed, with the reviewee doing most of the talking.

## Learning and development

Employee development is the main route followed by most organisations to improved organisational performance, which in turn requires an understanding of
the processes and techniques of organisational, team and individual learning.
Performance reviews can be regarded as learning events, in which individuals can
be encouraged to think about how and in which ways they want to develop. This
can lead to the drawing up of a personal development plan (PDP) setting out the
actions they propose to take (with the help of others, not least their managers) to
develop themselves. To keep development separate from performance and salary
discussions, development reviews may be held at other times, for example, on the
anniversary of joining an organisation.
Increasing emphasis on talent management also means that many organisations
are re-defining performance management to align it to the need to identify, nurture and retain talent. Development programmes are reflecting the needs of succession plans and seeking to foster leadership skills. However, too much of an
emphasis on talent management may be damaging to overall development needs
and every effort needs to be made to ensure that development is inclusive, acces-
sible and focused on developing organisational capability.

## Objectives and performance standards

Objectives (some organisations prefer to use ‚goals‘) describe something to be accomplished by individuals, departments and organisations over a period of time.
They can be expressed as targets to be met (such as sales) and tasks to be completed by specified dates. They can be work-related, referring to the results to be at-
tained, or personal, taking the form of developmental objectives for individuals.
Objectives need to be defined and agreed. They will relate to the overall purpose
of the job and define performance areas - all the aspects of the job that contribute
to achieving its overall purpose. Targets then need to be set for each performance
area, for example, increase ‚sales by x per cent‘, ‚reduce wastage by y per cent‘ …

Alongside objectives are performance standards. They are used when it is not
possible to set time-based targets, or when there is a continuing objective which
does not change significantly from one review period to the next and is a standing
feature of the job. These should be spelled out in quantitative terms if possible, for
example, speed of response to requests or meeting defined standards of accuracy.

### Measurement

To management performance effectively, individuals should know on what basis
their performance will be measured. Measures should be transparent and applied fairly across the organisation. Ideally there should be a mix of individual
and team measures, and measures relevant to both the inputs and the outputs of

performance.

The following examples of performance measures are by no means exhaustive as performance measures are highly contextual and often job specific.

Individual output measures:

- Achievement of objectives.
- Achievement against agreed standards of performance, which might be descriptions of excellent, good, satisfactory or poor performance.
- Behaviour, measuring the extent to which individuals exhibit behaviours associated with performance such as respect for others, trust etc.
- Specific instances of performance for example commendations for specific pieces of work.

Individual input measures:

- Competence.
- Skills and experience and the extent to which news skills are applied in the job.
- Potential to develop and/or acquire new skills and progress to next career level.
- Behaviours associated with developing and knowledge sharing.
- Communication skills and other traits which enhance team roles.

Team measures:

- Individual contribution to the team through involvement in cross team projects.
- Support for other individuals to achieve their objectives and participation in cross organisation initiatives by providing timely input.
- Understanding of team role.
- Engagement scores.

Pay

Performance management is often linked with performance-related pay (PRP), although by no means all organisations claiming to use performance management have PRP. Nevertheless, PRP is an important element in many performance management schemes because it is believed to motivate; it is said to deliver the message that performance and competence are important, and it is thought to be fair to reward people according to their performance, contribution or competence. Others, though, believe that other factors are more important than PRP in motivation; that it is usually based on subjective assessments of performance, that it inhibits teamwork because of its individualistic nature, and that it leads to ‚short-termism'. See our factsheet for more information on performance pay.

An alternative to PRP is competence-related pay, which provides for pay progression to be linked to levels of competence that people have achieved, using a competence profile or framework. The difficulty here is measuring competence, and some organisations use a mix of PRP and competence-related pay. Further possible pay systems are team-based pay, a kind of PRP for teams; and contribution-related pay which means paying for results plus competence, and for past performance and future success.

Performance may be used to determine all or some aspects of pay. In many instances only non-consolidated bonus payments are linked to performance which tend to reflect organisational, team and individual performance whilst salary progression is linked to service, market rates and pay scales.

Many organisations believe that when performance management is linked to pay the quality of performance discussions will inevitably deteriorate.

### 360 degree feedback

360 degree feedback became increasingly talked about in the 1990s, if not widely used. It consists of performance data generated from a number of sources, who can include the person to whom the individual being assessed reports, people who report to them, peers (team colleagues or others in the organisation), and internal and external customers. It can also include self-assessment. 360 degree feedback is used mainly as part of a self-development or management development programme, and is felt to provide a more rounded view of people, with less bias than if an assessment is conducted by one individual. See our factsheet on 360 feedback for more information.

## The First Days in a Turn Around

Having completed a dozen turn-arounds – usually in the role of Interim CEO / COO / GM – I'm often asked, "Are there consistent actions you take the first week at each company?" to which I answer, "Yes…and no." 'No' because each company is unique, with it's own set of problems, strengths, and market constraints; therefore each company requires a unique set of actions. But 'Yes' because I have settled on a consistent process for the first week, a process that helps me determine the real problems and possible solutions.

That said, there is one action I always take the first day; although the companies I've helped turn around have been in very different industries – from electronic ink to wireless mesh to software (of many types) to heart defibrillators to video games – each company needed cash to survive. So the one action I always take the first day is……to tell the head of finance I want, within 36 hours, a detailed understanding of the sources and uses of cash. You can't turn a place around if you run out of cash.

So here's the process for the first week, pretty much no matter what the industry: Day Zero. Before the assignment starts I meet with board members, investors, and the CEO (if he's to remain) – the 'interested parties' – each of whom is either a proponent or opponent to my assignment. (The opponents are usually board members aligned with a founder who is at risk of being moved aside.) The 'good news' about these conversations is that each person has a very clear view of exactly what the problems are and exactly what solutions should be implemented. The 'bad news' is that these clear views of the problems and solutions are often diametrically opposed to the views of other board members! Therefore, as I approach Day One I do not reach any conclusions based on these conflicting conversations. Day One. When I meet one-on-one with each of the Vice Presidents during the first day, I still do not expect that these conversations will result in my finalizing any conclusions about either the problems or the solutions; each VP has their own agenda which clouds the overall picture. But I do conclude two things this first day: Which VPs are 'with me' and which are 'against me.' And which people – mostly outside of the VP ranks – are going to be the 'key players' to turn this company around. The 'with me' VPs are those who are not afraid to take their share of the blame for the company's ills. The 'key players' are determined by asking questions like, "If I told you that someone just quit – let's say Mary – and your reaction was, 'That's bad news. Of all the people in this company the last person I'd want to see quit is Mary,' who is Mary?" Though everyone wants to be able to name more than one 'Mary,' I insist on only one name. (Though once I have the name I ask them to give me a second name!) Sometimes they pick Mary because the company is only one-deep in her area of expertise (usually a problem), but mostly they pick Mary because she's a 'key player.'

Days Two and Three. These days are spent in one-on-one meetings with each of the 'key players.' I try to make this a low-key, casual conversation because many key players are individual contributors who have not previously been asked into the CEO's office to give their view on things. I seek to obtain (a) the names of other key players, (b) their views on the cause of the company's problems, ("So how did we ever get into such a mess?"), and (c) their views on possible solutions ("If you were CEO and could take any action, what specifically would you do to turn this place around?") During my first week, these people are a huge source of information; going forward they will be a huge part of the solution. I end each 'key player' session with a comment that keeps open the door for future one-on-one conversations, allowing me to bypass the layers of management between us. ("I see you spent three years at IBM. At some point I'd be interested in hearing your view on some of the best practices you learned at IBM that we should implement here.")
By the end of Day Three I've a good handle on the company's problems, I've identified and met with all the key players, and I've ideas – often conflicting – on how to solve things.

Days Four and Five. These days I 'test drive' the various conflicting problem-solving ideas on various people, without yet identifying the source. Only after we've settled on a set of solutions will I then give proper attribution to the sources.

("Someone suggested we sell off our best selling product to our main competitor so that we can focus our resources on our soon-to-be-released product which has the potential to open up many new markets. What's your take on that?")

End of the Week: By the end of Day Five I have a mental plan on WHAT needs to be done to turn the place around, though I usually do NOT yet know HOW we'll pull this off. ("We need to cut our expenses by $2 million per year and increase productivity by shutting down our London development center – which is in the middle of a huge product release – and reconstituting the operation in Dublin, all without missing more than one week in the development schedule. How are we going to pull this miracle off?") After a weekend contemplating the solutions, the challenge of Week Two will be to figure out the "HOW".

Satisfying and Fun: When these turn arounds are complete, what's most satisfying is that it is usually a group of existing 'key players' – some VPs, many individual contributors – who have pulled this off. These existing employees – when properly lead, and when augmented by a few new hires – are usually able to turn the company around quickly.

# 10 ways To Measure performance and Establish Where Your Turnaround Project Stands

Turnaround managing an organisation mean it's essential to regularly review your business plan and performance to ensure progress and correct strategic direction. If you don't, the warning sign that your strategy is getting stale could be falling sales or profitability, and in an already critical organisation, that can be lethal. Find out how to measure up and stay fresh.

1. Check your progress against objectives. It might be obvious to re-examine your strategi in a turnaround situation; but it's just as important to assess your objectives on an ongoing basis. Check your progress against targets and if you aren't hitting them consider whether you are pursuing the right goals.
2. Review financial targets. Consider whether poor sales or profitability can just be blamed on market conditions. Talk to your accountant or other professional adviser if you can't pin down the underlying cause of poor performance. It may be time re-assess prices, cut costs or rethink your offer and how you pitch it.
3. Carry out a new SWOT analysis. As trading, societal or market conditions evolve you need to reconsider your strengths, weaknesses, opportunities and threats. Look at your industry and consider what has changed since you last reviewed your business. For example, are you sure your offer is still fit for your market?
4. Assess staff levels and performance. If staff productivity is down, establish the cause. Consider whether you have all the skills you need in your team - it might be time to launch a downsizing drive or bring in some new talent.
5. Benchmark your firm. Weighing up your firm's position against competitors will help you identify gaps in your offer, as well as in your market generally.

Look at what's driving success in your sector - try to pinpoint what enables a successful local competitor to do so well. Is it price, customer service or a recent advertising campaign?

6. Establish whether your customers are satisfied. Talk to customers and you will quickly discover if you are keeping up with their expectations and demands. Even if the majority of feedback is positive, they will always highlight areas where you can improve. Take note and act quickly on anything important.

7. Encourage staff feedback. Listen to your employees — they can provide you with insight into where you are working well and where you are not performing, and why. Make sure you regularly ask them for feedback and ensure they are comfortable with any changes to the business model.

8. Tune into new trends. Keep your ear to the ground to see what trends you can exploit. As well as speaking to customers to see how their needs are changing, read industry news and network to stay current. If you don't know about the latest developments, you risk losing out to competitors who adapt to customer needs before you. However, clearly you shouldn't follow every trend — be wary of compromising your unique selling point.

9. Assess the benefits of new technology. Don't ignore advances in technology - adopting it may save you money, ease work processes or even force a change in your offer. Weigh up whether it's time to update your IT and how you use it - have you incorporated social media into your marketing, for example? Are you using VOIP to reduce call costs?

10. Schedule regular reviews. Your business plan should be a work in progress and reviewed regularly. Assess your objectives at least once a year, as well as whenever your market or operation changes.

# Turnaround Leadership: How to Inspire Creativity in Your Business

The Experts Up Close:

Michael J. Gelb is a creative-thinking expert and leads seminars at companies such as Microsoft and Nike. He is the author of several books, including How to Think Like Leonardo Da Vinci. His latest book is Innovate Like Edison.
Kevin Carroll is a speaker and expert in personal growth and human potential, the founder of Kevin Carroll Katalyst and the author of several books, including Rules of the Red Rubber Ball: Find and Sustain Your Life's Work.
Niurka is a speaker, a communication and influence expert and founder of Niurka Inc., a corporate-training company.

Q: How can I inspire a spirit of innovation in my team members?

Kevin Carroll: *For innovation to flourish within a team and an organization, it is imperative that an organization's work environment foster a culture of "permission,"* which allows employees to think about and share ideas without fear of ridicule and judgment. Employees need to feel unencumbered when it comes to problem-solving, using ingenuity and using their imaginations to innovate.

Preparing and arming your team members with tools, resources and training that gives them increased creative confidence will increase the likelihood of more breakthrough and inventive moments. Some organizations also create specific in-house programs and destinations to increase the overall creative confidence of the organization and to assist with product and brand innovation.
Some organizations go as far as to enlist the expertise of an outside creativity team to assist in redefining the business culture and, ultimately, allowing it to function with more deliberate and strategic intention to implement play and fun moments that have purpose and will enhance innovation.

Michael Gelb: Thomas Edison is the best example for those who wish to nurture the spirit of innovation in an organization. More than the light bulb, phonograph and motion picture camera, Edison's greatest invention was the process of systematic innovation. He created the world's first research and development laboratory and was the first to link R & D with production, manufacturing, marketing and sales.

In our book Innovate Like Edison: The Five-Step System for Breakthrough Business Success Sarah Miller Caldicott (Thomas Edison's great-grandniece) and I introduce five basic competencies for innovating like America's greatest inventive genius. These competencies represent a blueprint for cultivating a spirit and culture of innovation. They are:

1.  Solution-Centered Mindset—Align your goals and passions. Commit to continuous learning, persistent experimentation and optimism in the face of adversity. Balance your optimism for the future with disciplined, rigorous objectivity regarding the issues you confront on a daily basis.
2.  Kaleidoscopic Thinking—Like Edison, keep a notebook to record your creative ideas. Practice generating lots of ideas and then look for patterns and connections. Cultivate the ability to think visually by practicing mind-mapping.
3.  Full-Spectrum Engagement—Optimize your energy by balancing apparent opposites like seriousness and play, intensity and relaxation, solitude and team. For example, if you take a 10-minute relaxation break every 60-90 minutes through the course of your day, you will remember better, work smarter and increase your chances of a breakthrough idea. The first three competencies focus on the attitudes and skills necessary for individual innovation literacy. They set the stage for the last two, which focus on how to create an innovative culture.
4.  Mastermind Collaboration—Recruit and hire for chemistry and results, rather than résumé. Create a multidisciplinary team, encourage an environment of open-exchange, and reward collaboration.
5.  Super-Value Creation—Create new, sustainable customer value by tuning in to your target audience. Seek to identify gaps in the marketplace and encourage your team to think creatively about how to bridge those gaps. Focus on buil-

*ding an unforgettable market-moving brand.*

Q: When generating new business ideas, should I reach out to all associates to utilize my entire talent pool?

Niurka: *Good ideas can come from anywhere—sometimes from the people you least expect. If you want passionate, committed people who are excited to contribute to your vision, enroll them in the process of generating ideas. Not only will they feel they have a stake in the company direction, they will also be creatively energized as they share and refine ideas.*

*Be certain to give clear guidelines for submitting suggestions from the beginning. Be specific about what you are looking for and why. Everyone has an opinion about how business should be run, so ask for specific feedback about what could be even better. And remind them to be solution-focused. Everyone will have suggestions to share, so respect each one and honor the contributors while communicating that not every suggestion will be immediately (or ever!) implemented.*

*Your team will be especially eager to share great insights when you offer rewards and incentives for the implemented idea that generates the greatest results for the company. Once all ideas are collected, remind everyone that there is a time and place for idea generation and a time and place for implementing those ideas. So once you've decided on a direction, commit to it and archive the other ideas for possible future use. Have the core team filter through and distill all ideas into the most effective ones for final consideration. Then make the final decision in accordance with the organization's values, purpose and mission.*

Michael Gelb: *Get everyone involved. The most creative organizations encourage a democracy of ideas. Thomas Edison's employees knew that their boss was a world-class genius. Yet, he was renowned for his collegiality with all the people who worked for him. As his former employees and contemporaneous biographers Dyer and Martin wrote, "He conversed, argued and disputed with us all as if he were a colleague on the same footing." When people at all levels know that their thinking is valued and respected, as they did in Edison's laboratory, it encourages them to do more constructive thinking.*

Kevin Carroll: *I've heard it said more than a few times that "creativity is NOT the sole, exclusive property of those deemed to be "creative." It's important to realize that if the goal is to foster an innovative culture throughout your organization, then be sure to be inclusive in the process to unearth solutions, because you NEVER know where the next great idea may come from. An organization's ability to deliver beyond-the-box thinking and new ideas can be bolstered by reaching out to the larger talent pool and creating a much more inclusive ideation process.*

Q: Creativity is not my strong suit. I want to hire someone whose strength is creativity. How can I tell if I have the best candidate?

Niurka: *It's easy to be seduced by creativity, especially for those who think of themselves as creatively challenged. So, if you're seeking a creative person to magically make business more glamorous, successful or interesting, don't just hire the first artist who shows up!*

*First, get clear about exactly what results you expect. Define the position in detail, including what specifically you want the person to do. Creativity can be challenging to measure, so determine in advance how you will gauge their success and progress.*

*What do you have to see, hear and feel to know that this person is the right fit? Before you interview candidates, ask to see a portfolio. It will speak volumes about the candidate's creativity and ability to present ideas in a powerful, elegant and innovative way. Look beyond the hype—creativity isn't just about show; it's about communicating a clear message in a unique and captivating way. Does the work lead to a specific, desired result? Does it fit with your company vision, or have that potential? When hiring a creative person, you'll want someone not only creative, but who can communicate well with you, your team, and your audience of clients, customers, and stakeholders. Once you've narrowed it to a few candidates, ask for a proposal. It will illuminate if the candidate understands the company's vision, the scope of the project and their role within it. And of course, choose someone with a passion for the position!*

# Turnaround Leadership: How to Build Your Dream Team

I often hear from clients that they say I have a talent for building high-performance and high-reliability teams. To me, teamwork comes natural becasue I believe that nobody on his own is great enough to manage everything on his own, and that without the help of others you only get so far.

So if you are tired of infighting, conflict and less-than-productive team efforts, dealing with your team's dysfunctions can consume all your time and effort, if you let it. The answer is building habits that help form a unified front.

Teamwork gets a lot of lip service in business. Is teamwork really as critical for success relative to other disciplines like technology or marketing?
I honestly believe that the single biggest competitive advantage that a company can pursue today is getting its leaders on the same page. I'm not implying that other disciplines aren't important—they are. But the truth is that without effective teamwork, without a cohesive group of people leading an organization, a company cannot begin to tap into the potential that it has in any other areas.

What's the first step to building a strong team?
You need to make sure you hire people who are capable of being strong team players. Team members should fit the company's culture, be committed to the team and be capable of being genuinely vulnerable and selfless.

Once the team is in place, make teamwork an ongoing priority, not just a slogan. Front load the team-building process by scheduling a meaningful offsite gathering. But remember, effective team-building has to be done in the context of real work, not tree climbing exercises. That doesn't mean you shouldn't get to know one another on a personal level and understand people's different personalities and their life experiences though. Team-building exercises have to be grounded in the realities of doing our jobs. That's what makes the team-building process stick.

How does the current economic crisis change the way you go about building teams?
I don't think it changes the approach as much as it creates a new challenge.

We have to confront the misguided reluctance to focus on our teams during this crisis and realize that without it, we're not going to be able to effectively identify and implement new ways to survive and thrive.

How can a leader build a unified team?
I encourage leaders and their teams to address the five causes of team dysfunction. To start, teams must address the first and most important dysfunction: an absence of trust. This sounds obvious, I know. But the kind of trust I'm referring to has to do with the ability of team members to be vulnerable with each other. Team members need to be able to admit their weaknesses and their mistakes, to acknowledge the strengths of others and to apologize when they do something wrong. This is critical on any team, but in a small company, people hiding their weaknesses and covering up their mistakes is particularly lethal because there is nowhere to run or hide. If even one team member can't be vulnerable, the work environment will likely be uncomfortable and the team will have difficulty taking on the next dysfunction: fear of conflict.

You are encouraging conflict on teams?
Yes, the fact is that great teams argue. Not in a mean-spirited or personal way. But they disagree, and passionately, when important decisions are made. They argue about concepts and ideas and avoid personality-focused mean-spirited attacks. Of course, so many of us have been raised to avoid conflict and disagreement that we try to compromise and reach artificial consensus, and that only leads to mediocrity.

But can't conflict break apart a team?
Only if there is too little trust. And that's why I say that lack of trust is the most important of the dysfunctions to overcome and why it must be addressed first. When team members trust each other and know that everyone is capable of admitting when they're wrong, then conflict becomes nothing more than the pursuit of truth or the best possible answer. Without trust, conflict becomes politics.

Engaging in conflict is necessary to achieving commitment on a team, which brings us to the next dysfunction: lack of commitment. When team members openly and passionately share their opinions about a decision, they don't wonder whether anyone is holding back. Then, when the leader has to step in and make a decision because there is no easy consensus, team members will accept that decision because they know that their ideas were heard and considered.

What happens if members disagree with a leader's ultimate decision?
That's the amazing thing. Even if they still disagree, there is a very high likelihood that they'll do everything they can to support it. After all, most of us are fully capable of embracing something that we didn't choose, but only if we think the people who made the decision listened and considered our input. Leaders have to realize that employees have a great capacity for rallying around a decision and that they don't have to get their way. They just need to have their way heard and considered.

Assuming the team is able to commit to a decision, how does a leader ensure follow-through?
Teams need to overcome the fourth dysfunction: avoidance of accountability. The best kind of accountability on a team is peer-to- peer. Peer pressure is more efficient and effective than going to the leader, anonymously complaining and having them stop what they're doing to intervene. On great teams—the kind where people trust each other, engage in open conflict and then commit to decisions—team members have the courage and confidence to confront one another when they see something that isn't serving the team. The only way team members will be able to do this is if the leader can effectively demonstrate their willingness to hold people accountable first.

What is the fifth cause of team dysfunction?
It is inattention to results. Team members have to be focused on the collective good of the team. Too often, they focus their attention on their department, their budget, their career aspirations, their egos. Great teams put the tangible results of the team ahead of their individual needs. That might sound idealistic, but it is something that truly great teams do. Team members won't subjugate their own needs if they aren't held accountable. And they probably won't be held accountable if they haven't actively committed to the intended results. And they can't commit to those results if they haven't debated and weighed in on the decision. And they won't debate and weigh in if they don't have confidence that everyone on the team is vulnerable enough to be trustworthy.

How long does it take to build an effective team?
It depends. If a team works together over a relatively short period of time, they can achieve this kind of team dynamic in a matter of weeks. But that means they talk about being a team, both in terms of interpersonal dynamics and specifi c goals and results. The fact is, some teams can work together for years and still be dysfunctional, and others can come together over the course of a month and become remarkably cohesive.

Let me just add one important point. Building a team is a process that never ends. Like a marriage, it requires a constant investment of time and energy. For those entrepreneurs willing to make teamwork a priority, they will enjoy a powerful competitive advantage that is essential for maneuvering in today's marketplace.

# Turnaround Leadership: Are You a Travel Agent or a Tour Guide?

Mahatma Gandhi said: „Be the change you are trying to achieve". Everything we want to accomplish on a change programme starts with us.

You see, leaders are either travel agents or tour guides. A travel agent send people to places they themselves have never been. They give them a brochure and say „Bon voyage". Too few leaders are like tour guides, who take you to the places they have been and experienced. If you start by making the changes you need to make, you'll lead from experience, and that will give you greater confidence and influence.

Some changes you need to make may include taking better care of yourself. It's a matter of fact that if you are physically or emotionally depleted, you won't have anything to give to others. What do the flight attendants tell you to do if the cabin looses pressure? Before assisting children or other passengers, take the oxygen mask and put it on yourself first. The lesson  here is you cannot help others if you don't help yourself first.

# Turnaround Leadership: Delegation

Howe To Delegate Effectively

In a turnaround time is everything. When a business is in dire straits, you don't have time; you need to turn the ship around quickly before the worst happens. That's why efficiency and effectiveness is everything. It is logic that you can achieve more if you get more people to work on a task than doing it all by your own. To get other people working, you need to delegate. But you need to delegate professionally.

People rarely delegate efficiently. Mostly what happens is that people get told to do a job or take something on – that is not delegation.

The most frequent excuse for not delegating properly is: "It's easier to do it myself". All that happens here is overload for you and loss of morale for others. The reasons for not wishing to delegate properly usually are:

*   You do not understand the need to delegate or do not know how to do it
*   You lack confidence in team members, and therefore will not give them the

authority for decision-making

- You have tried to delegate in the past, but failed and so you will not try again
- You like doing a particular job that should be delegated, but will not delegate it even though you know the team-member would enjoy the job
- You do not understand the management role or how to go about it
- You are frightened of making yourself dispensable, so keep hold of every job

Delegation is a skill. Like most skills, they can be learned. Here are some tips for effective delegation:

- Plan delegation well in advance
- Think through exactly what you want done. Define a precise aim
- Consider the degree of guidance and support needed by delegate
- Pitch the briefing appropriately. Check understanding
- Establish review dates. Check understanding
- Establish a "buffer" period at the end, in which failings can be put right
- Delegate whole jobs wherever possible, rather than bits and pieces
- Inform others involved
- Having delegated, stand back. Do not "hover"
- Recognize that the work may not be done exactly as you would have done it
- Do not "nit-pick"
- Delegate, do not abdicate responsibility

Things that can be delegated

- Work that should be done by another person or in another department
- Time-consuming tasks not entailing much decision making
- Repetitive tasks that require decision making and could help develop a team member

Tasks that should not be delegated

- Seeking opportunities for the enterprise
- Setting strategic aims and objectives
- Creating high achievement plans for the department
- Co-ordinating activity – knowing the task that has to be done, the abilities and needs of the staff, the resources available and mixing them to achieve optimum results
- Communicating with staff and with senior managers and colleagues
- The training and development of your team

## How to delegate

Each task that has been chosen as suitable for delegation should have a specification. This should state clearly:

- The objective or intended goal of the job
- The method you have developed to do it
- Data requirements and where / who the information comes from
- Any aids or equipment needed to accomplish the task
- Definition of boundaries of responsibility
- Principal categories of decisions that have to be made
- Any limitations on authority where making these decisions are concerned

Delegation is often considered a one-way ticket, being helpful only to the person in charge. But it has a bonus effect: It is of considerable benefit to the member of staff to whom the work is delegated. Effective delegation is a huge boost to the development of individuals both practically and psychologically.

## Turnaround Leadership: Clarity of Message

In a change situation it is important to be very clear, because people are already in a stage of uncertainty, new leaders might have entered the scene, displaying different leadership styles and most of all: There is neither room for error nor for misunderstandings.

Recently my of my Australian clients told me about a performance problem. It seemed that the performance of his staff was an ever dramatically swing, from peak to trough, day by day, week by week, month by month, year by year --- for years on end. I decided to shadow him and soon found out what went wrong:

He constantly sent out mixed messages. For example, in a staff meeting where he delivered some straight talk about the pending crisis and the need for everybody to pull their weight he pinpointed the weaknesses and nonperformance of staff. So far so good. But a minute later he started to hand out performance awards, (they are themselves in the motivational products business, so the idea was double nice) and at the of the meeting every single one in the room had received an award - the very sames people who received a pep-talk about their under performance 10 minutes before. Failing to make sure that both, the performers AND the under performers were in the room, a perfectly good idea got wasted.

Later on staff hand to stand up and pledge the company values and principles, a very good idea to gain commitment, create team spirit and reinforce the company's values and attitudes. However, body language and attitude of the leader confused staff who was torn between taking this whole thing as a slapstick or a serious business meeting. Why? Because the boss tried to sprinkle some humor and started laughing and giggling, self-sabotaging his efforts in this crucial moment.

Praise and blame, humor and seriousness have an absolute place in business - but not at the same time. As a leader, it is important to be perceived as clear, authentic

and serious, and that means that you have to fine tune and align all your communication chancels, including your body language, rhetoric and verbatim.


# Handling the Press

The following article from January 2011 is a good example of bad PR. Not trained
on PR, statements easily become laughable and can do a lot of damage:

LONDON (AFP) – Kesa Electricals, which owns the Comet retail chain, warned
on Wednesday that annual profits will be at the low end of investor expectations
due to wintry weather and increased competition in its major markets.

„Adjusted profit before tax (is) currently expected to be ahead of last year and towards the lower end of market expectations," the group said in a trading update.
Market expectations are currently for annual profit of between 98 million and
119 million euros.

Kesa said group sales on a like-for-like basis, stripping out the effect of new floor
space, sank by four percent between November 1, 2010 and January 18, 2011.

The group, whose businesses include electrical retail chains Comet in Britain and
Darty in France, said adverse weather conditions in major markets had hit sales
by about two percent.

This is interesting, because weather conditions seem to have only affected Comet.
Apparently it snowed on them, but not on Tesco and on M&S, whose profits were
up.

It is a sign of maturity to accept responsibility and not to look for a scape goat.
Perhaps the reasons for Comet doing not so well is rather their lack of a clear
profile and their renown bad customer service.

„Against a background of increased competitiveness, Darty France and the other
established businesses delivered a robust performance, offset by softer trading at
Comet and the developing businesses," chief executive Thierry Falque-Pierrotin
said in the statement.

Let us translate this into plain English: „Competition is outperforming us but yet
we only lost out less than we feared".
„We remain confident in our strategy and committed to our plans to implement
the Darty concept in all our markets and we have put in place a number of additional measures to improve revenue and reduce costs," he added.

Plain English translation: „we stubbornly stick to our strategy (observe the choice
of word, not „improve" our strategy but „remain committed" to it) and will roll-

out bad customer service of faceless stores. Knowing this won't work, we are prepared to sack staff, because reducing costs is easier to do than increasing sales". (Watch the choice of words: „Revenue" will be improved, not „sales" - and revenue comes from slashing costs if it doesn't come from selling more).

But Comet was expected to perform badly this year, partly because of the British government's recent VAT sales tax hike.
„Since the introduction of the VAT increase on 4 January we have so far seen sales trends soften," Kesa said.

Again interesting, as many other retailers seem to be doing well despite the VAT increase.

„In the light of these factors we are now anticipating that Comet will deliver a small retail loss for the year."

Nota Bene Turnaround Managers: Finding a scape goat does not constitute a discharge of responsibilities, and announcing pending losses is not managing expectations and does not constitute an except for accountability.

## Sales Strategies For Turnaround Situations: Up Trading = Upgrading

A typical root cause for a getting into a turnaround situation is the fact that you either don't sell enough products or that you don't sell enough products at the prices you need to sell them at.
Reducing prices is a common strategy, but it's the most ill of all: Reducing prices means that you have to move more stock to achieve your break even. But moving more means producing more, selling more, servicing more, and „more" means also more resources, more money, more costs.
It is always easier to sell 10 Rolls Royce a year than 1 million bicycles. Furthermore, to grow by 10% next year means selling 1 care more but it means selling 100.000 bikes more. Plus, at some day in the future your market will be saturated, and that „some day" is coming sooner the more you sell (at low prices).
Think about the current economic crisis: The very first business that went bust was Woolworth, not Harrods. So why is that if price is everything? Because it's not!

IF I have a business, I rather make it rely on rich customers than on poor customers, because the rich tend to stay rich even during a crisis. Like it or not: Rich people get richer, poor people get poorer. That's why it makes sense to establish or re-position your business in the high-end rather than at the low, non-profitable end.
For example, even now Luxury Goods are booming. A taste for finer things will propel sales of luxury goods by 4 % in 2011. This will bring the industry close to,

but not above 2008 level. Future growth will be led by China's ravenous appetite for prestige brands, as well as new sales channels everywhere. Having only recently edged into cyberspace, the share of online luxury sales will rise to around 5% of total sales from 4% in 2010. Cosmetics, leather goods and prêt-a-portê collections will be easiest to buy by click; watches and jewellery will remain a largely offline affair. In General, luxury goods are a good bet: In tough times buying a new car or exotic holidays might be out of the question but most consumer can still feed their hedonistic needs by treating themselves to new luxury cosmetic, handbags, briefcases, pens or a bottle of fine wine or champagne.

Up trading, by the way, is not an exclusive option for those in the classic luxury goods line of business. I have even positioned manufacturers of mundane generic products such as charcoal in a high-end market, allowing them to claim three times as much as their nearest competitors.

Another option is to develop new products: Established products tend to price-erode and retailers achieve 90 % of their turnover with products that are newer than 5 years. To survive you need, to grow you should have a constant flow of new products. In a turnaround situation it's not an option, it's a must.
In 2011 the new product „Tablet Computers" will generate the most buzz in the IT world. Apple's iPad will sell 28 m units in 2011. Competitors will introduce rival products - HP, Samsung and Research in Motion among them - but Apple will retain a 70% share of the tablet market, another advantage if you are able to claim your fist-mover stake. Hint: There are yet no specialist online shops for tablet computers.

## Sales Strategies For Turnaround Situations: Quick, Profitable and Safe Sales

Usually people then tell me the name of their biggest client. But that's not what I asked for. I asked not "who is OUR largest client", I wanted to know who is THE largest customer for our product in the whole world. This is when people shrug shoulders. And this is when I get mad. I mean, how can you execute a powerful marketing strategy if you don't even know where your market is? To find out the key users for your product is an exercise so basic I expect an intern to o it, and yet 1 out of 1000 sales managers is clearly able to tell me which is the single-largest customer on the planet.
Because it's just after Christmas and I am still in a giving mood, I give you the answer, which is well and truly a million-dollar-answer because it is quite literarily worth millions of dollars: For approximately 75 % of all goods or services offered on this planet, the single largest customers is the US Government. It spends $ 1500 bn year on year and it buys everything from toilet rolls to houses, from pens to cars and from web design to travel agency services. The list is endless. Approximately half of this budget is spent on defence - $ 700 bn in 2011.
For those who are like me and find it hard to relate to big numbers: $ 1500 bn is

equivalent to the GDP of Canada. So if you feel its worthwhile exporting to Canada, you must feel its worthwhile to sell to the US Government.

Often I get a lot of ignorance from turnaround clients and hear prejudices such as selling to the government are cumbersome, unprofitable, and only possible when subscribing to bribe or worse. Perhaps it ignorance that contributed to the crisis in the first place because all that is not at all true when it comes to the US Government. Trust me, I know, I secure government contracts for my clients for almost 2 decades and have added hundreds of million dollar bottom line results and I am surely not agreeing to sell at a loss, bribing or wasting time and money on inefficient and unproductive tendering.

## Sales Strategies For Turnaround Situations: Leverageing Emerging Markets

This is one of the unforgivable sins, because every business person should know that you simply do not put all your eggs in one basket. Last time I counted there were 193 different markets out there and I have never heard of the fact that all of the broke away simultaneously.

When in the need to start developing export sales, it makes sense to start where it's easy. And that's where there is growth. After all, trying to enter a depressed market can only lead to frustration, a waste of time, immense costs and low profits as a result of decaying prices.

So let's focus on the growth regions. Where are they in 2011?

Right there:

| Rank: | Country: | GDP Growth in %: |
|-------|----------|------------------|
| 1. | Qatar | 15,9 |
| 2. | Ghana | 14,0 |
| 3. | Uzbekistan | 8,5 |
| 4. | China | 8,4 |
| 5. | India | 8,2 |

An additional benefit is the fact that a lot of companies will consider these places still somewhat"exotic", allowing you to claim first-mover benefits. Think of Pepsi: While Coca Cola has penetrated the traditional markets, Pepsi has always been the first one on markets that were on nobody else's radar at the time and it is earning good money with its strategy.

Market entry will be easier and cheaper. I bet in Ghana and China they are not yet asking for listing fees, rack space lease and marketing contribution when you try to get your new product listed at the large supermarket chains.

I have picked this example because of all products and services it will be consumer products that will be doing interestingly in 2011.

Rich-country consumers will be slightly more confident in 2011, although tight credit will limit spending. Retail sales in America will grow by 2,4 %, faster than the 1,1 % rate that Japanese spenders will muster. Shoppers in western Europe will be the most miserly, cutting their spendings by 1,8 %, throwing a number of suppliers into a turnaround situation, as sluggish economies and government austerity squeeze incomes.

Consumer spending in China will expand by a whopping 22%, driven by rising incomes and government efforts to diversify the economy - music in the ears of companies seeking new markets for their products. Banks are being asked to devote more of their resources to consumer lending in hopes of eroding deeply ingrained saving habits.

Although retailers will flock to China, India and Russia are also appealing, if the legal and cultural hurdles can be overcome. After years of sniffing around for a takeover, Wal-Mart should finally establish itself in Russia, blazing the trail for others to follow.

Online sales will be a universal bright spot for retailers. So, if you haven't been told yet, you are being told now: If you are selling a product or service and have not web shop, you should not be in business at all because your omission is criminal. E-Commerce in the US and western Europe will grow at annual rates of 10% and 11% respectively.

If you would like boost your Internet sales, you want to read this book: *307 Ways To Build a Successful Web-Shop*

# Sales Strategies For Turnaround Situations: How To Deal With Public Spending Cuts

A lot of businesses that depend on public sector customers are vulnerable and prone to the risk of entering a crisis, following public sector spending cuts of historic dimensions.

Now is the time to decide how you are going to deal with the new situation.
The £81 billion of cuts announced in October 2010 won't just affect those firms that directly supply Government departments, but will also be felt by many businesses further down the supply chain. Find out how you can minimise the effects of public spending cuts on your firm.

The Government cuts unveiled in the Comprehensive Spending Review will hit many small firms hard. All public sector suppliers, direct or indirect, should form a contingency plan — as while the details of some of the cuts have already been unveiled, the full effects are likely to continue to filter down the supply chain over the coming months.

If your contract is directly with a government department, you are probably aware that you could lose work. However, even more small firms will be hit by the knock-on effects further down the supply chain.

## Manage lost contracts

Small businesses which have already lost contracts may have to make tough decisions, particularly if they are heavily dependent on the public sector. If you haven't yet lost business, check when your contract is due to end and find out if you can charge any penalties if it is cut early.

Firms in the services sector and businesses that tend to rely on contract work - such as construction and IT firms - are most likely to be affected.

Most businesses which lose contracts will be forced to cut costs to survive. You could consider reducing staff hours to 20 a week and then expand later when you have a better measure of your finances. If you have taken all other possible steps, you may have to let people go as a last resort.

If you lose a contract, approach your finance provider as soon as possible. Try to mix good news in with the bad, take a business plan and explain what you need. If your turnover drops, the working capital requirement often also drops, so you might only need a temporary overdraft extension.

## Adapt your offer

The Government expects to save £800 million in 2011 by renegotiating contracts with suppliers, so even the contracts you retain may become less profitable. Pre-empt this by approaching government departments first.

Perhaps offer them something which has lower input costs, with less features or a reduced service. Otherwise, you could adapt your offer to appeal to private sector clients, as the public sector will not be a growing market for a while for most firms. You need to establish what private sector opportunities there are to explore, or even consider overseas markets.

## Plan for further cuts

To find out if your remaining contracts are vulnerable, maintain good communication with your contact manager at the relevant government department. Your sales staff should also look out for warning signs. Having informal conversations with customers often yields useful information about contracts.

By planning ahead, you can limit the damage the cuts have on your firm. If you have lost public sector contracts, or are about to, the key is to take a measured response and don't assume things will get better by themselves. If you demonstrate to customers and suppliers that you are dealing with the situation proactively, you are much more likely to survive it.

## Sales Strategies For Turnaround Situations: Pricing For Turnaround - Pricing For Profit

In a turnaround situation it is important to get back to profit. This sometimes is difficult because a lot of people will be scared of putting their prices up; they believe they have to be cheap in order to attract customers. These are people who still think that "it's all about price". They are wrong. Those sales people who say that it's all about price simply lack of sales skills and all they can do is sell on price because every other aspects of their sales skills sucks.

The first victim of the latest economic crisis was Woolworth, not Harrods. It was General Motors, not Rolls Royce. It was Air India, not Lufthansa. Evidence enough that it is not about price.

Would you regard a Rolls Royce in the same way if it cost the same as a Ford Ka? I think not.

Think of people who have recently regretted not spending more on insurance as they have bailed their houses out after the recent floods.

Price and value go together. Price is only important if it's the only thing and your product has absolutely nothing else to offer. In which case you should not be in business anyway.

For the most part, people do not want the cheapest thing available. Walk around any supermarket and you'll notice that the brand leaders are never the cheapest products.

Taking this advice to heart, here are some key pricing tactics:

- Avoid round figures: People seem to buy more when price is set just below round figures - £ 9.97 (nota bene: "7" is the new "9") seems less than £ 10.00. Similarly, £ 977 seems significantly less than £ 1.000. Do not worry about why this is; it may seem silly – but it works, so use it.
- Range quotes: In a business where exact costing may be impossible, a quote may say that costs will be between £ 3.000 and £ 4.000, and that a degree of uncertainty may be acceptable. A larger gap might not. Nor is going over the top limit; this can very often prevent reordering – "They always go over their estimate".
- Exact price for bespoke work: If you undertake work where what you propose is a unique method or approach for an individual client – like a computer system, printing or consultancy – then remember that it will not be seen as credible if it just happens to work out at exact £ 10.000. Such a price will certainly encourage resistance. It will seem like the figure is either a calculation you have rounded up, or that the service being offered is not, in fact, bespoke. And that may well devalue it when a tailored solution is wanted.
- When someone asks, "How much?" rather than turning to jelly, you have to say "Just £XYZ, and worth every penny and it includes..." and emphasize the value. People want value. They want certainty. Neil Armstrong, the first man to walk on the moon, was asked what he had thought about during take-off. He said to have recalled that there were hundreds of thousands of

components in the machine below him and in every case NASA had given the contract to the lowest bidder. I doubt that knowing this did much for his confidence!

- Amortize the costs (i.e. spread them over a period: Less than £ 100 a month or just under (say £96) sounds much more attractive than £1,150 for the year).
- Pack size: A number of food companies have been criticized for reducing the size of their products – like a chocolate bar – while retaining the same price. This is effectively a price increase.
- Extras: With some products the number of elements that need to be paid for in addition to the basic price is lengthy; motor cars are a good example. Even one element added beyond the basic price is effectively a price increase.
- Deluxe: Research shows that when a company offers two similar products, one the "Rolls Royce" version of the other at a premium price, the majority of customers chooses the higher priced. This is usually configured so that it is also the most profitable; the extra features do not cost as much as the price difference.
- Link to other factors: Many mobile phones are cheap or free, the cost of industrial equipment may be linked in a similar way to servicing and spare parts. Such links are possible with many products
- Trade discounts: While the price of a book, say, may be he same in a chain store and an independent book shop, they will likely have been given different discounts (the chain store will have obtained a greater discount); different outlets selling the same products therefore can produce different profits.
- Discounts can be given on a variety of bases (like the large and small retailer above), but in turnaround situations you need to see that, wherever possible, you gain something from the process. Quantity discounts is perhaps the prime example; the unit price is less, but only when more are bought; it is a deal that can suit both parties. Alternatively, discounts may be linked to other advantages such as a discount for a cash payment or the purchase of another (perhaps related) product.

In an overall process that brings in the business, a continuing focus on, and commitment to, marketing action is necessary at a time when the gut reaction is to cut indiscriminately at the first sign of trouble. Sales down? Cut advertising and promotion, cut the staff and the training budget and then what…hope that the business will continue unaffected?

So what to do? Torn between cutting down costs and the fear that cutting down costs will affect the business, many managers get stuck, do nothing at all and hope the problems will go away. But most often "waiting for things to get back to normal" is simply not an option. Especially not in a crisis.

A number of factors seem to us to be fundamental: action and attitudes designed to make it more likely that existing customers will be held, new ones still won, the organisation kept on track and profitability protected and ideally maintained.

Some of these actions are:

- Do save money but do keep orders coming in.
- Professional selling: selling is a final link with customers. It can be taken for granted in buoyant times and must be deployed in the best possible way in any other, and this includes -specifically in a turnaround situation- sales training, because you can no longer afford to not utilize your sales team to its fullest and do need improved sales "PDQ" (pretty darn quick), because it's not an order until the money is in the bank.
- Professional selling means selling at a profit: Bullish pricing. In a recession even a hint from a customer that prices are too high often tended to lead to instant and ill-considered discounting. Price is now better understood for its role as part of the marketing mix, not least as a sign of quality, and organisations are now more likely to set profitable prices with confidence, justifying them rather than trembling of they are challenged.
- Do the maths: If you do give discounts, it is easy to deceive yourself by making assumptions rather than calculations. Couple this with a tendency to immediately offer discounts when faced with tough times and you have a recipe for disaster.

Consider some simple figures: you sell something for £ 100 and with costs of £ 50, you are marking up by 100 % and making £ 50 profit. Say you feel you must offer a discount. You want to make it significant to customers and yet preserve your profitability as much as possible, so you discount by 10 %. Thus your selling price is £ 90 and with costs still £ 50 you make a profit of £ 40.

Now do one more calculation. What percentage of your profit has gone? £ 10 of your original £ 50 has gone – that's 20 %. This ratio gets even scarier when large discounts are given.

If you give 20% off that's £ 20 off the sales price but that's a 40% of your profit, 30 % discount equals 60% profit and if you reduce your sales price by 50 %, thinking you still make half the profit, you are sadly mistaken because your are now starting to loose money.

I am not saying price reductions cannot be part of your turnaround strategy; they may have to be. But…

- Charge for any necessary extras in the best way. Look no further than Ryanair if you want to see these opportunities maximised.
- It also means chase payments! In a recession, those you do business with will very likely be suffering the same difficulties you are, and will be actively delaying payment. Certainly payment to those who do not chase. Once you made sale and invested all that effort into closing it, make sure you get paid.
- Do not deal with people who cannot pay: Credit checks are always a sensible thing to do, more so in difficult times. Do not skimp them and even more important, do not ignore them. It is easy when every order counts to give someone the benefit of the doubt – you accept the order, knowing that the check is not as good as you would like and "hope for the best". Don't do it – it is better not to have the business than to have it and the attendant costs and

not get paid.

- Talk to your bank about how to improve the management of your cash flow and to others like debt collectors too. Most important: Talk to your bank before your bank talks to you.

## Customer Service Strategies For Turnaround Situations: How Excellence Will Save You Money

A lot of people think that high quality is expensive to deliver. But actually delivering high customer care quality is reducing the cost of sale. How come?

Typically it takes 7 impacts on a consumer until a sales is made. These impacts could look like that:

1. Promotional activity leads the way.
2. Some people seeing this contact the company for more information.
3. Some of those receiving more information in whatever way (from telephone contact, brochures or website) ask to see someone.
4. A sales person has a meeting with them (it could be more than one).
5. Some people will want a formal quotation or proposal (and there could be other stages such as a presentation, demonstration or sample depending on the nature of the product or service).
6. While some orders may come now (or earlier), other prospects need following up – by phone, email, in person or whatever is appropriate.
7. Finally, you can log the number of firm orders that come through the "system".

It should ne noted here that by its nature this process is wasteful. If prospects drop out at a late stage (at worst because they feel that something has been done inadequately) then the time and cost it took to get them that far is gone for ever, and a similar investment of time and efforts (and cost) needs to be made to get another prospect through. In turnaround time this kind of wastage is something very much to be avoided.

How do you avoid it? By maximising the customer care quality. Typically there are a lot of things that can go wrong, and often they actually will, such as

1. Stage – required information is not provided quick enough, not at all or wrong information is provided.
2. Stage – customer don't get through on the phone and hang up, it takes too long for them to see someone or the are being paired up with the wrong counterpart.
3. Stage – the salesperson does not perform.
4. Stage – the quotation is not provided at all (try to get a written quotation in this country, especially from insurance companies or lenders), not attracti-

ve, takes too long to be provided, doesn't meet the clients needs because the briefing was not taken properly since the sales person did not listen well, or is outcompeted.
5. Follow up is not carried out at all, is carried out late or not succesfully.

In all these cases your organisation's low quality of customer service has either hindered sales or reduced its value.

Investing a little in best practice customer service, a perfect customer journey and optimised workflow processes (six sigma) will require some investment but earn a multiple of it. It's a classic case of leverage. Saving on customer service quality is definitely the worst place to save money and a sure-fire killer that will put you out of business faster than you can spell the word "insolvency".

A great way of optimising your customer service is using the entire team: Getting each member to do some investigation and think about possible changes in discrete areas of the process is more manageable than one person struggling to review and change everything. Provided everything is pulled together and any changes well communicated (something that may involve formal changes to policy and practice), all this can result in significant and rapid change and hence in significant and rapid cost reduction and sales increases.

Most competitive companies today are geared towards customer satisfaction. They haven't looked at the tremendous competitive edge you get by delighting customers.

You don't know the difference? Imagine you partner, would you like him / her to just be satisfied with you as a spouse, or indeed delighted?
The same goes for customers. Yeah, they might be satisfied, but if someone comes along who delights them, they're gone. So why don't you be the one delighting them? Many companies could delight their customers if they only wanted to, but not seem to hear the sound of the competition busily sawing the legs off their obsolete business practices. They finally get it by hearing that sucking sound of market share rushing south.

"But how do I delight my customers?", I hear you ask. First and foremost through operational excellence. Operationally excellent companies depend for their success on processes honed to deliver high levels of reliability at low cost. Yes, I said HIGH reliability at LOW cost, and this is not a contradiction in terms but cause and effect.
Standart operating procedures, practiced over and over and tested rigorously to isolate glitches keep the costs of each of these procedures down.

How do you reduce the number and magnitude of glitches? By applying lean six sigma. Simplifying and slimming processes reduces the potential for glitches. According to statistics, 15 – 20 % of any industry's costs come from error, recovery from error and from cleaning up mistakes. So you need to cut out waste and simplify procedures, hence make them error free.

In addition, in every large organisation there is some 20% hidden unemployment. This means that the larger an organisation, the less visible are non-performers and the higher the number of staff who is getting paid but does not actually add value. That's why you need to apply lean methods and cut out dead wood. It will save you money, simplify things and drive efficiency at the same moment.

Nota Bene: I am not saying that you need to re-invent the wheel. "Reengineering" is a word often used by consultants who try to convince you that you need a complete new system, whilst what you really need is some very specific fine-tuning.

When I work with clients, all I do is to drive out errors and drive out defects. Then I look at the process, do it one more time, look again and do it a third time, by then it usually near perfect and error and waste free.

It's actually no rocket science: Create a "10 Most Wanted List" of quality defects. Every department should have one up their wall. Then assign teams to work on each item on the list, and when they corrected one of those defects, celebrate. In one of my recent assignments this was the exact process we used to achieve 125 major quality improvements. We also made it mandatory that every manager in the company has to listen in on customer service calls two hours per month. None of them were competent at handling them, but they have to at least listen and understand what people want.

A word about training at this point: Training helps people perform; performance boosts self worth; a sense of worth builds employees' loyalty to the team and customer. The benefits of this self-reinforcing approach to management show up in both happy employees and a robust set of profit figures.

Strangely enough, while everybody agrees that a good education and a sound training are foundation stones for success, directors and managers seem to suddenly consider investment in training a mere expense or even worse, some sort of incentive or recognition. They couldn't be more wrong.


## Finance in Turnaround: Valuating A Company

Almost every business owner or CEO I ever consulted wanted to know what his company is worth. In almost every case the owners ideas had been completely wild guesses, more based on wishful thinking than on sound economic valuation techniques.

Let me explain how the value of a company is determined and why:

The model is called the "Discounted Dividend Model". It was invented by John

William Burr in Harvard 1923. It goes like this:

Assume that ACME (for those of you who always wondered what these famous acronyms that appear in countless cartoons mean – it stands for the (fictional) "American Corporation Making Everything") Inc. is generating a net earnings (also called "owners earnings" or "Dividends" for better understanding) of £ 350.000 a year.

Now think about how much money you would have to put into the bank in order to receive £ 350.000 a year for ever. The interest in our example is 5 %. The answer is: £ 7 million. Because if you put £ 7 million into the bank and the bank pays you a 5 % interest, you'll get £ 350.000 a year.

So why isn't the company worth more?

Well, assume the owner thinks his company should be worth more and his asking price is £ 14 million. If you paid that price, you would pay £ 14 million in order to get £ 350.000 / year net profit in return. This is a 2,5 % (2,5 % from £ 14 million = £ 350.000). So why would anyone invest £ 14 million in a business that gives her 2,5 % in return when she could put the same amount of money risk-free into her bank account and get 5 % interest instead? Got it?

Isn't that just beautifully simple?

And why isn't the company worth less?

Aaah! That's the more interesting question!
In theory, if the company is fairly valued using the above principle, you would pay a fair price. BUT:

Any business bears inherent risks. You don't know whether the company will still be producing the same £ 350.000 in future. So in fact you would be better of putting your money into the bank which is risk free. If you still decide to buy the business, your willingness to accept a business risk should be honoured by a higher return (more risk = more return, less risk = less return).

So what you want is to negotiate a price that is below the fair market value of –in this example- below £ 7 million.

Now I hear you asking "How then do I negotiate the price down and how much should I really pay?" This is the billion dollar question and fortunes have been made by those buying companies far below their actual value and either re-selling them with a profit or achieving high yields over many years. Warren Buffet did just that for 40 years and became the world's richest person. So as you can imagine I don't have the answer, because if I had I would also be extremely rich and wouldn't need to earn my money consulting on company valuation.

But here is another question for you:

Using this formula, your company becomes worth more in a recession when interests are low. How come?

If like now, interest rates are very low, say 1 %, then you don't need to put £ 7 million into the bank in order to get £ 350.000 annual returns, but £ 35 million. On £ 35 million at 1 % interest you get £ 350.000 returns.

And vice versa, if interests go up and stand at, say 10%, your company is worth only £ 3,5 million, because your get £ 350.000 for £ 3,5 million put in the bank.

Is that fair?

Well – it is. Because if a company in times of austerity still produces a steady £ 350.000 income and not suffering, then it is doing very well indeed and this "doing very well" is reflected in a better price.

In boom-times however, when practically everybody is doing well and generating £ 350.000 returns is not a piece of art, the value of the company is lower.

Life IS pretty simple after all, isn't it?

# Finance in Turnaround: How to Read Between The Lines of Annual Reports and Financial Statements - a case study

Elbit Vision Systems Announces Turnaround in Third Quarter of 2010 – But is it Sustainable ?

This Israeli company, a global leader in the field of automatic in-line optical web inspection and quality monitoring systems, today announced its consolidated financial results for the three month period which ended September 30, 2010. A news article reads:

"The Company recorded a net profit of $5.3 million from the sale of its subsidiary ScanMaster Systems (IRT) Ltd. in June 2010.  A restructuring of the Company, which commenced with the sale and included debt arrangements with the Company's banks and investors, significantly improved its financial situation and reduced the Company's short-term debt by nearly 60%."

This piece of information reads positive on the first glance, but let us drill deeper: If an organisation has manoeuvred itself into troubled waters –for whatever reasons- then it needs to address the underlying issues and resolve them.

By simply selling off family silver and taking on new loans, the acute symptom might temporarily be removed, but the problems are not solved.

It is like a man who owns joinery but gives his customers bad service: he is constantly missing deadlines and his mediocre quality just doesn't cut it. His business goes down and he gets into the red. In order to settle the debt, he is selling his house and takes on some extra loans. But how is this supposed to solve the problem of mediocre service and lousy quality? As long as he doesn't change the ways he operates, he simply will get into the red again, and what will he be selling then? This is exactly the situation with Elbit. They have sold some assets and taken on new loans, but what they fail to report is how they are going to address and rectify the root causes that got the company into trouble in the first place.

Read on and observe how financial statements can create smoke and mirrors that can easily deceive the inexperienced shareholder:

"Third Quarter 2010 Results:

Revenues for the third quarter of 2010 were $1.1 million, representing an increase of 22% compared to $0.9 million for the third quarter of 2009."

Of course they do! When you sell off part of the company, revenues go up, but this says nothing about the quality of management and competitiveness of the business without the help of extra sales.

"Gross profit on a GAAP basis was $0.7 million, representing 63% of revenues, compared with $0.4 million or 44% of revenues for the third quarter of 2009. Gross margins increased substantially due to the reductions in the Company's fixed costs after the restructuring in June 2010."

Cross margins may be reduced but the problem with margins is that they say nothing about the company's liability. The margins may be superb, but if the company has a substantial loan to repay, even the best of margins are no guarantee that it can meet its obligations. If your loan repayment is $ 1 million and your turnover is $ 500 K, you can have a margin of 100% and it still won't help you. Read on:

"Operating profit on a GAAP basis was $167 thousand compared with an operating loss of $392 thousand in the third quarter of 2009. Operating profit on a non-GAAP basis for the third quarter of 2010 was $243 thousand, compared with a loss of $297 thousand in the third quarter of 2009. Operating expenses in the quarter decreased primarily due the restructuring plan which began in June 2010 and the reduction in the Company's fixed costs. The Company also increased its efficiency in operating expenses.

Net profit on a GAAP basis for the third quarter of 2010 was $34 thousand, compared to a net loss of $559 thousand in the third quarter of 2009. Net profit per share on a GAAP basis was zero. Net profit on a non-GAAP basis for the third quarter of 2010 was $109 thousand, compared to a net loss of $373 thousand in the third quarter of 2009.

EBITDA for the third quarter of 2010 was $243 thousand, compared to a loss of $282 thousand in the third quarter of 2009.

Sam Cohen, Chairman and CEO of EVS, commented, „We are beginning to see the positive impact of the Company's reorganization which commenced with the sale of ScanMaster in June 2010. By restructuring our debt with our banks, investors, and certain state institutions for repayment over a 5-10 year period, we have created a healthy and stable financial environment for growth. Furthermore, we believe that by showing a profit, regardless of size, represents proof of the effectiveness of our long term strategy."

Again, lots of positive looking figures but not a single word about the root causes leading to the crisis, how they are being remedied, and how the extra income needed to repay the loans will be generated. The CEO simply put off the problem for the next 5-10 years, probably because by the time the shit hits the fan he is no longer around and can't be held responsible. The climax of this cheeky piece is "Furthermore, we believe that by showing a profit, regardless of size, represents proof of the effectiveness of our long term strategy."

How exactly will "showing a profit" (remember that this has primarily be generated by selling off part of the company and repaying current, due liabilities with new ones) demonstrate any long term strategy at all and any effectiveness of it? What is the long term strategy? Stripping all assets and selling them off until nothing is left? But there is more to come:

„We believe the significant achievements in the percentage of gross and operating profits shown in these results, which are particularly high in relation to other companies in the markets in which we operate, provide additional validation of our accomplishments. This achievement has been the result of continual improvements in our development and production processes. We are encouraged that the Company has reclaimed its future after several years of stagnation and losses. We believe that these positive trends will be reflected in the financial results for the coming quarters," concluded Mr. Cohen.

What significant achievements? If there are any noteworthy ones, why are they not presented? Is it a significant achievement to sell off assets in order to settle a debt and to take on new loans?

I am not saying that Elbit has nothing else to show, but I am saying that you should carefully analyse and read between the lines when it comes to annual reports or quarterly statements, especially in a turnaround situation. The simple but key question is: Why is here no word about fundamental changes if there are any? What do they have to hide?

I don't have the answer, but I do encourage you to ask the question.


Now read and compare how  T-Mobile deals and communications in a similar situation and note in particular

- what mistakes the CEO admits
- the root causes identified
- the solutions suggested
- the speed of implementation

T-Mobile CEO Humm unveils turnaround plan, says 10% of churn caused by iPhone

During the company's annual investor day conference in New York, T-Mobile USA CEO Philipp Humm unveiled a comprehensive turnaround plan he said will revitalize the company. The strategy includes reducing churn, growing revenues, pursuing new markets such as the enterprise market and considering strategic alternatives such as network sharing, partnerships and even spectrum leasing. Interestingly, Humm said 10 percent of T-Mobile's churn is due to customers migrating to the iPhone. He said the company will combat the leakage by laun-

ching more Android-based devices. According to PCMag.com, T-Mobile will offer 4G HSPA+ versions the Sidekick and the Samsung Galaxy S. As for the iPhone, Humm said according to PCMag.com that T-Mobile's 1700Mhz 3G spectrum is the major barrier to it obtaining the iPhone. The iPhone currently does not support T-Mobile's 3G spectrum bands, only those of AT&T Mobility (NYSE:T). Humm added that the company plans to launch competitive iPad tablet offerings in March and April.

In one of his first public appearances as T-Mobile's new CEO, Humm admitted that T-Mobile's growth stalled starting in 2008 primarily because the company was late migrating to 3G. He added that the firm also had a poor branding strategy and distribution problems. Humm said he believes T-Mobile is well positioned to overcome those issues and is already closing the gap on the competition by taking advantage of its core assets. Specifically, Humm touted T-Mobile's quick deployment of HSPA+ 21, which covers 200 million POPs today, and its plans to upgrade to HSPA+ 42 this year. He also said that 50 percent of the firm's device sales today are smartphones, which indicates continued growth in data revenues. Approximately 39 percent of T-Mobile's existing customer base uses smartphones, he said.

Humm said the company will unveil 25 4G devices this year. T-Mobile has branded its HSPA+ network as 4G. Interestingly, AT&T has said it will debut 20 4G devices this year (AT&T brands its HSPA+ network and its forthcoming LTE network as 4G). T-Mobile hopes to continue to attract customers by positioning itself as the value leader, offering as many smartphones as possible under the $100 price point and providing an entry-level data package priced at $10 per month, Humm said.

Regarding T-Mobile's need to grow revenues, Humm said the company plans to drive $1 billion in savings by reducing customer care, migrating to a self-service and IVR system, simplifying rate plans and deploying an all IP network that includes building 1,000 more cell sites to reduce the company's roaming fees.

The company also will explore new MVNO relationships as well as rebuild its business-to-business sales program, which has atrophied during the past few years due to T-Mobile's focus on the consumer market.

Deutsche Telekom CEO Rene Obermann also spoke briefly about the parent company's commitment to T-Mobile USA. He said the firm is convinced that T-Mobile is a good asset, but noted DT is not opposed to exploring options such as forming partnerships with other firms, embarking on network-sharing arrangements or even selling non-core assets such as T-Mobile's tower portfolio. He said DT's goal is to make T-Mobile USA a self-funded entity.

## Finance in Turnaround: Reducing Tax Liability and Protecting Owner's Assets

Money matters, even more if an organisation is in a turnaround and every penny counts. But it is even more important to protect the owner(s) personal wealth, because in a crisis things can turn worse and the company can go bankrupt.

I work a lot with SME's that are owner managed and I often find that some risks associated with managing cash flow, taxes and asset protection are not managed well enough.

Last week I consulted a client on four very typical issues that probably concern most SME owners without them being aware of it:

- Tax investigation
- Tax planning
- Provisions
- Personal asset protection

Chances are that one fine day (although this article is specifically written for UK readers, the same might apply to other countries) the tax authorities (in the UK HMRC, in other countries the Inland Revenue etc.) might decide to audit you. This will, inevitable, incur a lot of expensive hours by your accountants and book-keepers. If you take out a Tax Investigation Insurance, the costs for these hours, which can add up fast and to substantial amounts of money, are covered by the insurance.

The insurance will not cost you more than some £ 270.- p.a. After I tried in vein to give my business to AVIVA, who turns out to be useless when called, and not even know what a Tax Investigation Insurance is, I googeld and discovered Solar Insurance, which I used to get quick and simple cover online, and which I therefore recommend.

Better than to pay taxes and to be covered for tax investigation still, is to pay little or no taxes at all. Many people do not know the difference between tax evasion (which is illegal) and tax avoidance (which is legal). For legal reasons I cannot give direct tax advice and I wouldn't even try, but there are of course professionals who should be consulted. There are only but a very few, though, who understand the complex and highly expertise matter of tax avoidance. In the UK there are legal ways to reduce corporate and personal income tax to near nil. I don't know about other countries, but assume there are similar tax planning schedules available, too.

Because I don't want to be responsible for red hot telephone lines in my tax advisor's office due to hundreds of people calling after reading this blog, I am more than happy to make a personal introduction if you drop me an email. These London based tax advisors are specialised in legal tax avoidance and two no obligation information meetings are completely free.

On the subject of taxes: Taxes are paid on profits, and so it's logical that the less profit your balance sheet shows, the less corporate tax is due. Provisions can be used to smooth profits in good years and improve them in bad years. Provision are –simply spoken- funds set aside for future losses or future expenses, and are quite a smart tool because they reduce your corporate tax liability while building financial buffers at the same time. See you tax advisor for more information.

Last but least I need to remove a common misconception about the assets in a LTD company: A lot of business owners I met have transferred personal assets such as property, into the possession of their LTD, to boost the company's worth or creditworthiness. This goes against the grain, because a LTD company is LIMITED in order to protect the owner's wealth. If the company has problems, it only is liable with the company assets, and if you transfer your personal asset into to company, it may be gone. Generally it's the other way round that owners do it: They build up wealth in the company and then take it over into their personal possession, where it is protected.

Especially if your company is in a turnaround situation and threatened, make sure you protect your personal assets by taking them out and transferring them into your private ownership.

## Protecting Your Business and Your Family in A Crisis

Running a successful business means constantly meeting and overcoming challenges. It's highly rewarding for you and your co-directors / partners when things go well.

But when something goes wrong, perhaps for reasons beyond your control, the financial security of you all, and of all your families, could be at risk.

The death of a partner / co-director can threaten all that hard work and is one of the most common root causes for a turnaround situation.

Let's look at the potential problems and more importantly, the solutions. The partners / directors of a business are its driving force and the reason for its success. What would happen if one is no longer there? If those shares end up with someone you don't know and who doesn't know your business, how would you feel? This is precisely what does happen if arrangements have not been put in place. Their share of the business passes on, either through inheritance or sale.

The problems for the remaining partners or directors are

- Find the money to buy the deceased partner's share
- Continue paying income to the family until that share is paid off (perhaps from already reduced profits)
- Learn to accept the widow(er) as your new partner, with all that entails
- Consider winding up the business
- Competitors taking advantage of the situation

So we've seen it from the survivor's point of view. But what if you died? Where does your own family stand in this? They've inherited your share of the business, but they're unlikely to be able to take over your role. Do they have your skills, knowledge and experience? And would remaining partner(s) be prepared to accept them?

Your family's options are:

- Take a share of the profits. This may not amount to much if the business is struggling because of your absence. For how long will your partners agree to this?
- Insist on winding up the business. Receive a share of its value. If the real value has fallen, they could receive little or nothing.
- Sell your share. This relies on finding a buyer who's prepared to pay the right price and that can be a long and difficult process.

The solution is a structured, pre-planned legal framework which ensures the succession of the business and protection for the families. A smart programme combines new agreements, wills, life assurances and a series of trusts. These provide funds to the right people at the right time, enabling the continuing partners / directors to buy out the widow(er). This is more than simply life assurance planning. By utilising the new agreements a range of trusts, inheritance tax mitigation and bloodline protection is given to all the families of the partners or directors.

- An agreed succession to the surviving partners / directors
- Capital just when it's needed
- A clean break with the family
- The business can continue to trade in its own right
- No need for the widow(er) to become embroiled in the business
- Your family benefits from the business you've built up
- Financial security for your family
- Valuable inheritance tax advantages
- Continuing protection for your children and their children for the next 125 years
- Bloodline and divorce protection for your children

But there are additional considerations in case of the loss of a key person. This could be one of the partners / directors, a senior manager or a technical whizz kid.

The death of a key person can lead to

- Loss of relationship – people like to deal with people they know. Losing a key person can mean losing customers and lower profits.
- Loss of professional expertise. Specialist skills can be difficult to replace and heir loss can affect your competitiveness.
- Cost of recruitment. Finding and training a replacement can be expensive and time-consuming.
- Bank loans. The death of a partner / director can cause the lender to call in the loan, often very suddenly, giving the business additional problems.

The best defence against a crisis is good preparation, and it is always easier to prepare before something happens.

# Finance in Turnaround: Solvency Ratio

Not just in a turnaround, but especially in a turnaround, it is vital to know how the organisation can meet its financial obligations. To calculate that, you use solvency ration.

And this is how it works:

One of many ratios used to measure a company's ability to meet long-term obligations, the solvency ratio measures the size of a company's after-tax income, excluding non-cash depreciation expenses, as compared to the firm's total debt obligations. It provides a measurement of how likely a company will be to continue meeting its debt obligations.

The measure is usually calculated as follows:

$$\text{Solvency Ratio} = \frac{\text{After Tax Net Profit} + \text{Depreciation}}{\text{Long Term Liabilities} + \text{Short Term Liabilities}}$$

Example: Your After Tax Net Profit is £ 750.000 and your depreciation 50.000, your combined short & long term liabilities are £ 400.000 In this case your solvency ratio is 2, because you are twice capable of meeting your liabilities.

If you ATNP + Dep. Is £ 800 K and your liabilities are £ 800 K, your solvency ration is 1, because you can pay your debt back once, then you have no reserves left.

Is your ATNP +Dep. £ 200 K and your liabilities are £ 400 K, your ration is 0,5 because it is only enough to pay back half of your liabilities.

# Finance in Turnaround: Increasing Cash

In a turnaround, cash is tight. If you need to improve your cash position, say you need to make sure you have enough money to pay your staff, your bank has available some tools they call „Supplier Finance".

Supplier finance consists of two different tools: Factoring and Reverse Factoring.

## What is Traditional Factoring?

Traditional Factoring is the selling of outstanding invoices by a supplier to a bank or factoring company in order to receive the money now. If company S (Supplier) sends company B (Buyer) an invoice over £ 100 and payment terms are 90 days net, S can sell its outstanding invoice to a bank who pays to S immediately the sum of £ 90 and collects the £ 100 due from B 90 days later at its normal due date. S got its money faster and accepted a discount, getting £ 90 instead of £ 100 but therefore immediately, and the bank made a £ 10 margin for waiting 90 days until they collect the £ 100 from B. The factoring customer is S.

Factoring is usually applied if outstanding debt are less than £ 1 m. The bank is in control and therefore factoring is sometimes unpopular with the distressed company: Their clients see that their supplier has sold the claim to the bank, which

a)      Gives away the situation the supplier is in
b)      Can damage the supplier-client relationship because the bank might not be taking a soft approach to the debtor in opposite to the supplier who might have personal relationships and views the affair with a perspective to future dealings

## What is Reverse Factoring?

With Reverse Factoring, early payment is provided by a bank or factoring company to a supplier based on invoices qualified by the buyer.

## Why Factoring (Traditional or Reverse)?

Buyers and Suppliers have contradictory objectives. Buyers want to optimize their cash flow by 'stretching the trade', maximize Days Payment Outstanding (late payment), while suppliers want to minimize their Days Sales Outstanding (early collection). Factoring addresses this conflict using the invoice, which in essence is an illiquid asset for seller until payment is received, as the basis to generate working capital.

## The difference between Factoring and Reverse Factoring

While Factoring uses an invoice as the underlying asset for financing, Reverse Factoring brings the qualified invoice into play.

In essence, Traditional Factoring deals with the supplier's receivables from many 'unknown' buyers; Reverse Factoring deals with the payables of one well-known buyer.

Traditional factoring can be done by one supplier individually; Reverse Factoring also involves the buyer (performing the invoice qualification).

Unlike Reverse Factoring, with Traditional Factoring the factor company does not know whether the supplier really delivered said goods or services or whether the delivered goods or sent invoice will be contested by the buyer, …

…. as a result, Traditional Financing will on average provide financing of around 70% of the invoice value, while Reverse Factoring can provide up to 100% of the invoice value (minus the interest & service fee).

Traditional Factoring is not a suitable financing instrument in environments with weak contract enforcement institutions, incomplete credit information or frequent fraud; in such circumstances, Reverse Factoring could be a solution.

Many business owners and managers are uncomfortable seeking to discuss their finance needs with their bank. Partly this is because they don't understand that the bank has tools available to help them, partly it is because even if they know that such service products are available they don't know how they work and feel embarrassed to ask.

Knowing how these things work and what they mean makes it easier to speak to your bank, which is something you should do timely and not when crisis is already at your doorstep.

Under certain circumstances pension provisions can also be used as collateral to raise working capital.

# Finance in Turnaround: Managing Tax Debt

When you have HMRC arrears, it's a sure sign of financial distress within your business, and let's face it, HMRC isn't operational cash that helps to generate new sales. They are therefore usually one of the first places that companies go to when they have to make difficult choices of who they don't pay.

In November 2008, HMRC in the UK started to give unprecedented amounts of leniency to companies who were struggling with cash flow under a programme called the Business Payment Support Service (BPSS). This was part of the governments way of helping companies stay solvent and it has to be said that it worked as despite that fact that we have experienced the worst recession of the past century, the aftermath hasn't been felt in the number of companies filing for Administration or Liquidation.

By July 2009, HMRC had agreed to £3.1bn in deferred payments with 177,000 companies under agreements called "Time To Pay (TTP)" arrangements. In December 2009, Alistair Darling extended the programme until 5 April 2011 but did state that when the HMRC annual tax bill exceeds £1m, then an Independent Business Review (IBR) will be required to validate the proposal. By March 2010, the amount of debt effectively lent by HMRC had risen to over £5bn. However, since that time, there's been a blackout of information that could be a sign that the taxman is tightening up their BPSS policy which some now argue was too relaxed.

However, there are some things that can be done to make things more predictable and therefore retain control.

In November 2008, HMRC in the UK started to give unprecedented amounts of leniency to companies who were struggling with cash flow under a programme called the Business Payment Support Service (BPSS) (see our article „HMRC Time to Pay arrangements" for more information). It's generally agreed amongst the turnaround community that the BPSS ended in November 2009. Since that time, it's been much more difficult to obtain and agree a Time to Pay (TTP) arrangement. HMRC are notoriously difficult to deal with and your experience varies according to who you manage to get to speak to. There are however, many things that can be done to increase your chances of obtaining either your first TTP, or re-negotiating an existing TTP.

- Tip 1: Find out who you are talking to, get there name, telephone number, and then write to them confirming the content of the conversation and also what you agreed. HMRC's record keeping isn't all that it ought to be. You're likely to deal with up to 3 different offices during the life of a TTP arrangement, and they can't always see the information about your previous conversations. Therefore, if you keep good records, it will demonstrate to them that you've been upholding your end of the bargin and it's actually HMRC who keep moving goal posts.
- Tip 2: You must talk fluently about your business issues and ensure that the story stacks up. They are going to want to hear that you're doing something about the root causes of your cash flow issues. If you give the message that it's simply trading conditions and they are the only creditor who is not being paid, then they are not likely to agree to your plans.
- Tip 3: You must make them an offer. You should have your proposed payment plan ready and you need to be sure that you can stick to it. If possible, promise to pay them some cash now, and then make sure that you do it. This always helps to sweeten a deal. They may of course ask for more than you offered, so having 1 or 2 different proposals is usually sensible.
- Tip 4: Underpin your proposed payment plan with a cash flow forecast. The key point here is that you need to demonstrate that you are paying what you can afford to pay. Not too much – you need to be sure that you can meet the proposed payments, and not too little – if you show a growing cash balance, HMRC are likely to ask for more money.
- Tip 5: If you can't meet your agreed payment plan, tell them and start the process again but make sure that your story is stronger, and that the information that you provide is more robust. If you didn't provide a cash flow forecast initially, make sure that you do if you need a negotiate a revision.
- Tip 6: Always submit your PAYE/NI and VAT returns. Even if you know that you can't make the payments, you will be in a much better position if you submit your returns and HMRC know what you're your liability is. If you don't submit your returns, this will make the situation much worse.

## Finance in Turnaround: Cash Flow Management - Best Practice Cash Flow Management

Successful businesses are very meticulous when it comes to managing their cash flow. Especially when they are facing tough times, their payroll continues to be met, invoices are settled and the organisation can still manage (selectively) to move forward. How does this happen?

By applying sound cash flow management skills.

Pay-late companies will often ask for a net 30 day term when purchasing from a supplier. When someone is supposed to pay you, a cheque rarely turns up the day after you've sent the invoice. Part of this is due to accounting controls but the other part involves effectively managing cash flow.

You can easily take advantage of the same approach. Whenever you get a bill, whether it's for utilities, internet, credit card or office supplies, make a note of when payment is due. The payment is likely to be due between two and four weeks after you've received the invoice. When you pay a bill promptly you may get a warm satisfying glow, but you'll also have a hole in your bank account. The best advice is to pay the bill as close to the due date as possible without being late. During this time you could transfer the money into a savings account to earn interest. Another way of taking advantage of delayed payment is to pay as many bills as you can with accredit card. If it's possible, control the statement date of your credit card to align with the due date of the bill. With a bit of luck and if you use the grace period offered by both your creditor and your credit card company, you could delay writing the cheque for 45-60 days after the service has been invoiced and provided.

You need to use that time frame to earn interest on your money and collect in some additional payments owned to you in order to build up your cash flow.

It takes time to organise, but once you've got the hang of it it makes total sense.

If you intend to get a real grip on what state the organisation's finances are in, there are three steps that you need to take: Review, monitor and act. First you need to review tour financial position every six months. Then you must monitor on a monthly basis exactly where the money goes. That includes doing a bank reconciliation to see that there aren't any errors. Banks do make mistakes sometimes. Finally, based on a study of that expenditure, you need to act to ensure that you either make savings or economies to ease cash flow, or you work with your money (if you have a surplus) so that it earns interest while it is sitting in the bank.

## Finance in Turnaround: Private Equity

According to the British Venture Capital Association, the industry trade body, private equity is: "medium to long-term finance provided in return for an equity stake in potentially high growth companies, which are usually privately owned." Private equity firms are essentially fund managers who invest money on behalf of large financial institutions in private businesses with the objective of selling those businesses later for a large profit.

And already at this point a lot of wannabe entrepreneurs are getting it wrong because they think that private equity is easily available to fund start-ups, and the idea of putting together a business plan and then meeting a kind stranger who gives them private equity money is still very common among the start-up community. But they couldn't not be more wrong. Because PE firms are investing other people's money, they need to invest it into organisations that provide little risk and high returns, and by the sheer definition this excluded start-ups, because they are neither secure investments (1 our of 2 start ups fails in the first 2 years) nor offer they a high return (in takes sometimes years to achieve break-even, not to mention high yields). So let's be straight: PE is for the big boys – and for the turnaround community! Why for the turnaround community? "Simpelst" says the meerkat, because after a successful turnaround profits shoot up and a steep incline in yields is displayed, offering a high yield within a short period of time. This is usually done through a management buy-out transaction (MBO). The private equity fund invests alongside management to acquire the business from its shareholders, and helps management to deliver a high growth business plan. Most private equity funds aim to sell or 'exit' after three to five years, realising their investment. In reality this is often more like four to seven years as business plans usually have at least one kink in them that can delay the exit.

So why does private equity generate such high returns for its backers? The answer is a combination of financial structuring, good business and financial disciplines, and picking the right investment (better known as a good dose of luck).
Private equity transactions usually occur because a change is needed in a business. This will usually be a change in ownership – for example retiring shareholders passing on the reins to the managers – but is often much more than that and typically heralds a step change in the business size or performance.

The management team that takes over the business (another reason why it's unsuitable for start-ups, because no start-up entrepreneur let's easily go control of his baby) will normally want to stamp its mark on the company strategy and may need investment to access a new market, acquire a competitor or develop new products. It could be recognition by the former owners that they had driven the business as far as they could. It could also be that the business had not performed to its full potential and needed a more professional set of managers with stronger financial controls.

Whatever the underlying reason, truly successful private equity investments all experience this step change in growth and as a result can normally be sold a few years later for much more than they were bought for. Without private equity funding it is likely that some businesses would never reach their full potential. Good private equity firms are those that can achieve these results across their portfolio of investments.

How do the managers make their money?

One of the key principles of private equity is that it is the management team who runs the business, and therefore the private equity executives are as much gauging the quality of the CEO and his team as they are analysing the potential performance of the company. The investors sit on the board and contribute to the high level strategy of the business, but they are reliant on the management delivering what they have set out in their business plan. (This is another reason why PE is unsuitable for start-ups: Start-ups miss the necessary management experience). Deal structures are all about goal congruence and that means that the management team needs to be properly incentivised. This is done through equity. In other words the management team become co-owners of the business with the private equity firm. In an MBO, the management team has the opportunity to acquire shares in the company, and as shareholders, their best chance of making serious money is to increase the value of the business they run. They will be paid a decent enough salary but most of their earnings potential over the investment period is skewed to creating and then realising shareholder value by achieving the following:

- Increase the company's profits and cash flows
- Pay down the bank debt
- Position the business as an attractive acquisition target on exit

Managers can earn many times their initial investment from a successful MBO and this is why the opportunity to be part of a buy-out is often seen as a once in a lifetime deal. Running a private equity portfolio business successfully and selling for a large sum requires an enormous amount of hard work and talent. These deals are not guaranteed successes as many business owners know to their cost.

An MBO is a leveraged transaction. This means that the private equity fund uses bank debt to 'leverage' its own equity funding to allow it to buy businesses but invest as little of its own money as possible. In most cases bank debt will comprise more than 50 per cent of the total funding. When a business is saddled with a lot of bank debt, its financial flexibility is much reduced and it does not take many things to go wrong (for example, a couple of large bad debts or the cancellation of a large contract) before a company can be in default of its banking commitments. The real challenge is to extract synergies from each deal and to create a unified business that is strategically attractive to a larger trade buyer.

## Cost Cutting Strategies For Turnaround Situations: 18 Ideas You Can Implement Right Away

### Watch your finances

An in-depth and up-to-date awareness of your finances is crucial. Use financial tools to help you keep track. If your finger is firmly on the pulse you'll be more able to identify cost rises – such as rising energy costs, interest or currency rates – and react to them quickly. The all-important key tool you must have is a cash flow forecast. Start with that, start now.

## Make every penny count

It's easy to get wrapped up in the big costs and forget about the little ones. Go through budgets, line-by-line, examining each individual cost. For each, identify waste and areas where costs can be trimmed. I have saved my clients small fortunes doing simple but effective things like:

- Install a central PC shutdown to kick in at the end of play
- Set all printers on double-sided printing as default
- Refill cartridges instead of buying new ones
- Cancel non-essential memberships and subscriptions
- Consolidate or cancel leasing contracts
- Consolidate or cancel business insurances
- Sell off surplus inventory and business equipment (you will be surprised how much clutter your offices have gathered)
- Make provisions and through it reduce your taxable profit
- Sub-let office space not used
- Re-use paper as notepaper or for incoming faxes

## Set targets

Once you've identified areas for potential cost savings: set reduction targets. Be ambitious but realistic, so that you don't impact the quality and effectiveness of your business. Goals that are written down have the tendency to get achieved. Do write them down, do it now.

## Consult your employees

Every employee, from top to bottom, has their own area of expertise. Ask them to look within their world and identify where money is wasted and how costs could be cut. Make sure your cost-cutting moves are seen as positive steps to reduce waste rather than desperate attempts to raise cash. Don't put that off, do it now.

## Pick your battles

The adage goes that 80 per cent of your costs come from 20 per cent of your spending. Identify high-value cost positions and make it your priority to reduce them. Don't concentrate on saving pennies while you still loose pounds.

## Shop around

Suppliers – from gas companies to professional services firms – might be reducing prices to boost sales, so shop around to find the best value. Your current suppliers might also be open to price negotiations to retain your loyal custom. Be careful not to push too far; changing to an inferior supplier or demotivating your existing one could impact quality.

## Save energy

Look at your carbon footprint and work out ways to cut it. Every tonne of carbon cut saves the environment and saves your money.

- Switch off lights
- Reduce the central heating by 1 degree
- Shutdown PCs and monitors at the end of the working day
- Close windows
- Install double glazed windows
- Install energy saving light bulbs
- Take public transport for business trips where possible
- Have staff car-sharing when on business trips and public transport is not an option
- Install a hippo for all toilet cisterns
- Refill printer cartridges using syringes and cheap Tesco ink rather than buying new ones each time

## Get people talking

Customer recommendations and word-of-mouth are incredibly valuable marketing tools. If you have a satisfied and loyal customer base, figuring out ways to get them talking (such as refer a friend schemes or viral email campaigns) could help cut more costly acquisition marketing activities.

## Review your IT

Consider ways to cut IT costs. For example: Could open source or hosted cloud software services reduce IT hardware and software costs without reducing reliability and security? Could a paperless office cut stationary costs?

## Enable mobile working

Nowadays many employees who regularly attend offsite meetings are equipped with portable computers. Adding the ability to get online – via mobile broadband connections, for example – could enable employees to work remotely in-between remote meetings, thus minimising travel expenses and maximising profitability.

## Tighten up your supply chain

Work closely with suppliers and partners to improve your supply chain. This could lead to better managed logistics, improved and more efficient processes, or a reduction in waste of stocks or raw materials. Use Lean Six Sigma Principles.

## Cut recruitment costs

Your current employees might already know the perfect candidate, so try referral schemes to source job applicants. Recruit direct (but be sure your recruitment practices are up to scratch) and/or advertise on online job websites. Recruit internally by developing existing staff into new roles. Average recruitment costs are around 20% of the annual salary of the candidate – a very expensive convenience!

## Work with students

Students crave experience, are hungry to do well, and come from their studies brimming with ideas. They are a valuable and cost-effective talent pool. Make it a student project or competition and offer £ 100 for the best answers when you need ideas, market research or design, rather than using expensive professional consultants.

## Show employees you care

If employees feel valued they are more likely to be motivated, productive and loyal. That translates into increased efficiencies and reduced recruitment costs. Buying pizzas once a week won't cost much but is priceless in terms of motivation and loyalty.

## Offer benefits in kind

If you can't afford to give pay rises: explore benefits in kind. You could offer benefits such as gym membership, luncheon vouchers or health insurance; or you could even distribute share capital to key talent.

## Conduct virtual meetings

Use voice over IP, webcams or video-conferencing to conduct virtual meetings. Explore online collaborative tools which let participants simultaneously work on documents in real time. Such services offer benefits which counter-act the lack of face to face contact, and also help minimise travel costs.

## Bootstrap projects

The term bootstrapping is often used to characterise how many 'dot com' ventures develop new, early-stage ideas. It's the art of proving a concept with next to no cash, and usually encourages lots of imagination and ingenuity. Not a suitable approach for all projects, but for some it may reduce risk, minimise cost and spur innovation.

Innovate

A new idea (or an old idea that is new to you) which solves a costly problem could help improve the cost-efficiency of your processes. Innovation could also improve the quality of your products and services, thus delivering competitive advantage.

## Cost Cutting Strategies For Turnaround Situations: Flextime and Telecommuting

How to allow employees this benefit and help your bottom line at the same time.

Allowing employees to work flexible hours or work from home is one of today's most popular perks, benefiting both employees and employers. According to data from the Telework Research Network, a telecommuting resource site, 72 percent of employees say flexible work arrangements would cause them to choose one job over another. "Even half-time telecommuting can save a company $10,000 per employee per year," says Telework co-founder Kate Lister.

Enabling telecommuting is easier than ever. Most technology you'll need is available as open source (Google Chat, Google Groups, Skype and a host of others), SAAS (Google Docs), freeware (Dropbox, Doodle, Evernote), or inexpensive Web-based pay-per-use tools (Citrix GoToMeeting). Both Apple and Microsoft have tools that provide remote collaboration, remote monitoring and remote fix options. And with more companies using SAAS solutions, compatibility is less of an issue than it once was.

Communication is crucial to successful telecommuting. Lister recommends your communications tools include both synchronous (telephone, instant chat, texting) and asynchronous (e-mail, message boards, forums) choices. More important than your tools is your attitude. "It's essential to manage by results rather than presence," Lister warns. "You have to be of a mindset that if someone gets the job done, who cares when and how they do it?"

If not everyone in your company can work from home, Lister suggests considering alternatives like flextime, job-sharing, compressed workweeks or reduced hours.

## Cost Cutting Strategies For Turnaround Situations: Effective Savings In Niche Areas Often Overlooked

In any turnaround situation, saving money and cutting costs is paramount to survival. While it is easy to spot the big savings, once these have been looked at, it becomes harder to squeeze out additional cuts.

Here a few ideas often overlooked but highly efficient:

It may sound like an exercise in saving peanuts but it can actually contribute substantial savings: Go through the company's subscriptions and memberships. If the company is of considerable size and a lot of staff have paid memberships in Chambers, Clubs or are subscribed to expensive special interest magazines, you'd be surprised to what figures these often add up.

I have often saved thousands if no ten-thousands going through the list of memberships and subscriptions and cancelling them, often nobody even noticed because only very few people actively use their memberships and actually read all the mags that arrive every day.

Insurances are often the biggest post. They are expensive and a regular cash drain, provide no real value, do not build up assets and often are more expensive that paying for something when you need it. For example it is much cheaper to pay for the PC repair than taking out insurance, it is still cheaper to have the plumber come and fix your boiler than taking out boiler insurance. All insurances have been invented to make the insurance company rich, and not to make you rich. Remember that and vigorously cancel all those that are none-essential.

In marketing, strongly consider subcontracting: In other words, selecting marketing activities that you can get someone else to do. This seems easy, and it is also easy to decide (everyone votes for something that will not involve them in any personal hassle). A quarterly newsletter that can be produced externally, perhaps by a public relations consultancy, is a good example. Many companies have got locked into producing such a thing, rejoiced that it is easy to do, then found that it does not produce good returns.

Printer cartridges, phone bills, postages, taxi fares – the smaller the items, the less likely they are to be flagged up on the companies" financial radar.

I have once reduced a client's overheads by 55 % within just 2 months by doing nothing else but going through those items and eliminate waste and reduce spending line by line, cancel unnecessary insurances, memberships and subscriptions and consolidates a number of leasing contract.

Here are my personal top tips on how to save money without compromising the quality of your organisation:

- Cut the number of subscriptions you pay to trade associations, clubs and other organisations. There may be some (paid by direct debit) that you don't even realize you're paying for, let alone get any value from them.
- Cut the number of business and professional journals you receive. These may be paid by annual subscription in advance. Check how many of them are relevant to the operation of your organisation. Does anyone, you included, ever read them?

- Have a look at, or get someone else to do so if appropriate, the telecom contracts you are paying for. There are so many deals around these days, unless you know a lot about it or have time to do the research, you may be paying well over the odds for the services you need. Great savings could be made here.
- Send round a memo to all staff asking them to avoid dialling 0870 numbers. By using an alternative numbers (usually provided as the "calls from overseas") simply replace the + 44 with "0" and you will not be paying premium rates for these calls.
- Organize a review of the spending on business credit cards. Even a clamp down on the limit that can be spent on client hospitality (unless it has been approved higher up the organisation) could make serious budget savings.
- It would be a major decision to relocate your offices to a less expensive area in order to save money but there is a simple idea you could put into practice. Maybe there is an empty room in your offices that has become a dumping ground for junk. If you de-clutter it would be space available to rent to a micro-business / sole practitioner.

## Cost Cutting Strategies For Turnaround Situations: Should I Cut Down On Training Costs In A Turnaround?

Training is easily dismissed as a waste of money. Remember the old story of the manager saying, "I am not wasting money on training; what happens if people then leave?" To which the answer is simple: "What happens if you don't train them --- and they stay?" If you are still seeing training as a waste of money despite what has been said here, remember that training encompasses a great deal more than a formal course. Even reading a book can be regarded as low-cost training, and a host of different methodologies are available. Check tem out, make sure they do the job (poor training is worse than none and just wastes money), but think hard before you simply wipe out training as an option.

## Cost Cutting Strategies For Turnaround Situations: Outsourcing

One of the first things turnaround managers do, is look at fixed costs. Fixed costs are all costs that occur whether the cost generating services are actually needed or not. I have worked for large FMCG companies who entertained their own huge photo-studios and full-time photographers to do their products shots. In the old times this was a classic fixed overhead that has now been outsourced. Outsourcing means to commission someone externally to do the job so you just pay for the work you actually need done.

Is outsourcing just for big business?

Big business has been outsourcing aspects of their work for years, but could the format work well for small business owners?

For a small business or sole trader with a small team and limited time, outsourcing could be a blessing. It is now possible to outsource almost every part of your business, from IT to marketing, from finance to customer services. The main aim is to save time and expense.

The key is to play to your strengths and outsource where you can: Focus on what you do best — outsource the rest.

Why should you use outsourcing?

Outsourcing can reduce your overhead costs. For example, by using freelancers you can reduce the number of full-time workers you employ. As a result, you will save money by not paying National Insurance (NI) and full-time salaries. Employing suppliers on a project basis will make your finances more flexible.
However, another benefit is the reduction of time spent managing employees: If you're outsourcing to self-employed individuals, they have to do a good job because their business is based on you coming back and giving them more work. They're already self-motivated.

## Finding suppliers for outsourcing

A business owner who has never outsourced before may find it difficult to find suppliers — you will need to be secure in the knowledge that your work is being well-managed. For example, if you outsource your customer service, you want to be certain that customer calls will always be answered in a friendly manner. Set out strong terms and conditions at the outset.
A word-of-mouth recommendation from other business owners is always a good strategy for finding local people. Try going to offline networking events or searching business-to-business websites such as Bitsy, PeoplePerHour.comand Elance. While Bitsy is free to use, PeoplePerHour.com and Elance will take a percentage of the transaction between the buyer and the seller.
Let me tell you one thing: lots of people still thing the above websites are only used by small companies and for small service provider firms. This is not true! I have personally gained a client through www.Guru.com who is a $ 6 m business and whom I work for on a permanent basis, so it is NOT just about web designers, book-keepers and one-off jobs. If you are a company, reduce your overheads and do use this options.

## Managing outsourced suppliers

Although outsourcing can save you time, you may run the risk of having different teams working in isolation. Using a combination of online tools and regular face-to-face meetings will prevent this.

Tools such as Basecamp, Huddle and Glasscubes are online project management tools which are great for teams to stay involved virtually with what's going on. It's also good for those teams to come together once in a while. When you meet face-to-face you come up with new ideas, you get re-energised.

### Outsourcing overseas

Outsourcing overseas can work out even cheaper. However, if you decide to do so, consider carefully how you will manage your relationship with the supplier. You must also ensure that the supplier will adhere to UK laws, for example, the Data Protection Act.

If it's an accountant, a copywriter or a PR person, you generally want them to be based in the same country because you may need to meet them face-to-face. IT contracting is one where you can get away with outsourcing overseas, as they could access your computer remotely — there are some functions that could just as easily be picked up in a different time zone.

With many small firms struggling in the current economic climate, outsourcing is a solution that could reduce overhead costs, free up time and improve flexibility. It is time-effective to work with a virtual team, but you have to make sure all of you know what it is that you're working on, and that you're all going in the same direction.

## Turnaround Marketing Strategies - Making Impact

In a turnaround, every action must have an impact. You can't afford to be inefficient and you can't afford to loose time over trial and error or over re-doing things because they haven't been done properly the first time. Speed is of the essence. Remember:

- It is better to be first than to be better. Charles Lindbergh was the first to fly across the Atlantic. Bert Hinkler was the better pilot, flew faster and used less fuel, but, importantly, wasn't first. The Germans famously over-engineered their Fax machines and copier, but the Japanese came out onto the market first and improved their quality with each new generation of products, while the German waited until it was "perfect" --- and came too late.
- If you can't be first in a category, set up a new category you can be first in. Amelia Erhard was only the third person to fly solo across the Atlantic, but she was the first woman to do so. Richard Branson's Virgin Air wasn't he first one that offered first class experience, but it was the first one to offer on board massages, shoe-shines and manicure.
- The most powerful concept in marketing is owning a word in the prospect's mind: safety - Volvo; driving - BMW; engineering - Mercedes; technology - Audi. What's the word clients have in mind about your company?
- In the long run, every market becomes a two-horse race: Tesco / Wal-Mart,

Ford / GM, Coke / Pepsi, Burger King / McDonalds, Rolls Royce / Bentley, Procter & Gamble / Lever Sunlight.

- Two companies cannot own the same word in the prospect's mind: fast belongs to McDonald's, not Burger King – they have "flame grilled".

# Turnaround Branding

You've got a great product. Fair price. Solid service. Still you are in a crisis. What's the problem? You need a brand, experts say. "When businesses are trying to move from survive mode to thrive mode in a winter economy, the ones that break from the pack have branding on their side," says Roy Spence, advertising executive and co-author of the branding manifesto It's Not What You Sell, It's What You Stand For: Why Every Extraordinary Business Is Driven By Purpose.

Sounds good, but how do you define your brand? And once you do, so what? Until recently, successful brands afforded companies the ability to charge a premium, says Kevin Roberts, Saatchi & Saatchi Worldwide CEO. "It's not that brands have been dying, but that they've been commoditized," Roberts says. General Motors and Toyota have largely become interchangeable in many regards, as have Revlon and L'Oreal. Similar products, similar target customer, similar prices.

"The goal is to make your brand irreplaceable, and you do that with emotional connectivity: mystery, sensuality and intimacy," says Roberts, author of Lovemarks: The Future Beyond Brands. "You want loyalty beyond reason and loyalty beyond recession. For small-business owners, this is even more vital because they don't have the purchasing power that large corporations do."

Spence, GSD&M co-founder and CEO of Austin, Texas-based Idea City, puts it this way: "Every business needs to be in the business of improving customers' lives." In this, a brand is what he dubs a "sacred promise." Walmart promises to save shoppers money. Southwest Airlines promises the freedom to fly.

On the consumer side, iPods are a great example of loyalty beyond reason. All MP3 players offer the same promise of functionality and freedom of movement and choice. Yet iPod is the clear market winner as Apple's biggest money maker, proudly dominating 73 percent of the market and capable of commanding a premium price. Why? The industry-changing slick design and related advertising, reliable customer service via Apple's Genius Bars, and white ear buds that are so recognizable that "when you see them on the street, you feel as if you and the owner are part of the same tribe," Roberts says. "You want to take the iPod to bed with you—it makes you loyal beyond reason and price."

The emotional quotient of branding is not relegated to consumer goods, however. B2B companies have the opportunity to offer emotional connectivity by way of value and reliability. "It's very hard for the big guys to offer deep empathy," Roberts says. Adds Spence: "Everyone sells pretty much the same thing. The ones

that stand for something survive."
In the B2B world, the most important things are offering reliable customer service and close relationships to set a business apart from the rest.

An independent computer repair company, for example, competes with thousands of other small businesses in the same space. A computer repair company, however, that is committed to superior service offers the promise to improve the lives of frustrated computer owners on the brink of hurling their desktop off the roof. This promise, if fulfilled, has the potential to build a long-lasting successful brand—not just a profitable small company.

So how do you go about figuring out the essence of your brand, your promise, your emotional connectivity?
Idea City's Spence suggests starting out by examining why the business was started in the first place. What niche did the business fill? What need? And what do you have to offer the market that is unique? "Where your talent and the needs of the world cross, therein lies your purpose," Spence says.

Spence then suggests taking a survey of 10 stakeholders—five frank and honest employees and five frank and honest customers. Ask them, what are you doing right? What are you doing wrong? Where can you improve? What are you doing better than everyone else?

„You want loyalty beyond reason and loyalty beyond recession."
Many successful brands start with a positioning statement. This will identify the target audience, hone in on competitors, and pinpoint the business's most compelling benefit. From this, the promise can be formulated. The essence of the promise should be a guarantee that can be delivered now, but is also ambitious. "You can't make a promise you can't fulfill—it needs to deal with the moment," says Stan Richards, principal of Dallas-based The Richards Group advertising firm. "It also has to be aspirational."

An example of a killer positioning statement is that of The Richards Group client Motel 6:

Target audience: Anyone who is on the road and a budget traveler. "It doesn't matter how much money you have or if you're driving a BMW—if you are on the road and on a budget, you are a potential customer," Richards says. Competition: Other budget motels including Days Inn, Econo Lodge, Microtel and Super 8. Compelling benefit: "Always the lowest price of any national chain," and "always a comfortable place to stay." These are promises that are both actionable now, but also require planning to make sure they are true in the future. The sacred promise: Motel 6 offers anyone on the road who is a budget traveler a comfortable place to stay at the lowest price of any national chain.

Establishing the sacred promise is tougher than it may seem, experts agree. But once you've gotten it, then the real branding begins.

How do you build a brand that keeps on keeping on?

First, realize a brand is much more than a tagline or elevator pitch. In a general sense, a strong, successful brand will permeate every aspect of the company. "It is everything a company does," Richards says. "The way employees answer the phone, the way you greet customers, deal with constituents both internally and externally. Everyone in the business is, in effect, making a promise to customers, and everything you do will either enhance or detract from the brand."
The brand messaging must be consistent throughout all communication—PR, advertising, internal communications—and should be incorporated into every element of employee relations. "The internal audience is very, very important," Richards says. "The brand should affect the performance of everyone who comes in contact with it." Training, corporate communications and all business development should focus on this promise. Not only does this drive home the message, but an appropriate promise is inspiring and motivating for the entire company.

The key is to keep the brand alive for the long run. This requires a delicate balance of remaining true to the sacred promise while reinventing the product and messaging to address customers' ever-evolving needs.

An epic example of brand longevity is Coca-Cola. The company has fulfilled its promise of lighthearted fun for 124 years—with its bottle shape, logo and flavor remaining recognizable for nearly all of that time. Yet this branding powerhouse is constantly inventing new products, most recently Coke Zero with new types of artificial sweeteners, and Diet Coke Plus with vitamin additives.
Innovation is not relegated to product alone, but target markets as well. In 1935 Coca-Cola went Kosher to attract Jewish customers, and today the beverage is being peddled in developing countries that have booming populations with growing disposable incomes, like India and China. Such moves are expected to position the corporation to gross an astonishing $200 billion by 2020.

„Everyone sells pretty much the same thing. The ones that stand for something survive."
The brand is so successful, so ubiquitous, that few realize that the logo and graphics are in fact gently tweaked every three or four years to help retain a significant market edge over competitor Pepsi Co., which has had some of the most innovative advertising and product advancements in consumer products.

"Coca-Cola has combined the past, present and future in a brilliant way," says Saatchi & Saatchi's Roberts. "They've approached advertising and packaging in a way that it is always happy, always sociable, and always part of the local community."

These emotional promises, he adds, are what give the beverage maker its edge—not the bubbly black drink. "There is no technology in making a soft drink," Roberts quips.

Another example of staying current while remaining brand-true: Southwest Airlines' promise to keep costs down to afford customers the freedom to fly recently required a CEO-level decision to forgo the new industry movement to charge for all checked bags.

"They realized they were leaving hundreds of millions of dollars on the table, but by not charging, they stayed true to their purpose," Spence says. "[Southwest executives] decided that they were going to market the heck out of it, get the whole organization behind that decision, and attract new customers in order to stay true to their purpose."

## Turnaround Advertising

When you are in the business-to-consumer market, your sales grow in direct proportion to consumers knowing, loving and buying your product. Therefore, in this market, saving on marketing is definitely wrong. While cost cutting exercises are vital part of any turnaround situation, increasing advertising spend can be an equally vital part:

Hershey's fourth-quarter profit in 2010 rose 7% as the chocolate maker's major advertising push and new Hershey and Reese's products bolstered sales.

Net income hit $135.5 million, or 59 cents a share, up from $126.7 million, or 55 cents, earned during the fourth quarter of 2009. Sales rose 5.4% to $1.48 billion.

Confectionery sales growth was steady throughout 2010, Chief Executive David West said, noting that Hershey's U.S. retail takeaway was up 5.3% last year in channels that account for 80% of its business. Unlike other food categories, chocolate faces little competition from private-label brands.
West also said he expects the candy, gum and mint category to grow at its historical rate of 3% to 4% in 2011.

Once bashed by analysts for not spending enough to support its Hershey's and Reese's brands, Hershey has tripled its advertising spending from 2006 lows, making it one of the biggest spenders among major U.S. packaged-food companies. Indeed, Hershey boosted its 2010 ad budget by 62%.
Management's also focused on cutting costs, closing seven facilities since 2007, and on setting up partnerships in China, Brazil, and India. The company is stepping up advertising in these emerging middle-class countries as it rolls out its Hershey's and Hershey's Kisses brands.

With 85% of sales from U.S. consumers, Hershey has been knocked for its lack of international growth, but according to Janney Capital analyst Jonathan Feeney, the company's overseas sales have grown to $500 million from $100 million since 2007. At such a pace, he calculates this could add 23 cents to earnings by 2014.

Despite rising prices for cocoa and sugar, Hershey said it's confident that the cost cuts will keep gross margin at 2010 levels, or 42.8%. Sales for 2011 will grow an estimated 3% to 5% over 2010, while earnings are pegged to be 6% to 8% higher than last year, the company said.

What Happens When You Cut Advertising in a Crisis?

Well, for a while perhaps very little may change. The impact of what has been done in the past has a continuing effect and sales come in much as usual.
One major company – the makers of Oxo – once experimented by curtailing all of their advertisement to see what would happen. After a spall when little difference was seen, sales started to drop. New advertising was in the pipeline and was introduced before any further drop occurred, but it looked as if the next decline would be worse and occur more quickly.
So it would be for most businesses, but the gut reaction to turnaround situations is to cut promotional budgets. The effect can be to make a bad situation worse. If sales are already down, then a lack of advertising can send them into steeper decline.

Another very interesting case study is Procter & Gamble.

Procter & Gamble (PG), the world's biggest advertiser, increased its ad budget 17.7% last year to $3.1 billion. Yet its sales over the last quarter were flat, up just 1.5 percent at $21.4 billion in Q4 2010 (the second quarter of P&G's fiscal year.) P&G's Death Star-sized ad budget is, in fact, damaging the company's profitability: net income was down over the last three and six months (to $3.3 billion and $6.4 billion, respectively) while selling costs were up in both periods.

The phrase "SG&A as a percentage of net sales increased" occurs six times in P&G's last 10-Q filing, and on five of those occasions "higher marketing spending" is blamed as the cause.

The global economy is recovering. P&G ought to be growing revenues while keeping a lid on the expenses required to obtain those sales, thus making higher profits. Yet P&G appears to be failing to take advantage of a rising economic tide. As the advertiser that all other advertisers watch, this is cause for concern.
There are two possible reasons P&G is failing to get its act together:

First: P&G is stuck on the wrong side of the digital media revolution. P&G is famous for its digital marketing innovation.

The Old Spice Guy campaign is hailed worldwide as a model for how to use digital media to reinvigorate and promote packaged goods, the most traditional and conservative of all the ad categories.

Yet Old Spice is really an exception that proves the rule. What's the online presence of Tide? Have you downloaded a Febreze app? When was the last time you checked out a viral video for Dawn?

The problem is that outside the supermarket and the kitchen cupboard consumers don't spend a lot of time thinking about house cleaner and soap. Packaged goods don't drive a lot of search traffic.

At the same time, these products are used by everyone. Toothpaste, soap, shampoo, toilet paper — it's hard to get through the day without using a P&G product. So P&G must reach everyone with its marketing, and that means paying for exposure in old fashioned, expensive, old media. Old Spice Guy may be the darling of the web, but his TV commercials still run on cable every night.
Second: P&G is stuck on the wrong side of commodity price inflation: P&G charges a premium price, compared to competing brands, for its products. The company believes its brands are the best, it wants to be No.1 in every category, and it wants to charge more for that positioning.

But the price of oil and food are going through the roof. The phrase "higher commodity costs" occurs eight times in its most recent earnings release. P&G's goods are staples, but it is stuck asking consumers for more money in a world where many shoppers — particularly outside the U.S. — are searching for cheap food. Again, to justify those prices, P&G must keep its foot on the floor in terms of advertising, giving consumers new stories about its brands — and crushing margins in the process.

Combined, the two factors leave P&G a victim of its own success: P&G is unable to stop doing the two things — advertising and raising prices — that both made it the standout consumer marketer on the planet and now are hurting its bottom line. Worse, these problems have been around for a while and P&G shows no signs of addressing either of them.

## Quick-Change Promotion

Major companies do not repeat their advertising nightly on television or put their posters on every street corner without purpose; seeing things again and again gets the message home.

But there are some kinds of promotion where this principle is not so valid. Consider a shop. It may be well-located and have the same people walking by every day, say on their way to work. They look at the window display. As they go past the next day they look again. Repeated looking reinforces whatever message is presented there; but this effect is one of diminishing returns. All too soon they are not really looking any more, certainly not if a glance tells them that they have seen it all before. Once the window is changed, in whole or part, then the effect re-starts, and the changes of someone being prompted to enter the shop are increased.
How quickly must things change? For many shops it might be sensible to do so

weekly, and, yes, it is a chore (albeit not a very expensive one) but it is worthwhile. In one bookshop I know they have a number of display stands on wheels. Every day they turn them ninety degrees so that what faces the front of the shop is different. That's very easy to do and yes, they say it makes a measurable difference to sales.

The same is true of something like a website. If you sell that way, even to a small degree, have a look at one of your favourites. Certainly this is true of Amazon if we stick with books for the moment. Every time you log in there is something new to see: new displays, new recommendations, new products and more. Why? For precisely the reasons just explained: they are increasing the chance of prompting new business, the purchase of something other than what someone logged on for.

In order to increase effectiveness in a turnaround this is an area that can have an immediate effect. Check was goes on in your business. Do you have a shop window, a reception area, a showroom, leaflets, newsletter or a website? Any of these can do more for you if more people find them new and different more of the time. If you find something like a window display or newsletter difficult to refresh on so regular a basis there are several things you can do:

- Do some research; see what others are doing and whether any ideas they have could work for you. Look at both competitive and non-competitive areas and consider asking others how things are working.
- Collaborate. Window displays are a good example of this; you will often see something like a deck-chair in the travel agent's window that is borrowed from (or swapped with) another retailer.
- In addition, check with your suppliers: they may have ways to help you beef up this sort of promotion and to help you keep ringing the changes, both in terms of ideas and resources.

Whatever you do, make sure that you never delude yourself that it does the job for ever. If you want to change the market, then you may have to change something first (and continue doing so).

## Thou Shalt Not Save On Marketing

In a turnaround it's all about managing money. But nobody ever has saved himself into a market. Even the most excellent shop cannot regard opening the doors at 9 am as promotion, and we treasure the apocryphal story of the business that opened with the proprietor saying that "With such an excellent product, no promotion is necessary", they prevailed in this belief right up to the time they had to erect a "For Sale" sign outside their premises.

If you too believe that "our product / our service speaks for itself" – then just send your product or service to a client meeting next time and stay at home. If the client still buys, you were right, your product did speak for itself. If he doesn't, you were wrong.

# Turnaround PR 10 ways to…Generate Free Publicity

In turnaround situations budgets are tight. Getting the biggest bang for your buck is the challenge. Whether you are a small, medium or large company, it doesn't matter: The following techniques can be applied by organisations great and small, just make sure you execute professionally.

10 ways to…Generate free publicity

Media coverage is a blessing for small businesses — as your profile goes up, so will your sales. Marketing campaigns can be costly, but free publicity is a great way to increase the profile of your small business. In a world of "viral" marketing and social media, what options are out there?

## 1. Focus your coverage

Choose carefully exactly what you want to cover and your target media. Whether it's the launch of a new product, a significant anniversary or a competition win, make sure it is relevant to the readership of your targeted media — be it traditional or online.

## 2. Use social media for free PR

You can set up a Facebook page or a Twitter account at no cost. Social media is an excellent way to build relationships with your customers and create word–of–mouth publicity, but be aware of how much time you spend running online profiles. If few of your target customers are online, limit your resources.

## 3. Viral marketing

Whether it's a YouTube video with thousands of views, or a photo that is tweeted and retweeted, if your promotional material goes 'viral' it can give your public profile a huge boost. There is no magic formula to viral marketing — but something quirky, interesting and funny is more likely to capture people's imaginations.

## 4. Write a great press release

Press releases serve two purposes — you can add them to the news section of your site, link to them from your social media accounts and send them to journalists. Ensure you have an eye–catching headline and a strong, summarising opening paragraph before getting into the details.

## 5. Get back to basics

Traditionally small firms aimed to get editorial coverage by sending press releases to newspapers or magazines in the hope that journalists would write about their new product or service. Journalists want to write about something that is newsworthy, particularly if it will appeal to their readership. If it's linked with famous people or places, controversial or amusing, you are more likely to get the coverage you want.

## 6. Advertising promotions

These can be a double-edged sword — although you are guaranteed editorial coverage, paid promotions can be expensive and potential customers may skip the feature. Weigh up whether the potential results are worth the cost.

## 7. Go for gold

Winning an award is a fantastic way to get publicity — not only does it recognise your talent and increase your prestige, award ceremonies are a good place to network and are usually covered by trade or local press. Many awards are free to enter. Look for one that is well respected in your industry and is likely to generate press coverage.

## 8. Get philanthropic

You could get involved with a local charity to increase your standing in the community. Offer to speak at industry events or to write a column for a trade magazine or website.

## 9. Deal with bad publicity promptly

Swift, effective action can turn a negative comment into piece of good publicity. If a customer complains, contact them directly with a full apology and suggested solution. If you see negative and anonymous comments online, respond honestly in the same forum, explaining the situation from your perspective. Do not ignore negative feedback — it may be the first thing a prospective customer sees if they decide to search for you online.

## 10. Keep it in perspective

Publicity is a great way to increase footfall but don't neglect other aspects of your business in a bid to boost your profile. If you are spending a lot of time and energy on PR without much success, sit back and work out another strategy.

# Turnaround Advertising and Gallantry

In an overall process that brings in the business, a continuing focus on, and commitment to, marketing action is necessary at a time when the gut reaction is to cut indiscriminately at the first sign of trouble. Sales down? Cut advertising and promotion, cut the staff and the training budget and then what…hope that the business will continue unaffected?

Especially if you are in the business-to-consumer market, your sales grows in direct proportion to consumers knowing, loving and buying your product. Therefore, in this market, saving on marketing is definitely wrong. Out of sight – out of mind is the rule here. While cost cutting exercises are vital part of any turnaround situation, increasing advertising spend can be even more key to survival, and it takes bold and brave decisions for a manager to do the right thing. A picture book example is the story of GoDaddy.

GoDaddy was a small group in the crowded internet domain name registration sector. Started in 1997, the company had grown mainly through word of mouth. By early 2005, GoDaddy had a 16 per cent market share, with about 7m domain names under management.
The challenge.
Although not underperforming, the compmay was not outperforming the market neither but wanted to turn it's situation around and take the organisation to the next dimension, a quantum leap was what it wanted. GoDaddy wanted to use more formal marketing to help it expand. How could it maximise the effectiveness of its advertising?

## The initial strategy

Bob Parsons, chief executive, made two key decisions. The first was to advertise during the Super Bowl, the most viewed television event in the US. With about 100m people in the US tuning in each year, the ad slots are also the most expensive. As such, they become a Super Bowl talking point.

In 2005, a standard 30-second spot cost about $2.4m – this year's rate was $2.8m–$3m – but GoDaddy purchased two spots, a huge investment for a small company.

Second, the ad was designed to be provocative. The 2005 spot comprised a spoof congressional hearing in which an attractive woman explained why she wanted to advertise GoDaddy during the Super Bowl. When she stood up to display the logo on her tight shirt, a strap snapped, forcing her to grab her chest.

The ad did not explain the company. The idea was to create excitement and interest in GoDaddy.com.

## What happened

After the first spot, Fox, the TV network airing the Super Bowl, dropped the second one after nervousness about negative public reaction. Panellists on the Kellogg School of Management's first Super Bowl Advertising Review, set up to assess strategic strengths and weaknesses, gave the ad a mediocre grade because it did not communicate a clear positioning or consumer benefit.

But GoDaddy says the controversy generated nearly $12m of free publicity. It experienced a significant jump in web traffic, followed by extra sales: the company's global market share rose to 25 per cent the week after the game.

## The subsequent strategy

Each year since 2005, GoDaddy has aimed to run one or two ads during the Super Bowl that feature a "GoDaddy girl". They have included race car driver Danica Patrick and fitness coach Jillian Michaels.

The aim has been to create a media buzz around the airing of the ad. For 2011 Super Bowl, the identity of the newest "GoDaddy girl" was a mystery, revealed on the night as Joan Rivers, the 77-year-old comedian. Her subsequent Tweets about her Photoshopped body in the ad are only adding to the publicity.

## The results

GoDaddy said this week that its 2011 Super Bowl ads drove record web traffic. According to GoDaddy, 15 minutes after its first Super Bowl commercial aired, its domain name registrations rose by more than 466 per cent compared with last year.

GoDaddy now manages more than 46m domain names and is four times the size of its nearest global competitor. Sales have grown from about $200m to an estimated $950m in 2010.

## The lessons

First, GoDaddy capitalised on the power of controversy and used the free publicity it generated to build its brand.

Second, marketers should make the most of integrated marketing. GoDaddy used its provocative advertising to drive traffic to its website, where it delivered product benefit.

Third, there is power in being different. GoDaddy's creative treatment does not appeal to everyone, and even offends some. But this gives the campaign energy. The brand is selling domain names, not milk, so controversy may be less problematic for this brand than for others.

Finally, if an idea works, stick with it. Marketers often tire of their advertising before consumers do. As Mr Parsons has commented: "I'll keep doing it until it stops working."

Exercises:

1. Research what turnover GoDaddy generated in 2005
2. What were the risk for GoDaddy investing $ 6 m into just2 commercials?
3. Which traditional rule did the compmay violate by doing so?
4. How would you as the marketing director of GoDaddy convince the board of such an investment?
5. How could the risk(s) be mitigated?
6. How much of it's revenues should a corporation invest in marketing?
7. How much of its total marketing budget should an organisation put onto a single ad?
8. What was the result of GoDaddy's strategy?
9. Could these results be achieved using alternative strategies? If so. Which strategies do you suggest?
10. How would you celebrate a success like GoDaddy's one in your organisation if you were the CEO?

## The Role Of Customer Service in Turnaround

Bad Customer Service to me is the most inexcusable of all management short-comings. Inexcusable, because in 99,97 % of all cases it is down to downright sloppiness. Someone simply has not done his or her job or is competent, in which case the line manager is also to blame for either putting the wrong person in charge of the job, for not training, motivating, monitoring or performance managing him / her.

Examples:

In the 2011 census a telephone helpline was supposed to answer your questions. If you went through three menus pressing buttons, and at last found one that would put you on to a human being, you could hear the answer "There is no one available to answer your question. Goodbye."
It is beyond me how any organisation can manage to mess it up so utterly when there must be at least half a dozen controls be in the process.
I suppose there was someone in charge of writing the scripts for the telephone menu. Does that someone not have any clue as to what customers expect and how to talk to them?
How about the project manager, quality assurance, testing, marketing? Certainly these functions must exist within a project as huge and as important and politi-

cally sensitive as a census?

Someone or a whole bunch of people clearly did simply not do their jobs and certainly a lot of people simply did not control those who did not do their job. Period. Therefore: Inexcusable.

Thai Square Restaurant, Mansion House, London. I finished my main course and waived to the waitress because I wanted to order the dessert. She could not be bothered to come to my table so assumed wrongly I wanted to check out and brought me the bill. I did not order desert and coffee as I wanted, so they lost out on business. Why? Because the waitress was too lazy to walk over. Inexcusable for both her and the manager in charge of training.

Angus Steak House, Piccadilly, London. I finished my main and wanted desert and coffee. Being the only guest it should not have been too difficult to please me. However, the waitress, apparently untrained and lazy, cleared my desk without even bothering to ask how it was and never asked me if I'd desire anything else. I waited for 30 minutes before giving up. Why? Because she was lazy and untrained, inexcusable for both her and the line manager supposed to manage the restaurant staff.

In turnaround situations you need each and every order and each and every customer possible. It is a truism that it is easier to sell something more to existing customers than find new ones. And nothing is more likely to prompt repeat orders than good and preferably excellent service. So it follows that you need to work hard at ensuring this is so.

- Never ever use call centres. Do you know a single person who lobes being called by call centres? Do you? – Surprise, surprise, your customers don't like it either. Being able to operate a telephone does not make the person operating it a competent, trained expert in customer service, sales or complaint management. Given the fact that there is no second chance for the first impression, calling your customers is your business card and there is nothing worse than a cheap, outsourced call centre in India with people who speak an accent that British customers hardly understand, have no training and upset customers by sheer incompetence.

- Oh, yes, there is still one thing even worse: These latest automated calls. If you really really think that insulting your potential customers by basically telling them "I can't even be bothered to have somebody talking to you in person and you are just worth an impersonal, automated machine", you are – in my book – not fit to run a business and should rather dust books in a library, part time.

- Do I really need to talk about automated telephone systems? I mean the ones that quote you options – press one – play you horrid music and spew out trite little phrases like "Calls may be recorded to help us provide excellent service", when just getting through to them is the very reverse of excellent service. I recently spent long minutes listening to options and pressing buttons only to be told, "We're currently closed." Tell us that at once! This sort of thing has become part of life, the butt of jukes and yet affects choice very directly. How many people opt out part way through such a labyrinth and go elsewhere so that business is lost by whoever was in fact their first choice? It bears thinking about.

- First, make sure that your customer handling activities and system are as they should be and are guided by customers rather than internal convenience and bureaucracy. What this involves will vary depending on the nature of your organisation, but time spent here is worthwhile.

- Second, look too at your complaint handling procedures. If service is good you won't get too many, but if / when you do, regard them as an opportunity – if they can be sorted efficiently then the end result can be that customers are actually more likely to do business with you again than if nothing untoward had happened (though don't encourage complaints for that reason!).

# Turnaround Information Technology (I.T.)

There are always a certain amount of corporations that have found themselves in a situation of negative profitability and/or declining sales. If these cases are prolonged they are in need of a fundamental business change and infusion of cash in order to survive - A Corporate Turnaround. In the last couple of years the number of companies in this situation has increased significantly. The common approaches to address these situations are:

1. Assemble a finance team get a cash infusion from a bank, finance company or investor
2. Assemble a team to arrange the sale of all or part of the company
3. Cut expenditures and employees across the board in the company
4. Bring in a consultant to address the revenue side of the business
5. Re-organize under bankruptcy protection

While I agree that some or all of these approaches may be necessary in any given situation, I believe that except for the cases in which the company is liquidated, Information Technology also plays a vital role.

I have been working with several clients in the last couple of years that find themselves in the situation where revenue is down, cash flow is down, cash is hard to find and the company is in serious trouble. In one situation the client had already attempted to sell the company 3 times and was unable to come to terms with a buyer. In another, they had already brought in management consultants to address the issues and increase sales. In another the company was still in good position but the owner knew there were big bumps in the road and wanted to address them before they became serious. In all cases the biggest hindrance to management was the lack of information, financial, sales and production about what was happening in the business so that productive decisions could be made. Why was there such a lack of basic information? In all cases the root of the problem consisted of the following:

- Computer systems which were not integrated - each company utilized a minimum of 2 major systems in the business and sometimes more
- Significant manual processes that prevented timely and accurate information from being processed in the computer systems
- Inadequate and untimely reporting regarding financial and operational results
- Lack of an adequate system to track sales performance
- Because of the above Information Technology problems, the companies were unable to answer the following basic business questions:
- How much are sales down over previous years and in what product lines, customers or geographic areas?
- What sales do we have in the pipeline and what are the expected future revenues?
- Where are sales coming from in terms of products, customers and geographic regions?
- What is the productivity of operational staff and how can we increase the productivity?
- Where are the greatest expenses and what are the best cuts to make?
- What is the projected cash flow for the next month, quarter and year?
- What is the status of AR and collections, if collections are down why?

Now I know what most people would say - hire a staff of accountants to come in and generate those reports. Ok let's say we do that. First, these types of reports are not static. Management needs these reports on a daily or weekly basis. How many accountants and how much time will be required to compile this information on an ongoing basis? In most cases it would be unrealistic. So what can Information Technology do?

First, there are numerous Business Intelligence (BI) systems available today that can be used to gather data from multiple systems and create reports, trend analysis, dashboards for management to have meaningful information as soon as data is entered into the systems. This is especially important when analyzing sales and production data. The majority of these systems can access Excel spreadsheets and any ODBC data base. So even if there is no CRM (Customer Relationship Management) system and sales information is in spreadsheets, important management reports may be obtained from them.

Then the next question is 'Aren't BI systems expensive and difficult to implement?' Traditionally that has been the case but today there are several systems that are very inexpensive and they will build a dynamic data store from the raw data. These may not be a long term solution but can be implemented rather quickly to start providing management with critical information.

Second, in some situations the BI data can be used to create interfaces between systems that are not integrated. One of the biggest issues I see is operational systems that are not integrated with an accounting system. Some of the BI systems can be used to capture the operational transactions and generate Excel spreadsheets of the journal entries that can then be integrated to the accounting system.

Third, I.T. is no longer just an internal data gathering operation that is used to create financial statements and tax returns. Technology and automation are used to follow up on sales leads and prospects, survey customers, create new sales channels, provide customer and vendor self-service, provide for entry of data at the source, streamline operations and improve many other business functions. By effectively utilizing information technology and business process automation, many time consuming and inaccurate business processes can be streamlined and made more accurate. Much of this technology is relatively inexpensive. For example, there are many services offered by banks, financial institutions and vendors that are free or very low cost to implement. Many systems especially CRM (Customer Relationship Management) and prospect follow-up systems are available as a service at a low monthly cost.

By implementing timely management reporting, integrating systems and automating business processes many companies can find solutions to their business problems, provide better information to investors and lenders and even improve the chances for an acceptable sale of the business. Times are challenging and information technology is not a silver bullet but it is an arrow that should be in every executive's quiver.

## The Limits Of Turnaround Management

Very often I hear business people talking about the economy, the country, the government and especially about the NHS like this:
Once you understand UK Inc's main problems, the solutions become almost self-evident…

There's a lot that can be done to make UK Inc. operate like a well-run business. A corporate turnaround specialist would quickly hire an independent firm to conduct an audit of each business line…
I hope it's clear by now that UK Inc. has a spending problem, not a revenue problem…

In 25 years of studying tech companies and working in financial services, I've discovered that people will sacrifice if they have a clear idea of what their sacrifices can accomplish. I think the same goes for UK Inc…

UK Inc. needs to prime itself for renewal—and prepare for brutal decisions that change how we do business.
Actually, the solutions aren't self-evident. Try asking a corporate turnaround specialist to turn around a corporation run as a democracy, where every employee gets an equal vote.
Democracy might today be the only acceptable form to run a country, but it is not the best, and it is certainly not the best way to run a company:
In order to decide what's best, you need to be an expert; after all it's hard to decide what's best for an ill patient with stomach aches if you are a plumber and not a

doctor. Many of today's problems result from the fact that politicians are running the state economy, economists are running banks, public clerks run the NHS and everybody who has any opinion on something seems to be qualified running it. But this is not so. The problems we have are evidence. No director in his right mind would ask the workers in his steelworks about the best financial strategy, ask accountants to develop a marketing campaign or ask the office manager to suggest how the vehicle fleet should be managed. Yet, exactly that is the expectation of citizens when it comes to ruling a country. They all want to be heard and they all want their views to be considered, qualified or not.

And you can't really extrapolate from the rich and well-educated employees of technology and financial-services firms to Brits as a whole.

So, what's my point? My points are:

1.  When running a country, you can't run it like a business but what you can do is learn business best practices. If we suffer from a lousy public transport business, let's do what business managers do and what is called "best practice": Look at those who do better and learn. If Germany can run a perfectly well oiled public transport system, so can we.
2.  Employ men to do a men's job. Don't let GP's run the business side of the NHS and don't let business managers operate on patients. Let business people run the business side of the NHS and let doctors do the surgery.
3.  In a business, lead strongly and do not be too democratic. Even John Lewis has a CEO and doesn't let the company be run by the staff of the perfumery department.
4.  In a turnaround, strong leadership is called for. Take the reigns and hold them tight, because it's no time for lengthy discussions and aligning interests. When the house is burning it's time for quick and decisive actions. You can discuss later, when the fire is out, how you can do better next time.

## The Turnaround Manager: Bedside Manners

I said it a million times: One of biggest enemies of common sense is ego. Remove your ego and you are successful, allow your ego to blossom and you loose ground contact, become detached and go down.

A better textbook example than the current downfall of Air India's turnaround COO has yet to be written:

Just when one thought all was well with the turnaround plan of Air India (AI), three key executives appointed to implement the plan were either asked to leave or left the airline. The last to go was the one who came first and was key in the turnaround plan — Chief Operating Officer (COO) Gustav Baldauf.

The other two were AI Express COO Pawan Arora and AI's Chief Training Officer Stephen Sukumar. AI Express is the low-cost international subsidiary of AI and operates mainly on routes to the West Asian and Southeast Asian countries. Baldauf's entry in April 2010 AI was historical, as he was the first COO and expat to have joined the airline, without many inside and outside the carrier welcoming him.

After Baldauf's appointment was cleared by a committee headed by then aviation secretary, M M Nambiar, eyebrows were raised on his huge salary package. The airline, under huge debt and seeking equity infusion from the government to keep it afloat, was paying him over £ 400 K annually.

Criticism of the Austrian COO hardened after he started working with the airline. His handling of the shift in AI's operations from Terminal 1 to 3 at the Delhi airport was labelled a disaster and Baldauf was never seen at the terminal during the transition. He, apparently, managed it from his office in Mumbai.

But Air India Chairman and Managing Director Arvind Jadhav, who had asked for a COO to keep himself away from the day-to-day operations of the airline, stationed himself at T3 to monitor the shift.

The shift of Kingfisher Airlines, Jet Airways and their low-cost subsidiaries to the new terminal was smooth. This brought Baldauf's inefficiency out in the open. Questions were also raised on Baldauf's frequent trips to his country.

The last nail in the coffin, however, was Baldauf's open criticism of the government — the promoter of the airline — for interfering in the day-to-day functioning of the airline and not letting him function independently.

Following the comment, he was served a showcase notice by the airline management for violating service conduct rules, asking him to explain his act. For want of a justification, Baldauf resigned on February 28, 2011.

Before joining AI, he worked with Aircraft Trading & Airline Consulting in Austria. He had also worked at Austrian Airlines, Jet Airways and had over 26 years of flying experience at Austrian Airlines AG.

With 14,000 hours of flying experience, Baldauf is an instructor and is qualified to launch cold and winter operations. He holds an engineering degree in electrical sciences and has also done an accident investigation course from the University of Southern California.

During his stint at Jet, he served as the vice-president of flight operations. His responsibilities included cockpit crew performance and productivity, flight operation planning, monitoring of operational performance metrics for existing, newly-inducted and proposed to be inducted aircraft in the fleet, restructuring the flight operations department to cope with future expansion and overseeing flight dispatch functions.

His colleagues at Jet Airways remember him as an intelligent and innovative man but a person who would not be very serious about following rules. They add the reason behind his contract with Jet not being extended was his lax attitude.

The classic mistakes Baldauf made were:

He was never seen at the Mumbai terminal during the transition. He, apparently, managed it from his office in Mumbai. This is a cardinal mistake. A leader always has to lead from the front, lead by example and the very least show up and demonstrate commitment and interest. Remote controlling a huge project such as a terminal change will inevitably result into lack of staff engagement and low morale, loss of credibility as a leader and most of all into loss of quality project management – a recipe for disaster.

He may have been asked by the Managing Director to stay away, but a real leader must recognise what's best practice and make a stand. Just following orders, especially when they seem not right, is not what a COO should do.

Questions were also raised on Baldauf's frequent trips to his country. When an airline boss, who certainly will do a lot of flying as part of his job, is blamed for too many trips, something must be seriously wrong. It's another classic: A leader who thinks just because he is at the top he can behave as he pleases with no regards for the political messages of his behaviour is doomed. The higher up you are, the more exposed you are, the more your behaviour will be scrutinized, and shamelessly making trips home paid by your employer and neglecting your performance is a very unwise habit indeed.

Open criticism of the government — the promoter of the airline — for interfering in the day-to-day functioning of the airline and not letting him function independently can only be described a stupid. You never bite the hand that feeds you, and given his incompetence, interfering in the day-to-day functioning of the airline and not letting him function independently was he only option the government had, being ultimately accountable for the Airline performance.

I believe that a root cause was that the wrong kind of manager has been chosen in the first place. Baldauf's background is a technical one, not a managerial one, but you need a business man to solve a business problem. I suspect that Baldauf was out of his dept from day one and just tried to hang in there as long as possible, raking in his high salary as long as possible, knowing he will sooner or later fail.

## Ethics in Turnaround

Especially in a crisis, transparency and communication are key. Best practise management means to practice an open book policy and keep staff informed about what's going on in the company, because only when people know what's going on, where they stand, what options they have and what is expected of them, can they choose the best strategy for the situation. Never insult people's intelligence by pretending, they are grown-up and can deal with the truth, have deserved the truth and will eventually find out anyway if you'd lie to them about the true picture of the company.

Really? No! I disagree. Sometime, openness can make organisations nervous, confuse their leaders and make a crisis worse rather than better. Especially in a crisis situation. This is called "negative transparency".

Sometime a "need to know" basis is much better. Sometimes, if people know too much or things they can't deal with, information cab become dangerous:
Would you get nervous or calm down if your neighbour's house would be made of glass and you could watch him polishing his gun-collection? What, if he did

nothing else but watching you?

The issue is closely linked with inter-company freedom of information. It is a wonderful feature of a free system, but in certain circumstances it can be dangerous if used by individuals to agitate or to aggravate secret negotiations that could prevent conflicts or shorten them – think of negotiations with trade unions or the preparations for mass redundancies.

As a turnaround leader you often are faced with difficult ethical conflicts. Should you strictly stick to ruthless honestly or is it sometimes kinder to keep your card to your chest? Is it kind to tell a dying man "your time has come, you'll die, good by" when he is asking "will I make it?" or is it kinder to lie to him?

I think the guideline has to be what's better for the greater good. In Germany, the law says that the wellbeing of the community always outranks the wellbeing of an individual. I think this is a wise law and one we should consider when making corporate decisions and when deciding about corporate behaviour.

Turnaround Reputation Management

An important aspect of how you and your business will be perceived when going through a rough patch is how you present yourself. Let's be clear: You need to inspire confidence. In you bankers, your stakeholders, your staff and your clients. Because if they loose confidence in you, you might loose them respectively what they can give you, that is to say their money and their business.

Within a few moments, assumptions and judgements are made. You know it-s true – we all do. However hard you try to avoid doing so, you (and anyone visiting your offices – be they customers, suppliers or others) are likely to make an instant decision about how things are going in the organisation because of the way its employees look, speak or dress. The statistics speak for themselves about what people notice when you meet them:

- 55 % of the impression made is how you look – posture and what you wear
- 38 % is the energy and enthusiasm – body language, tone of voice
- Only 7 % is what you actually say to a person

Visual impressions are more important than oral messages. You may be going to the bank manager or your financial backers or shareholders to report on the current state of business. Those first few seconds when you enter the room could be crucial. Looking scruffy and down at heel may be one way of going about it (if you think playing the sympathy card will work). But looking professional and well held-together is likely to get you off to a good start. Everything you do afterwards will become just that much easier. A positive beginning not only affects any business that may transpire, it affects your confidence too. Confidence requires preparation and needs to be actively worked on to ensure you achieve the right impact.

This isn't a matter of tricks of gimmicks. It's about being business-like and professional. People are more likely to respond positively to your requests if you look well presented.

## The Future Role of the Turnaround Specialist

Leaders do not always act rational. Or they act rational in a way that seems irrational to others. Especially in situations of crisis personal interests change quickly, and often the good of the organisation is scarified for personal protection or gain. I knew directors at Chemviron Carbon who, in the face of an approaching crisis, hired extra staff only because they knew that soon they will be asked to reduce overheads and make redundancies, and by making those redundant they just hired they got away with not touching those who had been there before, effectively cementing their status quo and ending up with exactly the same number of people they had before. This is irresponsible, despicable gambling with human chess figures.

I knew of directors at 4711 who, in the face of an approaching crisis, had to make suggestions about cost savings and instead of making real contributions, though about ideas that would sound great on the surface but could never been implemented. Their motivation was protect their fifhdoms and not end up with smaller budgets, less staff and reduced importancte.

I knew of directors at Chemviron Carbon who deliberately hired the second best person for a job because the best one was "too ambitious" and was perceived a threat to those less qualified but yet above him in hierarchy. If you deliberately hire the second best and deprive your company of the best resources because of personal interest, that's criminal.

All these behaviour patterns seem totally irrational to an outsider who doesn't see the underlying motivation of the leader (who, in this examples, hasn't deserved that title). It is therefore vital for any controlling organ such as a non-executive board or a CEO to understand what drives their leaders, especially in a crisis, and to to take them out of control temporarily and replace them with a neutral, external crisis manager who has no personal interests and no political agenda and acts for the best of the organisation without regard for personal gain or loss. The problem is, many organisations still feel bullet-proofed, even if they are already bleeding to death. Human nature promotes denial. Military analysts had long predicted a possible Japanese attack on Pearl Harbour, but America fell victim to complacency and megalomania and denied such a possibility. Over night, the opinion of many so called "experts" changed dramatically.

Similarly sad was the shock the US suffered on 9/11. America felt bulletproof because of its superior military power, but simply did not see that that an envelop with Andrax or a few suicide bombers could make their airplane-carriers and nuclear missiles redundant. Over night, perception changed.
Just because something is too horrible to even imagine does not mean it will not

happen.

Many commercial organisations are in a similar situation: They are highly vulnerable and perhaps disaster is already knocking at their door, yet they still think they are bulletproof. Why? Because the worst case scenario is so terrible that they simply deny the possibility that it might happen. They are blind and think that history can be projected into the future: "It has worked all the time in the past, so it will too work in the future". But as every stock investor has learned, past performance is no guarantee for future performance. Personal power is not stronger than life's reality.

How to change that and make managers see the risks? By changing views and perspectives. If you can't see around the corner, change your position. Step a few yards aside and all of a sudden you can see what's around the corner. For an organisation, this means to bring in external views, new ways of looking at things, adding external experience that does not exist in the current structure.

But this leads to the next problem: Why change a system that benefits yourself and do something that seems to disadvantage you? This is were we need a paradigm shift. As long as leaders are rewarded with bonuses based on 12 weeks results, all they will ever do is thinking in 12 weeks horizons. They give a damn investing in new technologies that saves 20% of the corporation's cost over the next 10 years but will reduce the cash flow position next quarter. They give a damn about hiring extra staff to deal with high growth if this means that profits take a short term dip because hiring means recruitment and training costs.

Only if leaders start being rewarded for long-term performance and when leaders are rotated and taken out of a job after a number of years regardless of their performance, their motivation to protect and cement their status quo will become superfluous and attitudes will change.

At this moment, most leaders treat their organisation like a tradesman bending and forming a work piece until it fits him, while what we need is a culture where leaders treat their organisations like gardeners, creating an environment where organic growth and development can take place, fertilising and enabling that organism that's called a company.

With impending defaults looming as the economy slows and executive teams that have never dealt with an economic downturn, today's CEO needs to be armed with the appropriate tools to efficiently handle the problems that seem destined to be a reality. By hiring a turnaround manager who is expert in the financial, operations and sales/marketing arenas, the CEO can feel confident that his/her company is getting the individual attention and expertise needed to ensure that the business remains viable.

## Signs of a Troubled Business

A company may require the services of a turnaround specialist for many reasons. Below are the most common signs of distress that troubled businesses often display:

## Market Changes

Changes in the marketplace may have bypassed a company, leaving it with lagging sales and lost market share.

## Operating without Controls

Managing a company without adequate reporting mechanisms is a recipe for disaster. If management is making decisions on old or inaccurate information, the company can easily head in the wrong direction.

## Over-diversification

Today, many businesses feel the pressure to diversify in order to reduce risk. However, too much diversification may cause them to spread themselves too thin.

## Corporate Growth

Companies are sometimes tempted to add value by engineering a growth spurt. However, growth often carries a very high price tag and leveraging a company to such a degree means that management must operate with little or no margin for error.

## Lack of a Sound Business Plan

A number of growing companies operate without a business plan or with a different business plan in every manager's head. The result is that plans are carried out according to individual interpretation.

## Ineffective Style of Management

The president and founder of a company may be unable to delegate authority. As a result, the rest of the management staff is without solid experience or any feeling of ownership.

## Poor Lender Relationships

Some companies develop an adversarial relationship with their financial lending institution. Fearing that their loan or loans may be in jeopardy, they attempt to hide financial information from the bank, and communications are stressed. Since money is the lifeblood of almost every business, this kind of lender relationship only leads to more trouble.

## The Turnaround Specialist

Turnaround specialists are a relatively new breed in the business world, but in this era of rapid and painful change, the market has placed an increased premium on their demand. Rising foreign competition, fastchanging technology and shifting financial markets have created a climate where no business can take economic stability for granted. The accelerated pace of change has turned once-successful CEOs into hesitant managers who are no longer able to provide strong leadership for their companies. While downsizing has trimmed payrolls and improved economic health, it has also robbed companies of management talent. Twenty years ago, companies hired and carefully groomed managers to assume positions of top management; today, many companies have little or no bench strength in their leadership ranks. Turnaround specialists, operating as either an interim manager or consultant, assist a company's CEO in the decision-making process to guide it back toward profitability. A turnaround management firm specializes in operational and financial restructuring for troubled companies. Armed with a broad base of industrial and financial experience, the firm can guide companies in a wide variety of industries, including manufacturing, retailing, distribution, wholesale and service.

The turnaround specialist enters a company with a fresh eye and enjoys complete objectivity. This professional is able to spot problems and create new solutions that may not be visible to company insiders simply because the latter are too close to the subject.

The turnaround manager has no political agenda or other obligations to color the decision-making process, allowing him or her to take the unpopular yet necessary steps for survival. A turnaround specialist brings experience into crisis situations. Like a paramedic, the talent lies in making critical decisions quickly in order for the patient to have the best chance at recovery. Operating in the eye of the storm. the turnaround specialist must deal equitably with angry creditors, scared employees, wary customers and a nervous board of directors.

Armed with fresh ideas and a wealth of experience, a turnaround management firm can breathe new life into a faltering company. As it analyzes and then attacks the problems at hand, it can make decisions with total objectivity because, as an outsider, it can set goals without a preconceived agenda. The turnaround specialist also brings credibility to a company. When an organization's problems become known, creditors are often angry and confused. Employees are scared. Customers look on with suspicion and uncertainty. Therefore, the first important step is to stabilize the climate surrounding a troubled business. Creditors and customers often breathe a sigh of relief upon the retention of a turnaround consultant because it shows that the company recognizes that there is a problem and that it intends to fix it. Creditors and customers alike would like to see the company prosper, as a viable company will provide them with either revenues or supplies for years to come. The prospect of bankruptcy leaves the unsecured creditor with cents on the dollar, whereas a turnaround means payment in full or payment at negotiated rates.

Once engaged by a troubled company, the turnaround specialist moves quickly to minimize damage and restore stability. He or she concentrates on one or more of the following areas:

Manufacturing and Operations-Productivity and efficiency improvement, cycle time optimization, Kaizen, SS programs, Six Sigma, cellular/continuous flow production, Just-In-Time (JIT), industrial engineering, reengineering, pull-through scheduling, production/inventory management, lean manufacturing, outsourcing, warehouse and logistics efficiency, Asset Management-Management and control of accounts receivable, inventory and fixed assets to enhance return on investment, Financial Management-Information systems effectiveness and implementation, financial and cash flow projections, costing systems, break-even analysis, budgeting, financial analysis, Sales and Marketing--Sales force development and training, incentive programs, market and competitor analysis, customer satisfaction enhancement, strategic development, new market analysis and development, Cost Control-Optimizing the cost of raw materials, purchased parts, freight, utilities, insurance and other products and services to provide the critical balance between lowest cost and most efficient operations, Vision and Success Planning-Vision development, success action plans, strategic plans, Employee Motivation and Effectiveness-Team building, empowerment, leadership training, incentive programs, organizational effectiveness.

The results of the turnaround specialist concentrating on the above areas are numerous, including:

Dramatic Improvements in Organizational Effectiveness-Clearly defined vision, clear benchmarks and goals, involved and empowered employees, leaders instead of managers, Improvement in Operational Effectiveness-Commitment to continuous improvement, on-time delivery, reduction of cycle time/non-value added activities, improved response systems, pull-through systems, Cost Reduction-Aggressive purchasing, alternative materials, control of waste, scrap and overtime, outsourcing to more efficient providers, consolidate facilities/reduce floor space, Reduction of Under-Performing Assets-- Slow moving, obsolete or defective inventory, delinquent accounts receivable, under performing divisions/product lines, equipment/building, Consistently satisfied customers Impressive increases in sales and market share, Major improvements in profitability, cash flow and return on investment.

The specialist brings an integrative and analytical approach to improve distressed companies by developing and implementing comprehensive turnaround plans. Our effective, hands-on approach produces verifiable, empirical data that yields realistic alternatives, allowing a company's stakeholders to make intelligent, prudent and timely decisions about their organization or investment.

## Choosing the Right Turnaround Specialist

### Experience

Experience is the most important credential. MBA degrees and CPA designations count for little if the turnaround manager has not been proven in the heat of battle. The candidate should be able to produce a portfolio of success stories and satisfied clients.

### Reputation

No turnaround manager can expect to succeed without quickly gaining the confidence of creditors as well as accessing new sources of credit. Check the candidate's reputation with leading bankers, attorneys, accountants, financial advisors, factors and trade creditors.

### Fee Structure

Make sure the fee structure of the turnaround specialist is clear and fair. A company should make sure it can afford such a service, or else it may be trading one set of problems for another. Find out if there is an incentive or performance arrangement in the contract.

### Professionalism and Ethics

Membership in the Turnaround Management Association helps to indicate the degree of professionalism and honesty of a candidate. TMA holds members to a strict code of ethics and encourages certification by the Association of Certified Turnaround Professionals.

### Conclusion

By hiring a turnaround specialist as soon as difficulties become evident, a CEO can save time and money. The sooner a specialist is hired, the sooner their ideas can be implemented. Whether the economy continues to struggle or picks up in the next two quarters, most turnaround firms also offer services that can help streamline operations, as well as other specialties, that can help a company run more efficiently and effectively.

# Epilogue: Prevention, Loss Control and Protection

I am not at all advocating that business owners, directors or who ever might be responsible and accountable for causing an organisation to get distressed will not be held accountable if the worst happens. Especially if through fraud, negligence or sheer incompetence people loose their jobs and livelihoods, suppliers are not being paid and might go out of business and customers are left without products they paid for, I have no sympathy and say that those responsible for creating disaster must face the consequences of their deeds or omissions.

However, the honest, law abiding, hardworking business owner has a right and a responsibility to himself and his family, to protect his personal assets. That's why the concept of a Limited Company has been created in the first place, and law and moral is completely at ease with the fact that entrepreneurs are able to protect their personal assets from the grasp of creditors and HMRC. After all, being an entrepreneur is a risky business and nobody would become one if with each business venture private assets would be at stake. Given the fact that the economy consists of SME's by 90%, such precautions are a sheer necessity.

I have often met clients who had substantial private property on their business books. Asked why they did that, the most frequent answer was that they wanted to enhance the reputation of their business and its financial standing. Although an honourable idea, it is very risky and I have always advised them to take personal property out of the company name, after all if you run a UK Ltd. you do so for a reason, and if you run a PLC or are a sole trader then there are equally good reasons for that.

But most people don't do more to protect their assets and increase their personal wealth. Perhaps because they don't know what else to do and how.

There are very sophisticated laws in the UK that allow you to plan and avoid taxes and protect your assets. There is a big difference between tax avoidance and tax evasion and a lot of people don't know the difference: Tax evasion is immoral and illegal. It means evading tax payments after becoming liable for tax. Tax avoidance, however, is completely legal and good common sense. When you buy second hand cars where there is no VAT on it, when you make a donation, when you write off equipment, when you reclaim VAT, you avoid taxes, and that's completely legal.

If you decide to have your business headquartered in another country because taxes are lower there, that's completely legal too. If you decide to have your business headquartered in a tax haven, it is still completely legal.

If you are a UK Ltd. Company director and pay yourself either a salary or dividends (or both), it is completely legal to use intelligent tax planning by using trusts in tax havens to avoid taxes. Rich people do it for decades, and more and more SMEs do it each year.

Even if you are a small business and have at least £ 100 K taxable income, you can reduce your taxes to zero and protect your personal property completely against all risks of loss, completely legal and at affordable costs.

I cannot go into details at this topic would burst the scope of this report, but if follow this link you will see a schematic illustration about the function of a re-muneration trust and a personal wealth management trust. Purpose built for UK Ltd. companies by one of the countries leading tax and law firms, it is the ultimate protection and peace of mind for business owners.

Readers have often written to me and asked me to publish the contact details of my tax advisor. I won't do that because I don't want the poor people to be inun-dated with hundreds of inquiries, but if you are seriously interested to meet them and learn about a personal asset protection scheme, I am more than happy to give out the contact details, just call, write or email me (all my contact details are on my website www.RemborPartners.com).